EXECUTIONERS

EXECUTIONERS

by
PHIL CLARKE
LIZ HARDY
and
ANNE WILLIAMS

Futura

A *Futura* Book

First published by Futura in 2008

Copyright © Omnipress 2008

ISBN: 978-0-70880-491-9

Produced by Omnipress, Eastbourne

Printed in Great Britain

Futura
An imprint of
Little, Brown Book Group
100 Victoria Embankmenet
London EC4Y 0DY

Photo credits: Getty Images

CONTENTS

PART THREE: THE WITCH HUNTERS

PART FOUR: IMPALEMENT

PART FIVE: NEWGATE PRISON

PART SIX: TYBURN

PART SEVEN: THE GUILLOTINE

INTRODUCTION

To kill in the name of one's country is a glorious feat, one rewarded by medals. But to kill in the name of the law, that is a gruesome, horrible function, rewarded with scorn, contempt and loathing by the public.

FRENCH EXECUTIONER,
HENRI ANATOLE DEIBLER

CHANGING PERCEPTIONS

Our ancestors believed that death was an occupational hazard for anyone found guilty of murder or treason. In fact, according to the Bloody Code of 1795, even minor crimes such as theft or the malicious maiming of cattle were punishable by death in England. The British, like the Aztecs, Greeks, Romans and Turks meted out sentences that were, by modern standards, disproportionate with the crimes committed to control the population. These severe punishments did not have their desired effect unless they contained some element of gory entertainment or grand theatre.

THE PERFORMANCE

Whatever the form of punishment – be it a simple beheading by axe, or a more elaborate death by burning, drowning or boiling in oil – there have always been people employed by the state to carry them out. Executioners are people with the technical expertise to design an execution from beginning to grisly end, demanding authority and respect while inflicting terrible pain and suffering, and simultaneously fulfilling the illusive 'entertainment factor' that makes a public execution an occasion – something people will travel for miles to witness.

Executioners are undoubtedly a rare breed and their varied responsiblities often sit uncomfortably on their shoulders. Talented technicians sometimes lack the star quality needed to turn an execution into an event, and often great performers lack the ability to kill cleanly and efficiently without unnecessary mess.

AN ANCIENT SOLUTION

The death penalty has existed since the earliest civilisation, in fact execution is probably the oldest form of law enforcement, and therefore the job of executioner is as old as that of a prostitute or priest. Before written laws, before prisons, before courtrooms, juries and judges, the most obvious, the cheapest and often the most convenient punishment was death. During these times an execution would have been an informal affair, the death penalty would have been meted out by an angry mob, and the accused could expect to be stoned to death, or even torn apart by the bare hands of local people in their own communities. Of course, this form of execution still happens in some parts of the world, but today we tend to see that kind of vigilante justice as a crime in itself, and not a state-approved form of punishment.

THE DRACONIAN CODE

In 621 BC, The Draconian Code of Athens declared that any crime, however minor, should be punishable by death. It's widely thought by historians that Dracon, the Athenian law giver responsible for the code, decided that the minor crimes deserved to be punished by execution, and he simply had no more severe punishments for those who had committed more serious crimes.

In ancient Greece, you could even be forced to become your own executioner. Most famously the philosopher Socrates was forced to drink hemlock by an Athenian jury after being found guilty of impiety. He was instructed to drink the poison and then to walk until his legs grew heavy. Hemlock causes numbness, paralysis and loss of speech followed by failure of the respiratory system and then death. Difficult as it may be to believe, he got off relatively lightly. This was a punishment given to someone from the upper echelons of society since, although death by hemlock is undoubtedly uncomfortable, it is also fairly dignified. Those from a less noble background would have suffered severe pain and humiliation, by either being stoned to death or being hurled from a high point behind the Acropolis into a pit of spikes and hooks.

EMPHASIS ON PAIN

The onus during these early forms of executions was most certainly on painful punishment, rather than painless euthanasia. The guilty were meant to suffer and only God could excuse them from their agonising fate. The executioner was employed to deliver the people's punishment, to vent the rage and grief of the victim and the victim's family upon the condemned in a manner that befitted the crime.

MISTAKES DO HAPPEN

Today, we generally consider ourselves more refined, and less bloodthirsty than our ancestors, but perhaps this is a misconception. Execution by electric chair or lethal injection can be extremely painful and gruesome, and the technicians employed to carry it out have to be aware of this when they take the job. When the electric chair is the method of choice, it is not uncommon for the victim's skin to bubble and burn or even to catch fire while the victim is still breathing. This is one of the main reasons why so many people oppose it as a form of capital punishment.

THE LEGEND OF YELLOW MAMA

On 22 June 1983, John Louis Evans, a convicted armed robber and murderer, was executed at Holman Prison near Atmore in Alabama. The chair used on this occasion was called Yellow Mama because of its coat of bright yellow paint. It had been built by an inmate in 1927. It was a very old device which hadn't been used since 1965 – in truth few rational people would happily use a hairdryer this old and decrepit – and yet Yellow Mama was still deemed suitable for executing a man.

At 8.30 p.m. the first jolt of 1,900 volts shot through Evans's body. Sparks and flames erupted from the electrode tied to Mr Evans's left leg and the electrode burst from the strap holding it in place. Then a large cloud of grey smoke and yellow sparks poured from under the hood covering Mr Evans's face, and the nauseating smell of burning flesh along with a sound like sizzling bacon, filled the room. He was still alive. A second jolt of electricity was administered – more smoke emanated from his leg and head – but he was still breathing. At 8.40 p.m. a third and final jolt of electricity was passed through Mr Evans's body. At 8.44 p.m. doctors finally pronounced him dead. It had taken 14 minutes to perform the execution. Is that really our definition of a relatively painless, modern and ethically sound punishment? Opinion is fiercely divided.

HANGMAN WANTED ...

The job description of an executioner has evolved over centuries and varies widely depending on the society that employs them. In pre-Columbian cultures, an executioner was a shaman, a performer of a grand ritual, the representative of divine judgement on the earth – even a god. He was bestowed with the freedom of his community and would have certainly been revered (if not actually worshipped) by his followers.

In some Middle Eastern cultures, an executioner would have been a member of the victim's family – a brother or father of the wronged party who was granted the right to visit his rage upon the accused in the form of violent lashes administered using whips or chains. In some parts of Iran, the family of the victim, or the wronged party themselves, still have the opportunity of administering lashes to the accused.

In Ali Pasha's Turkey, the condemned were sometimes impaled on a stake and slowly roasted over a fire and the close family of the accused were forced to turn the spit – so a person could be made to act as executioner for his or her own kin.

BILLY–NO-MATES

Professional executioners are often shunned by society. They are usually feared, hated and avoided by their peers, which is why so many of them opt for anonymity over notoriety. The Australian executioners, who had usually been transported to the colonies for committing a crime themselves and were living in communities of people from the same criminal background, did everything in their power to conceal their true identities – often wearing false humpbacks and thick black beards – this explains why they are all nicknamed 'blackbeard' in surviving historical records. In Britain, many executioners chose to operate under the moniker 'Jack Ketch'.

Some executioners have remained almost anonymous while others rose to celebrity status. The Pierrepoints of England are still celebrated as a famous family of hangmen, producing three generations of executioners for the crown. The business of execution in many parts of the world is largely the domain of various families. The children are indoctrinated into the profession early in life and employed as assistants to their more experienced fathers and grandfathers. Their responsibilities might involve setting up the guillotine or gallows, holding a prisoner's neck in place while the blade is hoisted, or simply cleaning up the mess afterwards. They will continue in such a role until they have learnt the trade well enough to take over as head executioner, hence you will often find that a family name reoccurs again and again during the course of this book.

TODAY'S EXECUTIONERS

Today, most executions are conducted in private and therefore executioners are more like technicians than entertainers. Their primary responsibility is to make sure the process is conducted with decorum and scientific precision. In the province of Yunnan in China, mobile execution teams travel in vans converted from 24 seat buses, administering lethal injections at all times of the day or night. The windowless execution chamber contains a stretcher where the prisoner is strapped down. When the needle is attached by a doctor, a police officer presses a button which releases an automatic syringe, administering the lethal drug into the prisoner's vein. The execution can be watched on a video monitor and can be recorded if necessary. When the procedure is complete, the van simply drives away with its newly deceased cargo. The prisoner will be quickly cremated or, it is often claimed, harvested for viable body parts. This sinister development in China's capital punishment programme has been called 'progress', but others regard the execution bus as the modern equivalent of the phantom coach and horses of popular legend, arriving as if out of nowhere to transport their unwitting passenger into the afterlife, for better or worse.

This book explores the incredible lives and careers of the men and women employed to kill on behalf of the state, as well as those leaders who were ultimately responsible for ordering torture and execution and dreaming up new and creative methods of punishment. We investigate various techniques and the people who championed them, as well as the lives of the victims who, through their own evil-doing or through sheer misfortune, endured the most terrible pain and suffering ever inflicted by man. What, if anything, did they do to deserve it? And what went through the executioner's mind as he delivered the fatal blow?

PART ONE

EARLY FORMS OF EXECUTION

CRUCIFIXION

Crucifixion stands out as one of the most infamous punishments in our history. One that symbolises a religion and is best remembered for one specific act that took place upon a hill named Golgotha outside the walls of Jerusalem about 2,000 years ago: the crucifixion of Jesus of Nazareth. Yet this torturous penalty was a common practice long before the time of Jesus, dating back as far as Babylonian and Egyptian times almost 2,000 years earlier.

Indeed, it was carried out in huge numbers. The Persian emperor, Darius The Great, crucified 3,000 Babylonian captives in 519 BC. Alexander the Great continued the custom during his siege of Tyre in 332 BC executing 2,000 of his enemies. These mass crucifixions pale in comparison, however, with events following the end of the Third Servile War in 71 BC. Two years before, a band of rebel slaves, led by ex-gladiator Spartacus, was successful in threatening the Roman Republic. In retaliation, the senate sent Commander Marcus Licinius Crassus to crush the revolt, resulting in the capture of approximately 6,000 rebels. Crassus ordered them to be executed by way of crucifixion along a 200-kilometre (124-mile) stretch of the Appian Way from Rome to Capua.

Rome, it is thought, acquired this capital punishment from the Carthaginians, who applied the penalty for relatively minor offences. In Carthage, nobody was exempt from the cross. Even their own generals would be nailed to wood following defeat on the battlefield. Rome, however, did not crucify its citizens unless they were convicted of high treason. The punishment was reserved for those most despised by the state. Slaves, rebels, traitors were fodder for the cross. So, too, were the Jews, who were severely persecuted under Roman rule.

Much of what we know about Roman crucifixion comes from the writings of one particular Jew: Josephus – a Judean diarist and historian who later defected to Rome around AD 71. He describes the punishment as, 'the most wretched of deaths' believing suicide to be a more preferable way to die. It was such a feared method that just the threat of crucifixion caused an entire garrison at Machaeus to surrender. Another account from the records of Josephus tells of the Roman siege of Jerusalem in AD 70 in which more than one million people died, the majority of them Jewish. The Romans surrounded the city walls and crucified around 500 Jews a day stopping only when they found they had no more wood for crosses.

Even animals were liable to fall foul of the cross. Pliny the Elder, in his work *Naturalis Historia*, tells of the Battle of the Allia in around 387 BC when a Gallic army was able to invade via the Capitoline Hill due to the lack of warning from the guard dogs of Rome. The Romans were so furious that the dogs were crucified for their lack of vigilance and, from then on, mass canine crucifixions were held upon the hill every year in remembrance.

PRELUDE TO THE CROSS – THE BEGINNING OF THE END

The punishment did not begin with the crucifixion. Before the agony of the cross, the condemned were forced to carry the horizontal cross-beam or *patibulum* weighing approximately 45.3 kilograms (100 pounds) from the prison to beyond the city walls and the execution site. On this final journey past crowds that flocked to jeer the disgraced criminal on their way, the condemned were struck by their guards using whips with small pieces of metal or bone at the tips which ripped chunks of flesh from their bodies, causing heavy loss of blood and, in many cases, severe shock. This was called scourging and many died from this preliminary punishment before even reaching their destination.

On their arrival, the victims were stripped naked and their clothes divided among the unit of soldiers that had led the procession carrying the titulus or small sign on a staff stating the felon's crime. Nailed above the victim's head, this sign would join the condemned upon the cross for all to see.

Before the nailing, the victim would be offered a medicinal brew called 'the sopor' to numb the pain. Far from a miracle aid, its ingredients consisted purely of a cup of vinegar mixed with gall and myrrh. While this seems to conflict with the desire for prolonged suffering, it should be considered that such a potion providing anaesthetic qualities would have potentially forestalled premature death and therefore allowed the condemned to remain conscious during his sentence. This fits the common belief that torture played a large part in crucifixion. Far from just a death penalty, the plan was to subject the body to as much pro-longed physical pain as possible.

NAILED

The victim was then made to stretch out his arms which were then affixed to the cross-beam either by rope or nails. These nails were in fact tapered spikes

21

of up to 18 centimetres (7 inches) in length. They were made of iron – an expensive material at this time – and so were often removed from the dead and re-used or sold as healing amulets.

There are several schools of thought regarding how these nails were applied. The usual depiction of those on the cross has the nails through the hands of the victim, but for this to be feasible there would need to be some method of support by ropes or the inclusion of a footrest or *sedile*; a small seat attached halfway down the vertical beam. Without this, the nails would simply rip through the hands as the weight of the body would be too great. Another belief is that the nails were entered through the wrists between the four carpal bones and two forearm bones as depicted in the Shroud of Turin. Another consideration combines the previous two suggesting the nails went in at the hand at a downward angle passing through the carpal tunnel and, from there, entered the olive post. Whatever the technique, the pain would have been excruciating. Adding insult to injury, it is a distinct possibility that even the victim's genitals were nailed to the *sedile* – far from an aid to support but purely to increase the agony and indeed the shame of the condemned.

THE CROSS

The cross evolved from simple origins. Early crucifixions used trees to crucify their criminals and this was actually called 'fastening to a tree'. It is thought that the Gibeonites' tree-hanging of King Saul's seven children was an early form of crucifixion. It then developed into a single wooden stake planted in the ground, much as Jehovah's witnesses describe Christ's crucifixion. There then came the addition of the horizontal beam which was either fixed at the top of the vertical 'stipes' to form a T-shaped cross (known as the Tau or St Anthony's Cross) or attached slightly further down to create the more familiar Latin cross that became the symbol of Christianity.

In fact, crucifixes were constructed in many different shapes. In addition to the 'T', there existed both 'Y' and 'X'-shaped crosses. The positions in which a victim could be crucified seem to be limited only by the imaginations of the cruel and sadistic rulers of the time. If the usual method of crucifixion was not deemed torturous enough, Roman executioners later took to crucifying the condemned upside down! This is known as the Cross of St Peter after the disciple who requested this amendment because he did not feel worthy enough to die in the same way as Jesus.

DEATH

Death on the cross was far from instantaneous. If the victim managed to survive the scourging along the journey to the execution site followed by the brutal penetration of the nails through extremities, he was in for hours or even days of unbearable suffering.

The cause of death has been a matter of debate. It is widely believed that death came from asphyxiation due to the hyper-expansion of the lungs. To assist breathing, the victim would endeavour to raise his body up by his arms or use the footrest to take the body's weight. This theory has since come under question after experiments apparently showed no inhalation problems while suspended by the arms.

There are accounts of those who survived the cross in the face of such immense pain. Josephus tells of two friends he saw being crucified and, using his sway with the state, managed to obtain the necessary reprieves. During the English Civil War, when crucifixion allegedly made an alarming return under Oliver Cromwell's government, a woman called Agnes Griffin was reported to have been nailed to a tree and forced to eat her own flesh and drink her own blood. Despite enduring such torment, she survived and was even given money by the justices.

However, these cases were few and far between. Crucifixion was intended to be a capital punishment and so death to the condemned was, for the most part, inevitable. The bodies would be allowed to decay upon the cross. This was the final insult. In ancient times, burial was an act assigning honour to the dead. To be left above the earth to endure the weather and mutilation from the circling vultures was deemed a great dishonour and, to a Jew, would mean the dead remained 'under God's curse'.

Crucifixion, then, was a comprehensive method of punishment intending not only to humiliate and inflict pain upon the condemned but with the public nature of the whole process. From carrying the crossbeam past the heckling crowds to the slow deaths beyond the city walls, it acted as a deterrent to all would-be dissenters and wrongdoers of the time. It also provided a lawful avenue for the savage degenerate to create imaginative methods of inducing the most amount of pain. This avenue was finally closed with the eventual abolition of crucifixion during the reign of Constantine I when, in c.337 AD, Christianity became the state religion.

STONING

'He that is without sin among you,
let him cast the first stone'
JOHN: 8.7

Born out of a need for community justice, stoning, or lapidation is the oldest form of capital punishment. It is at least as old as written language and the most common method of execution meted out in the Bible. It is mentioned in Greek history as well as Christian, Jewish and Islamic texts.

STONING IN JUDAISM

There is evidence to suggest that the Jews were the first people to practise stoning. The Torah, like the Koran, describes God-approved punishments for particular sins. The punishment known as 'sekila' (or stoning) is set aside in the Torah for serious sexual and religious crimes such as incest, bestiality, idolatry, sourcery and witchcraft. Lewis's *Origins of the Hebrews*, describes the following horrific execution from biblical times:

When the offender came within four cubits of the place of execution he was stripped naked, only leaving a place before, and his hands being bound, he was led up to the fatal place, which was in eminence twice a man's height. The first executioners were the witnesses, who generally pulled off their clothes for the purpose: one of them threw him down with great violence upon his loins; if he rolled upon his breast, he was rolled upon his loins again, and if he died by the fall there was an end. But not if the other witnesses took a great stone, and dashed it upon his breast as he lay upon his back, and then if he was not dispatched, all the people who stood by threw stones at him until he was dead.'

Although Jewish religious law officially approves the use of sekila, no Rabbinal courts today administer sentences involving any form of capital punishment.

STONING IN CHRISTIANITY

Christians have come in for (and have also been responsible for) some pretty brutal executions throughout history. St Stephen was the first Christian to die for his faith, he was tried by the Sanhedin for blaspheming against Moses and God, and stoned to death by an angry mob outside the city walls. As a result, he is often depicted in art clutching three stones in his palm.

In seventeenth century Italy, Giovanni Pelanchion refused to convert to Papism, and as a result he was tied by one leg to the tail of a mule and dragged through the streets of Lucerne while being stoned by the townspeople. They believed that the devil possessed him and kept him alive using evil powers, so they took Giovanni to the riverside and chopped off his head, whereby the devil promptly gave him up. Giovanni died on the riverbank and was left there to rot, unburied.

DEATH IN THE PILLORY

Although stoning has never been widely practised in Britain, sometimes an hour in the pillory amounted to the same thing. During the seventeenth, eighteenth and nineteenth centuries, prisoners who were sentenced to a spell in the pillory had more to worry about than rotten tomatoes. Criminals convicted of attempted sodomy, seditious words, extortion, fraud and perjury were punished pubicly in an attempt to discredit their reputations. Pillories were built in busy places such as Charing Cross in London, where crowds could easily gather. The prisoner was placed on a raised platform with his head and arms secured in a wooden structure.

The pillory was positioned so that crowds could gather on all sides of the platform and pelt their victim with various missiles including rotten vegetables and eggs, blood and guts from slaughterhouses, dead animals, mud, excrement and even bricks and stones. Many people died as a result. The highwaymen and murderers Egan and Salmon were subjected to the pillory on Park Lane in London in March 1756. This account is given in the *Newgate Calendar*:

Egan and Salmon were taken to Smithfield amidst a surprising concourse of people, who no sooner saw the offenders exposed on the pillory, than they pelted them with stones, brickbats, potatoes, dead dogs and cats, oyster shells and other things. The constables now interposed but, being soon overpowered the offenders were left to the mercy of the enraged mob. The blows they received occasioned their heads to swell to an enormous size; and by the people hanging on to the skirts of their clothing they were near strangled. They had been on the pillory for about half an hour when a stone struck Egan on the head, and he immediately expired.

It is interesting to note that Salmon, Egan's partner in crime, was not much luckier than him. On that occasion the ordeal in the pillory halted with Egan's violent death, but Salmon died in squalor at Newgate Gaol soon afterwards.

STONING: THE TECHNIQUE

Stoning is an unusual method of execution because it involves the community directly in the kill instead of a single executioner. For this reason it bares some similarities with the most contemporary form of execution: lethal injection.

DEATH BY COLLECTIVE

Lethal injection involves as many as three technicians but only one of them actually administers the fatal dose – the other two carry dummy doses. None of the technicians will ever find out which one of them administered the poison. In the same way, the 'inclusive' nature of stoning means that none of the participants will ever know which stone struck the fatal blow. If a judge and jury can be said to deliver the 'people's' verdict, than death by stoning ensures that the people, rather than the court, the government or the prison warden, literally deliver the sentence. The problem with this is that it implicates the entire community – making murderers out of everybody, even if it does so with the approval of God himself.

THE FESTIVAL OF GOTMAR MELA

The festival of Gotmar is staged the day after the Krishna Paksha 'amavasya', during the Hindu month of Bhadon. It is a festival 'celebrated' by the inhabitants of Savargoan and Pandhurna near the city of Chindwara, India. Gotmar literally translates as 'hitting with pellets', and the name describes exactly what happens during the festival. Over 5,000 people gather to throw stones at each other. The story behind the festival is an ancient and a fascinating one:

In olden times (the exact period is unknown), the ruler of Pandhurna got to hear about the beautiful daughter of the raja of the nighbouring town of Savagaon on the other side of the river Jam. He successfully crossed the river and abducted this lady from the palace of Savagaon. But the people of Savagaon became aware of this and chased the abductor, pelting him with rocks as he crossed the river. The people of Pandhurna were gathered on the riverside and, seeing their leader attacked with rocks, began retaliating. The raja of Pandhurna was success-ful in reaching the other side of the river, and for this reason it is thought that he had the protection of the goddess Chandi.

The Gotmar festival is held each year to com-memorate the incident. It is estimated that between

750 and 900 people are injured in the skirmishes every year and inevitably some are killed, the violence being fuelled with illegal alcohol. In recent years, attempts have been made to ban the festival, or at least to ensure that alcohol is not available to buy on the day, but still the people of Pandhurna and Savargaon insist on celebrating Gotmar. The injured go immediately to a local temple hoping to be miraculously healed by the goddess Chandi.

WIDESPREAD CONDEMNATION

Many human rights organisations such as Amnesty International have long condemned the use of stoning as particularly barbaric, and the fact that it is most often employed as a punishment for so-called moral crimes (such as prostitution or adultery) rather than those most would consider to be serious crimes (such as murder, drug dealing or rape) makes this form of punishment even more controversial in the eyes of western governments. International pressure means that often in these cases a stoning sentence is passed, but later quashed or commuted to a lesser punishment such as lashes or a prison sentence.

There are no non-religious courts left in the world that legally recognise this form of punishment. The United Nations has concluded that treating adultery or consensual fornication as a criminal offence goes against international standards of human rights. However, it has been, and is to a lesser extent, still in use in areas of the Middle East and sub-Saharan Africa where sharia law is practised.

STONING IN SHARIA LAW

Sharia law literally translates as 'The Path to the Water Source' and it denotes a system of criminal justice, but it is actually meant as a code for living. Many Muslims believe that sharia law is a necessary factor in the life of a good Muslim. Under sharia there are a number of crimes known as Hadd offences. These are crimes which carry certain pre-ordained penalties such as stoning, lashes or amputation. These penalties have apparently been laid out in the Koran by the prophet Mohammed, and they apply to crimes such as unlawful intercourse, false accusation of unlawful intercourse, the drinking of alcohol, theft and highway robbery. More women than men tend to be accused, tried and found guilty of unlawful inter-course and therefore they are more likely to fall victim to this most violent punishment.

STONING OR CRUSHING?

Some historical references to stoning actually pertain to the practise of crushing a victim to death using large, heavy stones. This technique was once used for torture in British prisons, but for the purpose of the book we have covered executions of this type in *Piene Forte Et Dure* on pages 274–83.

The most common stoning method puts the emphasis well and truly on a slow and painful death, rather than quick and painless euthanasia. It is important that the prisoner does suffer. Typically the victim's hands are tied behind their back and they are wrapped head to toe in white cloth. Then they are partially buried in the ground in order to keep them still. A male prisoner is buried up to the waist and a female is usually buried up to her shoulders or her neck. Then a circle is drawn around the prisoner and the congregation are asked to select stones which are small enough that they could not cause death with a single blow, but big enough to inflict significant harm. The congregation take their positions on the outside of the circle, and the victim is then pelted with stones until they are obviously dead. Death is eventually caused either by excessive blood loss or serious head trauma. The process is extremely painful and it can take up to an hour for death to occur. Sometimes the victims parents, their spouse and even their children are forced to witness the killing.

IRAQ

Stoning was still in use in some parts of Iraq as recently as May 2007. 17-year-old Du'a Khalil Aswad had been born and brought up within a Kurdish religious group called Yezidi. She had the misfortune to meet and fall in love with a boy from a sunni- muslim background. As a result of this relationship, Du'a was condemend to death by male members of her family and hard-line religious leaders, in the belief that she had shamed them by failing to return home one night. Some reports suggested she had also converted to Islam in order to be closer to her boyfriend. Du'a sought shelter in the house of a Yezidi tribal leader in Bashika, a Kurdish town near the northern capital of Mosul. A large crowd gathered to watch as eight or nine men stormed the house and dragged the young woman out into the street. They pelted her with rocks for half an hour until she was killed. A month later a video of the execution appeared on the Internet.

IRAN

Officially, the administration in Tehran called a

moratorium on stoning in 2002, but Ammesty International and other human-rights groups claim that the practise continues to this day. In 2005, the organisation Women Against Fundamentalism in Iran, claimed that there had been ten stonings during the first six months of 2002, and a further twenty-six reported cases of stoning between 2002 and 2005 – seventeen of those victims were women and the majority were convicted of unlawful intercourse.

According to the Women Against Fundamentalism website, article 99 of the Islamic Punishment Act stipulates that:

Whenever the act of adultery is confirmed based on his or her own testimony, during the stoning process, the religious judge should throw the first stone and the others follow. But if adultery is confirmed based on the testimony of witnesses, first the witnessness throw stones and then the religious judge and subsequently the others.

The act stipulates that no less than three believers should be present while the sentence is carried out. Interestingly, it also states that, in the unlikely event that the prisoner manages to pull themselves out of the ditch, the stoning should be called off. In some countries if this happens the condmened is usually shot dead as they make their escape.

In October 2004, it was reported in the international press that thirteen-year-old Zhila Izadi from the north-western city of Marivan in Iran, had been condemned to death by stoning having been raped by her fifteen-year-old brother, Bakhtiar. She was found to be pregnant with his child, and her devout father, believing that her daughter had bought shame on the family, turned her in to the local authorities. Campaigning by organisations such as Amnesty International and the International Commitee Against Stoning saw her sentence reduced from death by stoning to fifty-five lashes, matching her brother's sentence, though she received these while she was heavily pregnant. The young woman gave birth to her child days later while in prison.

NIGERIA

Sharia law was introduced in some areas of Northern Nigeria in 2002. The most famous case involving stoning in Nigeria is that of Amina Lawal who was found guilty under sharia law of having unlawful sex when she conceived a child out of wedlock. The case was eventually quashed at appeal when it was established that Amina was already pregnant when the law came into force. Lawal's case became the focus of human-rights organisations all over the world. Despite the fact that Amina's freedom was actually secured on a technicality, rather than an ideological U-turn, Lawal's lawyer hailed the result as a victory for justice. There were some spectators at the trial who disagreed with the court's verdict. One man who had come to hear the ruling said: 'I would have preferred Amina to be stoned to death. She deserves it.'

HUMAN SACRIFICE

Today we see human sacrifice as the stuff of old-fashioned children's picture books. The enduring image of a safari-suit-clad explorer crouched, sweating and petrified in an oversized cauldron, has come to represent an anachronisitc and bigoted western view of indigenous peoples and their customs.

In fact, human sacrifice has been practised by people in many parts of the world. It was not reserved for 'bloodthirsty primitives', but formed an important part of sophisticated belief systems within many societies, including those that have evolved to form our own.

It would not be outlandish to claim that any war motivated by religion also involves an element of human sacrifice because blood is inevitably spilled in order to strengthen a belief system or a way of life. The Crusades of the middle ages, the holocaust of World War II, the attacks of 11 September 2001 on the USA and the subsequent invasion of Iraq and Afghanistan all involved the sacrifice of human life. At least some of those who died in the wake of these terrible events believed that they would be rewarded in the afterlife, just as an Mayan slave whose heart was ripped from his body in a sacrificial ceremony believed he would bypass many phases of the Aztec purgatory and be transported directly to paradise.

In many cases, the line between execution for the sake of punishment and execution for ritual sacrifice has become blurred. Criminals and captives were often chosen for religious sacrifice simply because they were the members of any society most easily disposed of, as were (sadly) illegitimate children and unmarried men and women. On the other hand, many victims of punishment executions died purely because of their religious beliefs and refusal to deny their faith – even on pain of death. The Christian martyrs come under this category.

The following pages explore human sacrifice of various types. For the purpose of this book a human sacrifice is defined according to the motives of the executioner and the society or group that condones the killing. In a human sacrifice, the executioner is almost always a religious leader, a highly respected member of the community rather than an employee of the government or prison system. He or she occupies a completely different position in the community from one who executed his victims according to the will of a judge and jury. Instead of a life of isolation and secrecy, the life of one of these religious leaders was often one of privilege and power and although the names of many of these priests and holy men have been erased over the centuries – their many brutal acts have become legendary.

There are three main types of human sacrifice evident in history. They are ritual, cannibalistic and retainer sacrifice.

RITUAL HUMAN SACRIFICE

Ritual human sacrifice involves the killing of a human being in order that the victim's body or lifeblood can be offered to a supernatural force. Most participants believing that the strength and happiness of their gods, and consequently that of the people, depend upon human bloodshed. The Meso-Americans were prolific in their ritual sacrifice of captives and commoners to their vast pantheon of gods, and it was looked upon as an integral part of their worship. The ancient Chinese and the Celts believed likewise.

EAT YOUR HEART OUT

Cannibalistic human sacrifice involves killing a person in order to invoke the powers of the Gods or ancestors through the consumption of various body parts, or to punish an evil-doer. The reasons for consuming human organs are usually spiritual, but in societies where people rely on hunting for meat and do not keep livestock, human meat from sacrificial victims might form the main source of protein and animal fats for those privileged enough to receive it. The people of the Kombai who live in the jungles of Papua have been known to kill and cannibalise people they deem to be witches, or Khakhua-Kumu. They believe that these people eat the souls of their victims, and the only way to punish them properly is to kill and eat them. As the soul is perceived to dwell in the brain and in the stomach, it is these body parts which must be eaten. There are men still living within the Kombai tribe who have killed and eaten male witches.

TAKING ONE FOR THE TEAM

Retainer sacrifice involves killing important or useful members of the household belonging to a dead patriarch, king or nobleman in order that they might continue to serve him in the next world. This was perhaps the most widely practised form of human sacrifice – many cultures adopted the practise, including the Vikings, the Egyptians, the Romans and the Greeks. Servants, concubines, wives and employees considered it a great honour to accompany their lord and master into the afterlife, and were willing to die in order to continue serving him. Perhaps they were so willing because the alternative was often a future of slavery, extreme poverty and eventual death through malnutrition or disease.

PROPAGANDA?

It is important to remember that stories of human sacrifice often come from invaders of that particular society. These people would have been keen to portray themselves as vastly more civilised and superior to the 'primitive natives' they had come to conquer. Therefore many historians are sceptical about the true role of human sacrifice within these ancient civilisations. In the years following their invasion of Britain, the Romans invested a lot of energy in accusing the Druids of incredible evil towards the Celts. Stories of enormous fires on which were thrown women and children for the appeasement of the pagan gods filtered back to Rome, in the same manner that Polish immigrants to Britain were occasionally accused of eating babies in the years following World War II. It is also worth noting that during a large-scale invasion, religious scriptures, ceremonial artefacts and other important cultural items were often wiped from the face of the earth. When the Spanish Conquistadors invaded South America they burnt as many sacred books as they could get their hands on, obliterating centuries of history because they believed them to be the work of Satan. The Romans destroyed or bastardised Pagan religious sites in order to introduce their religion of choice: Christianity. Therefore the real role played by human sacrifice within these long-dead civilisations can never be fully understood.

Hard evidence of these practises does exist in many places. One thing is for certain; the concept of human sacrifice is certainly ancient and has its roots in reality, even if the actual occurrences were in fact more rare than we've previously been led to believe.

THE BINDING OF ISAAC

All three abrahmic religions (Christianity, Judaism and Islam) feature the story of the binding of Isaac. According to this story God (also called Yanweh or Allah, depending on the chosen version) ordered Abraham to slaughter his favourite son Isaac in the land of Moriah. Abraham and Isaac travelled for three days until they came to a hill. Their servant remained at the foot of the hill while Abraham and Isaac proceeded alone, Isaac carrying the wood upon which he was due to be sacrificed. During the journey Isaac repeatedly asked Abraham where the animal for the burnt offering was. Abraham then replied (somewhat ominously) that God would provide one. Just as Abraham was about to kill Isaac, he was stopped by an angel and given a ram which he sacrificed in place of his precious son. Thus it is said, 'On the mountain the Lord provides' (Genesis 22). As a reward for his obedience he received a promise of numerous seed and abundant prosperity. Many followers of the abrahmic religions consider it important that God stayed the hand of Abraham and did not actually require him to go ahead with Issac's murder. For believers, this proves that theirs is a merciful and gentle God who does not harm his followers unecessarily. However, the very fact that

Abraham of the story was not utterly dumbfounded by God's demand for blood demonstrates that it was once a commonly held belief that the sacrifice of an eldest son or virgin daughter may place you firmly in the Lord's good books.

Perhaps the most important human sacrifice included in the Bible is that of Jesus himself, who Christians believe gave his life to ease the debt of human sin. Many believers would not consider this a true human sacrifice because Jesus was not human as such, but rather an incarnation of God in human form. Also, his tormentors were not of the conviction that God would be appeased by the death of his only son – so they were not conciously offering up his soul to a supernatural being, merely punishing him in the same manner as they punished common criminals. Nevertheless there was certainly an exchange of sorts taking place in the eyes of Christians. According to the Bible's teachings Jesus went to his death at the hands of the Roman authorities so that God could forgive humankind of our sins against him (See 'Crucifixion' on pages 18–25).

The Christian ritual partaking of the holy communion, or eucharist, is a symbolic re-enactment of this momentous exchange. During communion, Christians eat of the body and drink of the blood of Christ in exchange for God's absolution, and as a reminder of his supreme sacrifice for our sins. This ritual could be interpreted as having roots in cannibalistic sacrifice because in consuming the body and blood of Christ, Christians expect to embibe something of his spirit.

Of course, over the centuries many Christians, Jews and Muslims have sacrificed themselves and others in the name of religion – and some continue to do so to this day. How this differs fundamentally from the examples we are about to explore, or whether the latter-day al-Qaeda suicide bomber is really very different from a Medieval Catholic martyr or a Mayan sacrificial victim is a controversial subject more suitable for discussion in another book.

THE CELTS

There is strong evidence that ritual human sacrifice took place in ancient Celtic society. It should be pointed out that much of the surviving written evidence comes from the Roman invaders, who would have had a political agenda. Nevertheless, writers such as Strabo and Diodorus Siculus maintained that a normal Celtic sacrifice involved striking a man who had been consecrated for sacrifice in the back with a sword, and making prophecies based on his death throes. These killings would not have been carried out unless a druid (a Celtic priest) was present to officiate, though it is unclear whether the druid himself would strike the death blow. According to Strabo other methods of sacrifice involved shooting with arrows, impalement, or the burning of humans on a huge fire of wood and straw, along with livestock and various wild animals.

It is certainly worth noting that no evidence for the Celtic use of bows and arrows has ever been found by archaeologists. The Celts were not keen archers and the Celtic words for bow and arrow were adopted from Latin and Norse, so it is likely that this was an invented rumour based in Roman political propaganda.

THE WICKER MAN – FACT OR FICTION?

Julius Caesar personally accused the people of Gaul of building huge human effegies from wood, the limbs of which were filled up with living people and set alight. In *Commentarii de Bello Gallico* (Commentary on the Gallic Wars) written between 58 and 45 BC, he claimed that those chosen for such a fate were usually thieves and petty criminals as these pleased the gods most, but when stocks of petty criminals ran low, innocents were sacrificed in the same manner. There is more actual evidence for this method of sacrifice than for Strabo's bow and arrow nonsense.

The notion of a 'wicker man' has become an enduring part of Celtic heritage – the image of a large god-like effigy turning up in blockbuster films, poetry, folk art and scuplture as well as neopagan festivals. This symbol of Celtic heritage has been enjoying something of a resurgence for sometime now – leading many to believe that the wicker man is just a sensational invention by the Victorians to romanticise our shared past. In fact, a variation on the wicker man can be found in many places, including Irish and Welsh legend.

A story included in the second branch of the ancient Welsh book, *The Mabinogi*, describes an unusually cruel form of punishment whereby the victims were enclosed in an iron chamber and given an abundance of alcohol. While the victims were getting drunk, the village blacksmiths gathered to build a huge charcoal fire around the chamber, gradually heating the iron chamber until it became white-hot – slowly roasting the unfortunate inhabitants.

Whether this method was ever actually employed is a matter for debate. One imagines that the building of an iron chamber large enough to house a human would be expensive and elaborate in the extreme, not to mention the effort involved in gathering enough local blacksmiths to build and feed the fire until it was hot enough to cook people alive! However, evidence for the existence of the Brazen Bull (see Phalaris on pages 65–69) suggests that similar contraptions were built and used by other cultures, so perhaps it is not beyond the realms of possibility.

TERANIS: GOD OF THUNDER

The Celts worshipped three main gods and each required a different kind of sacrifice. According to ancient Celtic legend, Teranis, the god of thunder, required his sacrifical victims to be burnt alive in giant wicker cages. It is not a huge leap from giant wicker baskets to wicker 'men', built as a likeness of Teranis. This seems a more likely form of punishment than the iron chamber described in *The Mabinogi*.

THE LINDOW BOGMAN

The strongest evidence that the Celts were exponants of ritual human sacrifice was dicovered in 1983, when a English man named Andy Mould found the body of a man buried in Lindow bog during the first century AD. The body was so well preserved that it was possible to ascertain his last meal and the nature of his death. The Lindow bogman was struck three times on the head with a blunt object (probably an axe), strangled using a thin cord which closed the windpipe and broke two upper vertebrae, and had his throat cut in quick succession before being thrown into the bog. This pattern fits with the threefold method of human sacrifice often described in Celtic legend. The Celts believed, as Christians do, that the number three was a sacred number, coinciding with their three most powerful Gods, Teranis, Esus and Teutates. Teranis required his victims to be burnt to death, but sometimes a weapon like an axe made a suitable substitute. Esus was the god of the underworld – his sacrificial victims were usually hung from trees, stabbed to death or strangled in some manner, Teutates was the god of the tribe and required his victim to be drowned. The manner of Lindow bogman's death may have been planned as a sacrifice to all three gods at once. His throat was most likely cut immediately after death in order to drain the blood from his body – another sign that his death was carefully planned and executed for ritual purposes. The blood was probably collected in a vessel, whereby it was offered to the gods, or imbibed by the officiating druid.

UNUSUAL FINDINGS

During the investigation into the case of the Lindow bogman scientists made a number of other interesting discoveries. Firstly, the Lindow man had worn a beard – facial hair is almost unheard of in other bog bodies. His hair had been cut a few days before his death, his fingernails were clean and he was taller than average – 170 centimetres (5 ft 7 in). These observations led scientists to believe that the bogman was a privileged member of society, the clean fingernails and evidence of grooming meant he was not a labourer, and the lack of injuries (apart from those he incurred during death) meant that he was not a warrior either. The archaeologists concluded that the Lindow bogman was either an aristocrat, a druid or a king who had probably been chosen for sacrifice during the summer festival of Beltane.

<u>BELTANE</u>

The Beltane festival took place on 1 May and marked the centre point on the Celtic calendar between the vernal equinox and the summer solstice, like the festival of Samhain (the ancient Celtic equivalent of halloween). The festival of Beltane was seen as a time of year when the other world and its inhabitants were particularly close at hand. It was treated as an ideal time for transition and purification. Traditionally, Beltane included a human sacrifice in order to ensure a good summer's harvest. Historians believe that the ceremony began with the building of a large bonfire. In the fire, an oatmeal cake called a *bannock* was baked and a small portion of it was deliberately charred. The bannock was broken into small pieces, put in a bag and passed around. The unfortunate person who chose the charred piece of bread became the sacrifical victim, and was usually burnt on the bonfire. The Lindow bog man's last meal was found to be a charred oatmeal substance, but he had escaped a death by fire – why?

Prominent archaeologist Anne Ross believes that the Lindow bogman was certainly a prominent member of society – either a druid priest or a king, who chose to be sacrificed in AD 60, in order to stave off violent attacks by the Romans who were attempting to wipe out the Celts around this time. Given his position in society, it is unlikely that he would have been sacrificed in the same manner as a commoner – and a more respectful execution was planned instead.

In a way, the Lindow bogman succeeded in his mission to ensure that the Celtic traditions lived on. If Andy Mould had not found the remains of the Lindlow bogman on that summer's day in 1983, perhaps an important element of Celtic history, that of the Beltane sacrificial ritual, would have been lost forever.

THE VIKINGS

The Vikings have lived on in the history books as a people committed to bloodthirsty and depraved violence. Life for a typical Viking was hard and short. The ancient Norse people worshipped a pantheon of war-like gods, and like many other civilisations, they believed in spilling human blood in order to ensure abundant crops, victory in battle and the continuing health and wealth of their people.

THE CULT OF THE VOLVAS

The volvas were a group of high priestesses who were considered by some to be higher in status even than the gods themselves. An old Norse story describes Odin (head of all Norse Gods) consulting a volva for advice, whereby she taunts him – unafraid of his wrath. The volvas are generally portrayed as aged women who dressed in white robes – a Viking forerunner to our witch, and one of their main roles was to predict the future. A human sacrifice, usually a prisoner of war, was awarded to the volva's. They would sprinkle his blood in order to prophesy coming events during a ceremony or 'Blot'.

BLOT

The blot was a sacramental meal or feast with a sacrifice at its centre, called a 'blota'. The oldest form of the word 'blot' means 'to summon with incantations', 'to worship with sacrifice' or 'to strengthen'. Often the sacrifice would have consisted of animals – a pig or a horse, but occasionally, perhaps when trouble was close at hand, or the gods were particularly needful, a prisoner would be sacrificed in the same manner. The meat was boiled in large cooking pits with heated stones, either indoors or out. As in many other cultures, the blood was thought to have special powers and was sprinkled on statues of the gods, on walls and on the attendees at the feast, using specially made blot-brushes. Such a festival must have been spectacularly grisly to behold.

The number nine had magical significance in Norse mythology, and although different regions practised blot in different ways, the number nine was significant for all, so every nine years all Viking communities would stage some form of sacrifice, often involving humans – sometimes as many as ninety-nine prisoners would be executed and their remains offered to one of the three major gods – Odin, Frey or Thor, depending on the particular circumstances.

THE ANCIENT CHINESE

The Chinese of the Shang dynasty (1600–1046 BC) and the Zhou dynasty (1122–255 BC), worshipped a combination of nature gods ranging from forest imps to hill gods, earth gods, sky gods, wind gods, river maidens and rain spirits.

THE BRIDES OF THE YELLOW RIVER

The kings of these early dynasties worshipped a special god named the 'Gatherer of the Clouds', otherwise known as a mighty rain god, who was often depicted in dragon form. This cloud gatherer required a sacrifice in order to guarantee good fishing for the year to come, along with an abundance of rain. A richly clad young girl would be made to lay in a raft of her bridal bed and be cast out into the Yellow River to perish alone. An traditional song was sung as the ceremony took place, the lyrics of which remain hauntingly resonant today.

You mount the white turtle, Oh!
your train is striped fish!
I rove with you, Oh!
by the aisles of the Ho.
In the chaos of the sweeping thaw, Oh!

down we shall go.
We join our hands, Oh!
as eastward we move.
They escort the lovely one, Oh!
to the south estuary.
Waves in steady surge, Oh!
come to welcome us –
Fish in swishing tumult, Oh!
are bridesmaids to me.

Regular sacrifices were also made to the gods of war in order to guarantee victory in battle, and in honour of long dead ancestors in order to gain a connection with the heavens. The executioners used a bronze yueh axe (a ceremonial weapon) to behead their victims. The axe featured a very large blade which was often assymetric in shape and elaborately decorated, sometimes inset with precious stones.

MAYAN HUMAN SACRIFICE

To understand the Mayan's use of ritual human sacrifice, and the individuals who were responsible for carrying it out, it's worth looking briefly at the unusual and complex structure of their universe.

THE MAYAN UNIVERSE

The Mayans believed that the earth was flat, something like the back of a crocodile resting in a pool of waterlilies. This mythical crocodile had a counterpart in the sky which took the form of a double-headed serpent. They believed that the sky itself was multi-layered, and that four strong and powerful gods called *bacabs* kept the sky suspended above the people, preventing it from falling in and destroying the earth beneath.

According to ancient Mayan teachings, their gods had already destroyed and recreated the universe a

number of times. This meant that any natural disaster –
such as a violent storm, a hurricane or a flood – struck
fear into the people because they thought that the gods
may have become angry or even bored, and decided
simply to wipe them out and start all over again.

OUT OF CONTROL

It's likely that the resulting atmosphere of mass-
hysteria, coupled with the shamans' use of mind-
altering substances such as pulque (an alcoholic drink
made from maize and agave), the leaves of wild tobacco
plants and hallucinogenic mushrooms led the Mayans
down the path of human sacrifice as a way of exerting
some control over the elements, or at least creating the
feeling that they were asserting themselves.

A PANTHEON OF GODS

The Mayans worshipped a large number of different
gods and goddesses – at least 166 named deities – and
each one required love and nourishment in order to
ensure the health and wealth of the people. The
people's devotion needed demonstrating. This could
take many forms, but the most extreme was that of
bloodletting and human sacrifice.

Mayan shamans controlled learning and ritual and

were in charge of calculating time, festivals and ceremonies, fateful days and events, curing disease, writing and genealogies. The priesthood were not celibate, and the role was usually passed down through the generations from father to son. The Mayan year was dictated by a 260-day sacred round calendar and their rituals were based around this calendar which was controlled, like most everything else, by members of the priesthood.

BLOODLETTING

Many Mayan rituals involved self mutilation and bloodletting in order to annoint religious objects. The motive for the ritual dictated where on the body blood was taken from, and what kind of sacrifice was made. The head of most Mayan households would give a small amount of blood every single night in order to stave off disaster.

The Mayan elite were obsessed with blood, both their own and that of their captives. As the Mayan civilisation began to fall, kings of various territories rushed from city to city performing desperate bloodletting rights in order to invoke the protection of their gods. Some have argued that the reason for this bloodlust lies with the fact that meat was extremely scarce, and the people malnourished to the point of lunacy. Human sacrifice may have provided the Mayan aristocracy with their only reliable source of protein.

FERTILITY RITUAL

In one particularly eyewatering fertility ritual, a king would use a stingray spine or an obsidian knife to make an incision in his penis before drawing a piece of rope through the wound in order to increase blood flow. He allowed the blood to collect on a piece of paper in a bowl. The paper would then be burnt, releasing human energy skyward and thus offering it as a sacrifice to the heavens in return for a son. It was believed that the gods could be seen in the smoke, communicating messages to their living subjects and issuing demands.

The Mayan kings were able to do this, not because they had extraordinarily high pain thresholds, but through the use of potent hallucinogenic drugs, which propelled them to a place where pain no longer mattered very much.

When a king acceded the throne, a captive would be sacrificed to the gods in order to cement the new king's position. This was the most important ritual in a king's life as it was the point at which he inherited the throne and became leader of his city.

Human sacrifice was routinely practised on prisoners, slaves, orphans and illegitimate children who were specifically purchased for this prupose. The priests would gather on elevated platforms or on top of pyramids so that the people could gather beneath them to witness the special event. The priests were assisted in the sacrifice by four older men called *chacs* (after the Mayan rain god). These men would hold the arms and legs of a sacrificial victim while another man called a *nacom* opened up the chest. A shaman or chilam was also in attendance – he conversed with the gods in a trance-like state and relayed messages which were interpreted by the gathered priests.

THE SACRIFICIAL VICTIM

In this most exotic of rituals, the prisoner was first painted blue, and held over a sacrificial table by the chacs. The position of the alter meant that the prisoners chest was thrust upwards, making the following procedure easier to carry out. The prisoner's chest was opened up, usually using a sharpened stone, and the heart was removed by the officiating priest. He then held it up above his head while it continued to beat, so that the crowd below could see it. Then h deposited the heart in a stone vessel which was h by another man who lay next to the sacrificial

PHALARIS

Some powerful men cast a shadow over history. In many circles, they are written about and spoken of as progressive, intellectual renaissance men who worked tirelessly towards technological advancement, and ultimately for the good of their people. They are sometimes even regarded as heroic figures in their nation's past, but scratch the surface and you will quickly unearth a different story, one of violence and cruelty involving cannibalism, ritual killing, genocide, institutionalised child molestation and a whole host of other bloodthirsty and depraved acts.

Occasionally the reverse happens. A historical figure we perceive to be a murderous maniac will be revealed as a secret opera fan or crochet addict. It is well known that Adolph Hitler was a vegetarian and a keen painter, and the reason we find this odd is because it's so difficult to marry Adolph the evil tyrant with Adolph the vegetable-loving, watercolourist. In these cases, it is often difficult to decipher which is truth and which fiction, but it's likely there are elements of truth in both versions.

THE HANNIBAL LECTAR EFFECT

Hannibal Lectar, the cannabilistic psychopath in *Silence of the Lambs*, is a fictional manifestation of one of these characters, made all the more terrifying and dangerous by his apparent sophistication and capacity for intellectual thought. Phalaris, the tyrant of Acragas, demonstrated the 'Hannibal Lectar effect'. Like Adolph Hitler, Vlad the Impaler, Ivan the Terrible and Saddam Hussein, Phalaris was a wolf in sheep's clothing – a monster disguised as a diplomat.

PHALARIS: THE DIPLOMAT

Phalaris has been credited with some very significant achievements. He was entrusted with the building of the Temple of Zeus Polieus in the citadel of the city, and took advantage of this position to rise to power in this part of Sicily. According to a later story, told by Polyaenus, Phalaris actually armed his labourers, effectively turning them into an army that occupied the citadel. It is however true that, once under his leadership, the city of Acragas enjoyed relative prosperity. He single-handedly supplied the city with water by building an aquaduct, adorned it with other fine buildings and built defensive walls around Acragas in order to keep it safe from invaders. On the northern coast of the island he was elected general with absolute power – and by adopting an expansionist foreign policy (invading other Sicilian towns and cities) he eventually succeeded in making himself ruler of the whole island.

PHALARIS: THE MONSTER

However, despite his many achievements, Phalaris has become infamous as the prototype evil dictator who, among other things, enjoyed feasting on the flesh of suckling babies. Of course, it is very possible that these rumours of cannibalism were the invention of political enemies of Phalaris, who were attempting to cast him as nothing more than a bloodthirsty barbarian. It is also possible that Phalaris himself encouraged others to think of him in this light – afterall it takes a brave man to willingly attack someone mad enough to eat human baby flesh! One thing is for sure – cannibal or not – Phalaris definitely seems to have had a taste for the exotic when it came to torture and execution.

THE BRAZEN BULL

As ruler of Sicily, Phalaris commissioned Perilaus, a well-known bronze-worker from Athens, to invent for him a new form of punishment. The result has gone down in legend as the Brazen Bull of Phalaris, and is still included in countless on-line lists of 'the most horrible way a human being can die'. Perilaus cast a life-sized brazen bull with a door in the side. The victim was forced to climb into the contraption, and then the bull was locked up and a large fire was built around its base. The fire was lit and continuously fed while the prisoner slowly roasted to death. Perilous indeed!

In a stroke of sheer engineering genius, the nostrils of the bull were so contrived with acoustic mechanisms that the groans of the sufferer resembled the bellows of a mad bull. Phalaris commended the invention, and then ordered Perilaus to be the first to test it out. When the bronze-worker climbed inside the Brazen Bull, Phalaris is said to have slammed the hatch shut behind him and lit a fire. Some stories claim that Phalaris took pity on the half-dead artisan and removed him from the bull, throwing him off a nearby cliff to finish the job in a quick and efficient manner. Others end this harrowing story with Phalaris enjoying the death-cries of Perilaus as he roasted alive within the white-hot walls of his own design.

It is quite likely that the Brazen Bull was used by Phalaris to sacrifice prisoners to his gods. It is true that human sacrifice was not uncommon in Carthage and Western Sicily. Sicilian rivers were often represented as bulls with human heads, so it would follow that Phalaris used his brazen bull to sacrifice people to a local river god. It is also true that the Pheonician Baal (Zeus Atabyrius), was sometimes worshipped in the form of a bull.

The fate of Phalaris was much like that of other tyrants such as Saddam, Adolph and Vlad. He was eventually overthrown in an uprising headed by Telemachus and put to death. He was apparently roasted alive in the very contraption that would make him so infamous.

BURIED ALIVE

To die is natural; but the living death
Of those who waken into conciousness,
Though for a moment only, ay, or less,
To find a coffin stifling their last breath,
Surpasses every horror underneath,
The sun of heaven, and should surely check,
Haste in the living to remove the wreck,
Of what was just before, the soul's fair sheath,
How many have been smothered in their shroud!
How many have sustained this awful woe!
Humanity would shudder could we know
How many have cried to God in anguish loud
Accusing those whose haste a wrong had wrought,
Beyond the worst that ever devil thought.

PERCY RUSSELL, **1906**

DEAD RINGERS

Many more live burials have occurred quite by
accident than intentionally. In the days before the

wonders of modern medicine, when victims of disease or injury could easily slip into an undiagnosed coma, it was relatively common for people to be buried too hastily by friends and relatives, concerned about the spread of deadly infection. It was not unusual to find deep scratch marks on the inside of exhumed coffins, evidence that the unsuspecting victim had struggled desperately in a bid to free themselves from their premature resting place.

In order to reduce the frequency of such accidents, Victorian coffins were occasionally buried with a rope attached to a bell above ground. If the deceased miraculously 'awoke', he or she could then pull on the rope, thus ringing the bell and alerting the grave-diggers to their plight. The effectiveness of such a device is a matter for debate, since the idea that a gravedigger could hear a bell ringing, decipher the position of the 'dead ringer' and muster enough help to dig up the coffin and free the victim before they ran out of air, is a long shot to say the least. The unwitting victim had somewhere between five and fifteen minutes before air disappeared from the coffin and asphyxiation killed them. Permanent brain damage could occur after only two minutes. This is probably the reason why some societies refer to those who have 'risen from the dead' in this manner as 'zombies'.

PRIMAL FEAR

For most of us the thought of being buried alive comes pretty high on our list of the most horrifying deaths we can imagine. The root of this horror comes not only from an obvious fear of death by asphyxiation, dehydration, starvation or (in cold climates) exposure, but also the innate fear we all have of being left alone in the dark and simply forgotten about by our fellow man.

Most of us will have experienced at least one nightmare in which we try to scream, but the noise is stifled, or the noise comes out but we are ignored. Being buried alive, whether on purpose or by accident, must be the agonising real-life equivalent of this imagined scenario. As a form of punishment, it has to be among the very worst there is.

INTERMENT:
A PUNISHMENT FOR WOMEN

In many societies, live burial was reserved for the punishment of women and children, particularly for crimes against religion. One theory behind this is that during such an execution, more sensitive spectators would not have to endure the gory reality of the victim's demise. In most cases, the dying prisoner was either hidden entirely from view, or at the very worst, only their head was visible while the body was submerged in earth, sand or concrete. Perhaps this is another reason why interment can seem even more cruel a punishment than burning, hanging or drowning, since this method leaves enough territory unknown to allow the victim's imagination to run riot.

Live burial was, according to most experts, never popular in Britain, perhaps because, being a small island, land is generally perceived as precious – not something to be wasted for the disposal of criminals. As a result, there is only one official instance recorded in the ancient annals. It occured in 1222:

A Prouinciall councell was holden at Oxforde by Stephen Langton, Archbyshoppe of Canterburie, and his bishops and others. There was a young man and two women brought before them, the young man would not come into any church, nor be partaker of the Sacraments, but had suffered himselfe to be crucified, in whom the scars of all ye wounds were to be seene, in his hands, head, side and feete, and he rioyed to be called Jesus by these women and others.

One of the women, being olde, was accused of bewitching the young man unto such madness, and also, altering her owne name, procured herself to be called Mary the mother of Christ; They being convict of these crimes and others, were adiudged to be closed up between two walled of stone, where they ended their lives in misery. The other woman, being sister to the young man, was let go, because she revealed the wicked fact.

In ancient Rome, vestal virgins who broke their vows of chastity could expect to suffer a similar fate. The Greek essayist and biographer Plutarch described the practice thus:

A narrow room is constructed, to which a descent is made by stairs; here they prepare a bed and light a lamp and leave a small quantity of victuals, such as bread and water, a pail of milk and some oil; so that a body which had been consecrated and devoted to the most sacred service of religion might not be said to perish by such a death as famine. The culprit herself is put in a litter, which they cover over, and tie her down with cords on it, so that nothing she utters can be heard. Then they take her to the forum . . . When they come to the place of execution, the officers loose the cords, and then the high priest lifting his hands to heaven, pronounces certain prayers to himself before the act; then he brings out the prisoner, being still covered, and placing her on the steps that lead down to the cell, turns away his face... the stairs are drawn up after she had gone down, and a quantity of earth is heaped up over the entrance to the cell . . . This is the punishment of those who break their vows of virginity.

The Romans were not the only people to utilise this punishment for unchaste behaviour. It was quite common for nuns and monks to be bricked up alive within the walls of religious houses, as penance for sin. There is some actually strong archaeological evidence to suggest that punishment burials were carried out in Roman Britain. In some Roman cemetries, bodies have been found to have been buried 'prone', that is to say, dimembered, mutilated, bound, buried face down, decapitated, or with evidence of de-fleshing or exposure.

This has led some archaeologists to conclude that at least some of these people were buried alive with their limbs bound, or mortally wounded and simply thrown into a grave to die of blood loss or exposure. In London's eastern cemetry, where fourteen bodies (three per cent of the total buried there) had been buried lying face-down, two had large blocks of stone on thier lower backs, and another appeared to have had her arms tied behind her back. A cemetry at Alington Avenue in Dorchester, Dorset, contained a prone male whose lower right arm had been hacked off around the time of death, and at Butt Road in Colchester, two prone men buried outside the cemetry gates appeared to have been bound at the wrists, and their ankle bones had been gnawed as if their corpses were left partially exposed.

The question remains, if punishment burials were never a feature of ancient British law and order, why did these people go to such lengths to restrain, or weigh down corpses where they lay. It is true that the Romans believed resolutely in the existence of ghosts and may have adopted such measures in order to prevent the dead from walking once more among the living, but then why leave their ankles above ground to be nibbled by rats unless for purpose of torture? We will never know the truth.

BURIED ALIVE HEAD-FIRST

Many other civilizations besides the Romans have used live burial as a form of torture or execution. In seventeenth-century Japan, prisoners could be suspended by their ankles from a gallows erected over a large hole dug in the earth, with the length of the rope being adjusted so that the prisoner's upper body was suspended below ground level, leaving one arm free to move. Shaped boards were then placed around his body to cover the hole and pegged to the ground so that very little light and air could penetrate. The victim was able to signal with his free arm when he wished to do as he was told. If he chose not to, he was simply left there to die before being cut down and buried in the hole. There is some anecdotal evidence to suggest that the Japanese employed similar techniques in the execution of enemy soldiers during World War II, burying soldiers alive, leaving only their feet exposed so that their fellow Americans could locate and identify them.

LIVE BURIAL IN INDIA

The two younger sons of Guru Gobind Singh (the last guru of the Sikhs) were buried alive because they refused to accept Islam. Nine-year-old Zorowar Singh and seven-year-old Fateh Singh were accompanying their mother, Mata Gujri, on a perilous journey to Sahedi in India in order to stay with the family of a servant. Unbeknown to them, members of this family accepted a bribe from the Mughals and turned them in to the enemy. The two boys were offered passage to freedom if they became Muslims, but they refused, and were bricked up alive. As a result of their bravery, these two young boys have become the most hallowed martyrs in Sikhism.

More recently in 2007, a newborn baby girl was found partially buried in a field 150 kilometres (93 miles) south of Hyderabad. Her maternal grandfather

PART TWO

THE SPANISH INQUISITION

THE PAPAL INQUISITION

This infamous institution of the Medieval Age was responsible for the sentencing to death of many religious separatists who would burn at the stake for their non-conformist beliefs. The men who hunted down these heretics were known as inquisitors; appointed by the Pope himself, they created an inhospitable climate for the unorthodox religions that were spreading throughout Europe. While they may not have swung an axe or lit the combustible faggots beneath their unfortunate victims themselves, these inquisitors, fuelled by their fervent religious zeal, were the driving force behind so many fiery deaths. As God's representatives, they became holy executioners during the thirteenth and fourteenth centuries.

A NECESSITY

With the forging of new trade routes with the East, European merchants brought back more than silks and spices. New thoughts and ideas made the trip from far-off lands and helped initiate new religious belief systems in these trading nations that would soon demonstrate a threat to Christianity. The Catholic Church were quick to identify these unorthodox religions and excommunicate those found preaching in their favour. However, excommunication from the Church proved to be an unsatisfactory deterrent.

The followers of these heretical faiths had no desire to be linked to the Church which had, owing to years of unobstructed rule, grown corrupt and excessively egocentric. They saw themselves as truer, purer faiths and believed Christianity had invited the Devil into its fold through abuses of power and wealth. The extreme punishment of these religious dissenters was seen as fair judgement at the time. A deep religious conviction was prevalent in the hearts of medieval people and, in an age where all criminals were vigorously dealt with, heresy was just another crime to be punished. Due to the prominence of religion at this time, the Church believed the creation of one uniform faith was of utmost importance for ensuring stability. Any obstacles to this proposed stabilising faith, such as heresy with its infectious disease-like existence, must therefore be removed.

THE HERETICS

The two main heretical sects seen as a very real danger to Christianity were the Cathars and the Waldensians. The Cathars were a dualist faith believing in two gods, one good and one evil, which was in direct contrast with the Church's monotheism. The sect began in Bulgaria, taking their name from the Greek word *katharoi,* meaning 'pure', before spreading their polytheistic beliefs across Southern Europe. The Cathar *perfecti* or initiated priests acted as missionaries who aggressively converted Christians caught up in the Crusades at the end of the eleventh century. A century later, the Cathars' numbers had swelled and a high concentration had settled in Western Europe particularly in South-west France and the Languedoc region. These areas would soon come under attack from the Catholic Church as they unrelentingly pushed forward their plans to eradicate all non-conformist faiths.

The Waldensians would suffer a similar fate to the Cathars. They were a Christian fundamentalist sect known as the Poor Men of Lyon, but which later took the name of their founder, Peter Waldo, a rich merchant who gave his assets to the poor after becoming a radical Christian in 1160. Taking their teachings from a French translation of the Gospels, the

Waldensians advocated a simplified form of worship in comparison to the affluent, indulgent Catholic faith. These self-imposed indigents headed for Rome and were blessed by Pope Alexander III in 1179, although he allowed them to preach only after permission was granted by the local bishops. They disobeyed the papal instruction and began to openly preach a doctrine that would soon be mirrored by the papally recognised Mendicant Orders, who would play a major part in the Inquisition in years to come. The religious dissidents were not put off even with the excommunication of their leader, Waldo, by Pope Lucius III in 1184. With the deficient religious denunciations failing to make an impact on these rising beliefs, the Catholic authorities were called upon to find a repressive method that would ensure these menaces to Christian society would be forced to capitulate. Burning was seen as the ideal punishment for this flourish of heresy. Not only did it have ties with the fires of hell – the destination of all heretics – but it ensured the Church could severely punish without breaking their own code; that being never to spill blood.

THE EPISCOPAL INQUISITION

The first attempt to set up an Inquisition to staunch the flow of these heretical faiths occurred in the same year as the excommunication of the Waldensian founder. In 1184, Pope Lucius III issued the papal bull entitled *Ad Abolendam,* which ordered his bishops to make inquisition of heresy throughout Christendom. Unfortunately, by passing the responsibility of ridding their dioceses of heretics to the bishops, this first example of the Inquisition was doomed. The majority of these chief clergymen did not reside in their relevant bishoprics but lived in Rome. They rarely attended to their flock and were rather more concerned with their own status at the Holy See. This lack of centralisation, along with an indifference to the cause, ensured it would be a highly flawed prototype of the later forms of Inquisition. The proliferation of followers belonging to the unorthodox faiths remained unchecked and developments at the core of Catholicism were essential before the Inquisition would be capable of systematicly eradicating non-conformist faiths. The heretical religions of Catharism and Waldenism forced the Catholic Church to focus on piety and to move away from extravagance.

THE IDEAL INQUISITORS

Fortunately for Catholicism, the initial decades of the thirteenth century saw the creation of the Mendicant orders; a group of monastic fraternities that had taken a vow of poverty, preferring to dedicate their time and efforts to preaching the word of God. This fresh approach to Catholicism was welcomed with open arms by the Pope, who quickly saw the potential value of these orders in the fight against heresy. In 1210, Innocent III gave Francis of Assisi permission to officially create the Franciscans, or the Order of the Friars Minor, and six years later Dominic of Osma had his Order of Preachers formally recognised by Innocent's successor, Honorius III in 1216. These über-pious friars practised orthodox values while improving the position and reaffirming the status of the Catholic Church. They were the perfect counter agents to the Cathars and the Waldensians. Now, unsettled Christians could look within their own Church for a more virtuous path and not feel forced to search beyond the boundaries of Catholicism.

In these saviours of the orthodox church, the Pope had not just discovered a devout society capable of stealing the heretics' religious thunder, he had also found the right men to lead a new version of the failed Episcopal Inquisition. He had found his inquisitors who would be his permanent judges responsible for crimes against the one true faith. Unlike the egocentric bishops that had inefficiently ran the prototype, these men were, on the whole, unselfish and driven by a true love of God and the

Church. The members of the Dominican and Franciscan orders proved to possess the qualities needed to take on the heavy burden of such a role. They were well-educated and highly skilled in debate. These qualities were often considered by the religious writers of the time. The ideal inquisitor was called upon to not only have an unwavering zeal for the Catholic faith, but to enjoy saving souls and exterminating heresy. Coupled with an inherent compassion, it appeared the Mendicant brotherhoods lacked none of the characteristics deemed necessary for the upcoming fight against their religious opponents.

The papally controlled Inquisition was methodically brought into being through a series of bulls issued by Pope Gregory IX in the early years of his reign. Imperial decrees of 1220 and 1224 authorising the burning at the stake of all heretics were adopted into ecclesiastical criminal law in 1231, proving that, this time, the Church meant business. A steady stream of commissions were created throughout the 1230s and sent out to suppress the nonconformist traditions wherever they were at their worst. The priorship of the Dominicans at Friesbach received its orders on 27 November 1231, while the Convent of Strasburg got its call on 2 December 1232. That year, Dominicans had already been despatched into the Rhineland and on to Tarragona in Spain, and the following year, commissioned friars were posted to Auxerre, Bordeaux and Burgundy in France, all following the papal orders to destroy the heretical threat. By 1255, the Inquisition had its representatives working tirelessly for this one aim in almost every country in Central and Western Europe and as they reached the fourteenth century, the Inquisition was at its height, its grip tightening whenever a display of heresy reared its head.

THE PROCEDURE

The inquisitors were sent out by papal decree and led an almost nomadic existence, moving from town to town, seeking out heresy and handing out punishments to those found guilty of unorthodoxy. Along with their sizeable entourage, these inquisitorial judges took large crucifixes into their chosen town, no doubt attempting to appeal to the dutiful side of the inhabitants. They would invite the townspeople to gather in the main square for a mass confessional. Attendance was voluntary – however, those who failed to accept the invitation would run the risk of being suspected of heresy. The visiting inquisitor would then issue a period of grace – usually lasting a month – in which time all individuals who wished to confess any heretical guilt could come forward and receive a minimum penance before being welcomed back into the fold. Those who came clean were also encouraged to inform on their neighbours and even children were pushed to give details of their parents' heresies. Any two testimonies, even those provided by the despicable and disgraced, were enough to warrant a full enquiry by the Inquisition. This all helped the investigation get under way, stirring up suspicion and blame.

The focus of many an inquisitorial probe were the affluent members of a town. While such rich pickings usually ensured a higher profile arrest and therefore a more effective deterrent to heterodoxy, it was routine for those charged to have their property and assets seized by their religious interrogators. It was therefore in the inquisitors' best interests to find heretics that had money, revealing that the unselfish Dominicans and Franciscans were not wholly resistant to the drawing power of wealth. In fact, as the numbers of executed heretics swelled so did the coffers of their persecutors.

Once sufficient, if factually dubious, information had been gathered, the trial could then take place. This would be a fairly one-sided affair favouring the prosecution, for as far back as 1205 Innocent III had issued a bull entitled *Si Adversus vos,* forbidding any legal help for heretics. Despite this ruling, legal counsel was often permitted, although finding a willing representative was tricky as any defending lawyer losing a case ran the risk of losing his practice, as well as being considered a supporter of heresy. Witnesses for the defence were few and far between for much the same reason. The trials failed to follow the judicial process today. The Inquisition conducted their trials of heresy behind closed doors, where the bulk of the details were shrouded in secrecy. The suspected heretic would be arrested and imprisoned and kept in the dark – both literally and figuratively – while being forced to guess what charges had been brought against him. The accused would not be granted any opportunity to question their accusers during the trial, however they were afforded the chance to name those they believed possessed a 'mortal hatred' against them. If this list of enemies included their accuser then the charges – whatever they were – were dismissed and the prisoner would be given their freedom. The named foe would then face the possibility of life imprisonment for his grudge-bearing testimony.

This general obscurity promoted self-incrimination. The majority of inquisitors wished for heresies to be self-confessed without resorting to other more severe means, yet despite the threat of torture or even death, freely declared confessions were rare. It was far more common for the accused to remain stubborn and steadfast. While chaired by the Chief Inquisitor, the trial was required to be conducted in collaboration with the local bishop and they were both obliged to consult the *Boni Viri* – a number of experienced laymen and clergymen considered honest and true – to come to an informed decision as to the guilt of the charged. Anything up to 80 of these wise men were summoned to decide the fate of the prisoner, who could soon find himself facing execution.

Those prisoners who tenaciously denied any religious transgression and refused self-condemnation would force the inquisitor's judicial hand. The next step to elicit the truth was torture, which was made lawful on 15 May 1252, when Pope Innocent IV issued a papal bull entitled *Ad Exstirpanda*. Physical torment had been used on prisoners in the past but only by secular authorities and never the Inquisition. The bull authorising enforced confession through violence would be regularly affirmed throughout the thirteenth century by successive popes such as Alexander IV on 30 November 1259 and Clement IV on 3 November 1265. Naturally, the more devout and spiritual officials within the Church regulatory sector called for restrictions. They demanded there be no bloodshed, mutilation or death from these truth-extracting acts and that the torture sessions should be limited to only one. For the less principled inquisitors, this was an obstacle that was easily overcome. The single session would merely be suspended when the physical torments proved fruitless and when they returned to the pain-racked prisoner the agony would resume within what was officially, the same session.

Despite the restrictions requiring a bloodless torture session, the inquisitors still found many forms of torture to draw out a confession of heresy. Before resorting to any physical violence, the inquisitors would traditionally start with simple threats, intimidating the prisoner with thoughts of the unbearable pain that could await them at the stake. If this was unproductive, then the supposed heretic would be confined in a cell and often starved of food and water. The last non-violent method employed was the use of tried men; previously accused and investigated individuals who had experienced the pressure of an inquisitor. These first-hand accounts of inquisitorial justice were intended to persuade the prisoner to confess and if this failed to pay dividends, the preacher turned persecutor would have no choice but to make use of the gruesome contraptions that were at his disposal.

There were several established methods of physical torture used throughout the reign of the Papal Inquisition in the thirteenth and fourteenth centuries against the more doggedly determined deniers. These included the *strappado* and the rack; two ominous-looking devices which stretched and pulled the limbs to such a degree that dislocation often occurred. If stretching could be endured then thumbscrews and *brodequins* or *stivalettos* were introduced. These would crush and splinter bones, rendering hands and feet permanently mutilated.

Once the physical, mental and spiritual ordeals were exhausted, the verdict against the accused would be determined. However, this could still mean a lengthy stay in prison as the inquisition preferred to stockpile the cases for one mass sentencing. This religious reckoning called a *sermo generalis* would be scheduled on a Sunday, or traditional feast day, in order to attract the bigger crowds and would be a ceremonial event full of pomp and circumstance. The Church would want to take full advantage of such an affair which celebrated orthodox Christianity and denounced its captured heretical opponents. Amid the self-congratulatory glamour of the *sermo generalis* was the real business of the verdicts. Prisoners would finally be made aware of their charges before the crowds and the punishments were promptly assigned. These could often be fairly minor penalties such as enforced pilgrimages to demonstrate a renewed devotion to Christianity. Further confiscation of assets could be imposed, an unconvincing representation of the Mendicant rejection of worldly possessions. Some would escape with excommunication, others with imprisonment. And then there was the ultimate punishment for heresy – the stake. This was given to two groups considered the worst examples in the eyes of the Church; those who consistently chose an unorthodox path and those who remained unashamed of their non-conformist beliefs.

While the Inquisition was responsible for convicting the heretic, the completion of the sentence was outside the jurisdiction of this ecclesiastical body. Those who had been convicted as repeat offenders or unrepentant heretics and were therefore prescribed capital punishment, would be subject to *relictus culiae saeculari* and handed over to the secular court for execution within five days. This appears to have removed the inquisitors from the final act in the life of a condemned heretic, detaching them from responsibility. However, this relinquishing to the state authorities was just an official stance. The Church could not be seen to take the lives of these men and women, heretics or not. They needed to remain suitably disconnected from the burning so as not to further tarnish their reputation and religious values. Yet the Inquisition – as always – still managed to exert control. The civil authorities may well have had the last say in the life of a heretic, but if they failed to follow the inquisitors' recommendations, the officials involved could find themselves excommunicated. This was far more serious than it sounds, for ecclesiastical law stated that if they were unable to free themselves from the papal ban they would be labelled a heretic.

By 1325, after almost a century of official extirpation, the Inquisition saw the destruction of Catharism, the main threat to the Catholic Church, and so slowly relaxed its persecutory grip over the continent. The number of heretics burnt at the stake by the Papal Inquisition throughout the towns and cities of Europe has never been accurately calculated. The various figures reported show that relatively few heretics succumbed to the flames. At Pamiers, in South-west France between 1318 and 1324 five out of 24 heretics were placed under the control of the civil court to perish on the pyre and likewise, from 1308 to 1323, only 42 out of 930 in the Cathar capital of Toulouse, died at the stake. This confirms the Inquisition's desire to convert rather than execute in the main. Execution admitted defeat and was a loss for the Church. They wished for a nonconformist to admit their sins and repent, to see the error of his or her ways but a dead man could not confess. A dead man could not have his soul saved or freely understand the power of the one God and the authority that served Him – the Catholic Church. Despite this preference for conversion, favouring the redemption of a wayward soul rather than its extermination, which exemplified the beliefs of the Mendicant orders, there were unfortunately a number of inquisitors who were less keen to rescue a life and more devoted to the annihilation of all heretics. These rather unscrupulous souls would prove to be effective executioners.

CONRAD OF MARBURG

The actions of the papal inquisition effectively began with the appointment of one man: Conrad of Marburg. His reign of terror throughout the Rhineland in the early 1200s would single-handedly help the Inquisition become the force that has been so well-documented in modern times. A man of unequalled religious zeal, Conrad crusaded against the many heretical sects that existed throughout Germany with the full power of the Pope behind him, sending large numbers to the stake with his hard-line and hang-tough approach of recant or die.

The early life of this notorious inquisitor is shrouded in mystery. Little of note is known about his parentage or his schooling, however, it is widely believed he did complete a course at a university, possibly at Paris or Bologna, having been referred to as a magister – one involved in academia – in writings from the time. At some stage following completion of his scholastic studies he became a priest, though doubt surrounds which order he belonged to. Modern thinking suggests he was not attached to either the Dominican or the Franciscan orders but was a non-monastic or secular clergyman.

Conrad first came to prominence in 1213 when he spoke vehemently in favour of the religious crusades against heretics called for by Pope Innocent III. In turn, the Pope became a strong and vocal supporter of this austere priest. During these turbulent times, the Catholic Church was concerned with the piety of their own officials and Innocent's successor, Honorius III, saw Conrad as the right man to reform the errant convents and monasteries of Germany and to ensure its wayward clergy were brought back into line. During this tour of re-education, he encountered Ludwig, the Landgrave, or Count of Thuringia, who took to Conrad and made him a leading figure at court. Conrad became highly influential, with one of his many powers being to appoint ecclesiastical livings which was soon confirmed by Pope Gregory IX in June 1227. His significant role at the Thuringian court was that of spiritual counsel and confessor to Ludwig's wife, Elizabeth.

The relationship between Conrad and Elizabeth was a peculiar one. The Landgravine was a match for the strict priest's ascetic ways and willing to adhere to

Conrad's severe instruction. She took to wearing a hair shirt beneath her regal attire, was often separated from her three children and would regularly submit herself to violent physical attacks from her spiritual tutor in a bid to become worthy of the religion she held so dear. These correctional episodes may well have been too excessive to endure, as it is thought by some to have been the cause of her death on 19 November 1231. Her confessor may well have been her killer, and yet rather than suffer any reproach, Conrad was asked to look into and document the virtuous life of Elizabeth and assist in the application for her beatification. His efforts were a success and she was canonised four years later.

By the time Pope Gregory IX had commissioned him as the first papal inquisitor of Germany on 11 October 1231, Conrad had already built a reputation as a dedicated terroriser of the unorthodox sects. The first that we know of to fall before this fanatic was Heinrich Minnike, the Provost of Goslar in Lower Saxony, who was to suffer a trial lasting two years before he was found guilty of heresy and suffered the flames. Conrad's persistent endeavours were observed by all. Heretics and high officials within the Catholic Church alike followed his wicked work throughout Germany, generating two divergent factions: those that championed his efforts such as the archbishops of Trier and Mainz, who both wrote letters of praise to the Pope in 1231, and those who heavily criticised the enthusiastic manner in which he was allowed to wander districts and dioceses dispensing his own dubious justice.

Conrad's focus was fixed upon one specific group of heretics, a fantastical sect called the Luciferans. Conrad believed that these infidels shunned the word of God for the power of the fallen angel, their Lord of Light, Satan himself. For Conrad of Marburg, there could not be a faction of unorthodox believers more guilty of heresy than those that worshipped the Devil and, marauding through the towns of Thuringia and Hesse, he forced confessions and burnt those who failed to come clean. Conrad's ignorant assistants, Dominican friar Conrad Dorso of Tor, John Le Borgne and the Franciscan Gerhard Lutzelkolb, found heresy in all things. A look or word out of place would be sufficient for them to report back to their inquisitor with what they considered a solid accusation. And Conrad would listen.

With the Pope's blessing, Conrad enjoyed freedom from the restraints of the usual canonical procedure and so was allowed to dispense with the formality of a trial. The unfortunate accused were threatened and tortured by Conrad and his collaborators and found guilty of their crimes without legal counsel, judge or jury. The torments subjected to these religious prisoners would have been severe, for Conrad was not disinclined from administering various acts of torture upon himself as part of his own atonement. He would have raised the bar when it came to devil-worshippers as for him the more violent the punishment, the sooner these heretical sects would be destroyed. If a supposed heretic confessed under excruciating pain, the inquisitor would order for their head to be shaved and a penance undertaken. For those who withstood the agony without admitting their guilt, the punishment would be death. The fact that the apprehended may be innocent seems to have not concerned Conrad, whose twisted sense of justice is encapsulated in the motto he lived by:

We would gladly burn a hundred if just one of them was guilty.

Fear consumed the districts before the arrival of Conrad and his entourage, with even the kings and bishops of Rhineland fearing for their lives. And for good reason, for Conrad was not averse to accusing the aristocracy, for no one was above the law of God in his eyes. However, it would be the denunciation of one such noble that would lead to the downfall of this supposedly untouchable inquisitor. In 1233, Conrad of Marburg publicly accused Heinrich II, Count of Sayn, of participating in satanic orgies. Whether or not this was true, Conrad had chosen to point the finger at a very powerful target. Furious at this allegation, the count appealed to the Archbishop of Mainz demanding to be allowed a fair trial. This earnest entreaty for justice was approved and the archbishop convened a Synod on 25 July 1233, which was even attended by the young King Henry VII of Germany. For the first time since his papally appointed perogative, Conrad of Marburg was required to legally prosecute a supposed heretic and was, unsurprisingly, unable to do so. The bishops and nobles on the council all elected to find the count innocent of the charge of heresy, much to the chagrin of Conrad, who immediately called for a reversal of the verdict. The synod had made their decision and there would be no U-turn.

With this failure to prosecute, Inquisitor General Marburg made public his fury and assured those that would listen that he would focus his persecutory zeal on heretical noblemen and ensure such an injustice would not occur again. Conrad would not see another aristocrat escape the wrath of Catholicism nor see one burn, for only four days later, the much-hated inquisitor would be dead. Travelling back to Marburg with his satanist-spotting companion,

Gerhard Lutzelkolb, Conrad and his Franciscan aide were set upon by what were later thought to have been knights in the employ of the vindicated count.

The inquisitor's death was not mourned by the people of Germany. A collective sigh of relief must have swept across the Rhineland, thankful that, at last, true justice had been served. Back in Rome, Pope Gregory IX was incensed by the murder of his trusted weapon against the heretics. He wasted no time in proclaiming Conrad as a champion of the Christian faith and called for the castigation of his killers, but this was not forthcoming. The strength of the German people had been clearly shown by their endurance through interrogation and execution at the hands of Conrad so there was little hope of them surrendering the names of the inquisitor's executioners. The murder of Conrad of Marburg sent an unsubtle message to the Pope illustrating the general feeling towards the severity of persecution they had suffered and Gregory IX, along with his successors, would never apply such a heavy inquisitorial hand in Germany again.

The unerring brutality Conrad of Marburg inflicted upon the German people during the first half of the thirteenth century ensured his name was to live on through the centuries as a dark symbol of the Catholic religion and would be forever associated with extreme cruelty. Tales of the macabre surround him to this day. The exact spot where Conrad met his end, marked by a stone on private farmland in the village of Hof Kapelle near Marburg, is thought to be haunted by his ghost and there are reports that tell of Satan worshippers performing black rituals there. How ironic that the very people Conrad wished to exterminate come to carry out their Luciferan rites at the scene of his death.

ROBERT LE BOUGRE

By the time Conrad of Marburg was attacked on the road to his hometown in July 1233, another inquisitor was making a name for himself across the border in medieval France. He went by the name of Robert Le Bougre which came from *bulgarus*, the Latin for Bulgarian, a reference to his being a converted Cathar. It is also from this that we obtained the Modern English word 'bugger'. His actions as papal inquisitor would prove this a fitting moniker. If one nickname was not enough, Robert would soon receive an even more sinister soubriquet through his extermination of non-Catholic followers – that of *Malleus Haereticorum* or the Hammer of the Heretics.

In the year 1233, despite seeing his beloved Conrad assassinated, Pope Gregory IX had not lost any of his enthusiasm for ridding the world of followers of inferior religions. Turning his attention to northern France, where Catharism was known to be rife among its domains and principalities, the Pope called together a mass of Dominican priests hailing from Besançon in the east to 'make inquisition' in La Charité-sur-Loire; a small priory town which had become particularly stubborn in its resistance against the Catholic faith. The leader of these papally empowered priests was one Robert Le Bougre. The details of this trip are not known but by the following year, Le Bougre's zealous deeds and general conduct as an inquisitor were gaining ill favour with the bishops in whose dioceses he put 'the question'. In 1234, the bishops collectively made known their grievances towards this Cathar-turned-*converso* putting pressure on Gregory to remove him from office. The Pope reluctantly withdrew his licence – the French clergy had got their way. However, Robert's suspension was as temporary as the smug grins on the faces of fault-finding bishops, for the following year Gregory IX renewed the debarred Dominican's commission. Worse still for Robert's detractors, the Pope was to make it incontrovertibly clear exactly where his loyalty lay by making Le Bougre the Inquisitor General for the entire French kingdom. This appointment came with a further twist of the knife. Gregory IX ordered all bishops to extend all their support and assistance to Robert in his quest to exterminate the heretics from communes of France.

With full backing of the Pope, Robert Le Bougre was able to return to his ferocious ways, displaying his own special brand of persecution throughout such towns as Péronne, Cambrai and Lille. Rather than follow the surreptitious interrogation style and perform his duties in secret – as was the modus operandi of the Inquisition – Robert Le Bougre preferred a more public approach to obtaining a supposed heretic's confession. His technique involved humiliation before a crowd as opposed to solitary confined suffering. For example, on 2 March 1236, Le Bougre assembled ten convicted heretics in the centre of Douai, a river town near Lille. Along with the condemned, the Inquisitor General had invited prominent figures from the surrounding area including the bishops of Arras, Cambrai and Tournai, Countess Joan of Flanders and a select assembly of Flemish noblemen. These high society spectators watched as the unlucky ten bore the torture directed by Le Bougre and ultimately perished upon the pyre.

Bankrolled by Louis IX, King of France, who also granted Robert safe passage throughout his realm, the trail of terror and burnt corpses persisted and, with it, a growing reputation for Robert Le Bougre, who quickly became the subject of fantastical fiction. As his success rate climbed, so the rumour mill churned with the fearful French believing he achieved his high number of confessions through hypnotism. Maybe mind control was the manner in which he managed to achieve an outstanding result in May 1239, in what would be his most renowned victory over the heretics. In the town of Montwimer in the region of Champagne, a large Cathar community had developed under the guidance of their clergyman, Bishop Moranis, and when Robert received word of this heretical locale, he vouched to put an end to their religious deviation. What followed was a whistle-stop one-week crusade against the heretics. In only seven days, Robert Le Bougre investigated the town of Montwimer and brought charges of heresy against 183 inhabitants. As was his wont, Robert gathered another topnotch set of dignataries to watch the interrogation and execution. Fifteen bishops, the Archbishop of Rheims and even Theobald I, King of Navarre, were among the guests at the mass burning.

This swift and severe operation was too conspicuous an event to go unpunished. Robert was, again, suspended from his duties but this time there would be no quick return for the Hammer of the Heretics. He was brought before a trial of his own and found guilty of overindulgence during his sadistic attack in Champagne and sentenced to life imprisonment. There ended a short yet productive career of one of the most prominent inquisitors in France.

Dominicans. This association with the head of this most Catholic of denominations surely had some bearing on Peter's next move when, in about 1221, he joined the Dominican Order. Peter became a renowned preacher, spreading the faith in stirring sermons throughout northern and central Italy. He attempted to emulate St Dominic, who was well known for his thorough asceticism, wearing a hair shirt and *cilice* even during sleep. Peter became a radically austere Catholic, pulling no punches in his fanatical lectures within the cities of Rome, Florence, Bologna, Genoa and Como, where he called for a comprehensive persecution of the sacrilegious faiths. Crowds flocked to hear him speak of his hatred towards those Catholics who were all talk and no action, unlike himself, who ceaselessly demonstrated his devotion. Such a glowing example of Catholicism was Peter, that he managed to convert many of those in the crowds from their 'inferior' creeds.

This ardent fervour caught the attention of Pope Gregory IX who, in 1233, made Peter the inquisitor of Lombardy, which effectively meant he would be head of all inquisitorial matters throughout the whole of Northern Italy.

With the acquisition of the priorships of Asti and Piacenza – one of the richest cities in Europe at this time – by 1241, Peter's position was one of all-powerful oppressor of whom heretics should be fearful. The new Pope, Innocent IV, knew this and so despatched the Inquisitor General to Florence, where a considerable cluster of Cathar heretics existed thanks to the numerous counts – themselves supported by Emperor Frederick II – who allowed the Florentine heresy to flourish. Peter's arrival had an instant effect. After stirring up support from the Catholics in the area, Peter formed a religious society called *La Compagnia della Fede,* or The Company of the Faith, a glorified gang that sought out and regularly administered beatings to the rival Cathars. These bouts of religious street fighting were prevalent throughout August 1245 and La Compagnia became a hit with the Catholic Church as new societies, or *crocesegnati* as they eventually became known, sprang up in other areas of Italy to defend the inquisitors and attack the enemies of their faith.

After his innovative actions in Florence, Peter was sent to hunt the heretic in Cremona and, then, to Milan. During his almost twenty-year career as a papal inquisitor, Peter had amassed a good number of enemies, particularly among the Cathars, and it was a plot by a gang of Cathars that brought Peter of Verona's life to an end. Roughly halfway between Como and Milan in a forest near Barlassina, Peter and his friend, Dominic, were attacked by two assassins,

Carino and Porro, who had been paid forty lire to execute the inquisitor. Striking the Dominican in the head with an axe, they turned their attention to Dominic. Legend has it that while they stabbed his travel companion to death, Peter mustered the strength to write on the ground in his own blood the words *Credo In Unum Deum* – 'I believe in one God' – before receiving Carino's blade to the heart.

His remains made the rest of the trip to Milan, where they were placed in the Church of Saint Eustorgio by his Dominican brotherhood. His passing was mourned by many who saw him as a pure specimen of the Catholic faith. Even death could not diminish his ability to convert a heretic, for Carino, his killer, was eventually overcome with the horror of his actions and soon repented his heresy entering the Dominican Order at Forli. Less than a year later, on 9 March 1253, Peter of Verona was canonised by Pope Innocent IV becoming Saint Peter Martyr – the quickest papally appointed saint in history and patron saint of inquisitors.

THE SPANISH INQUISITION

Never has a religious organisation managed to terrorise a single nation quite like the Spanish Inquisition. Born during the late fifteenth century in an atmosphere of religious suspicion, the infamous Inquisition created a breeding ground for mistrust and betrayal within every district it visited, pitting neighbour against neighbour all in the name of religious conformity. This led to the persecution of thousands of non-Catholics and many found themselves condemned to death by fire. The Spanish Inquisition shrouded itself in secrecy and instilled a paranoiac fear into the people, spreading across the towns and cities of Spain for over 350 years.

A UNITED SPAIN

The marriage of Ferdinand and Isabella in the palace of John de Vivero in Valladolid on 19 October 1469 set the wheels in motion, leading Spain down a path of governmental and religious unity. Ten years later, the royal couple sat upon the thrones of two dominant territories which had previously remained distinctly separate. Isabella became queen of Castile in 1474 and her husband took the crown of Aragon in 1479, uniting Spain like never before. This new-found sense of unanimity saw the two sovereigns forge ahead with their desire to bring harmony to all areas of Spanish life; not just to law, order and the affairs of State, but to the core of Spanish society – religion. The belief was that a single, united faith would make for a stronger nation and so, with the desire to ensure all Spanish citizens followed the national religion of Catholicism, the Spanish Inquisition was created for the enforcement of this mono-doctrinal ideal.

On 1 November 1478, Pope Sixtus IV gave the Spanish potentates the authority to set up the Inquisition for the first time in Castile. Ferdinand's Aragon received permission a few years later, yet this was not the first instance of the dreaded Holy Office here. There had been an Aragonese Inquisition since 1232, when Pope Gregory IX sent the *bull declinante* to the Archbishop of Tarragona, which later allowed Nicholas Eymerich to persecute heretics throughout this kingdom. Yet, as the old-style Inquisition's tribunal in Aragon fell dormant, Eymerich's actions would soon be overshadowed by the deeds of the newly revived office of Catholic defenders. Particularly when the Inquisitions of both territories succumbed to the unifying wave created by Ferdinand and Isabella and merged under the *Consejo de la Suprema y General Inquisicion.*

This 'Supreme Council' was made up of five inquisitors with an accompanying staff of secretaries and consultants and at its head was the Grand Inquisitor or Inquisitor General, who was appointed by the Spanish monarchy and verified by Rome. This was a major difference from the Medieval Inquisition which was managed by the Pope. Pope Sixtus had granted Ferdinand and Isabella permission to appoint their own inquisitors, ensuring that the Inquisition was under monarchical rather than papal control. A further contrast with the old Inquisition concerned the archives of the office which were exhaustive, recording suspects' details from family background and financial status to listing their crimes and misdemeanours against the Church.

THE *CONVERSOS*

The Spanish Inquisition, then, was created to keep the Spanish people in religious check and to ensure spiritual harmony prevailed in Ferdinand and Isabella's newly unified Spain. But from what abominable and abhorrent evil was the Inquisition responsible for protecting the Catholic faith? The focus of the Inquisitors' zealous attention were the *conversos*. These were resident Jews and Moors whose ancestors had converted to Catholicism about 100 years before, following a wave of persecution and maltreatment.

Judaism had been present in Spain as far back as Biblical times, it is thought, when Tubal, the grandson of Noah, had settled on the Iberian peninsula. However, it was the arrival of King Nebuchadnezzar II during the sixth century BC who was responsible for the spread of the Jewish faith throughout the country with the building of many synagogues, guaranteeing a constant influx of Jews into Spain from that moment on. Despite such a lengthy period of residence, the followers of this faith were always considered a secondary race, inferior to the Catholics and indeed the Muslims who also had a period of religious rule in ancient Spain. The Jews were seen merely as visitors to the country rather than a permanent residents and, while they were tolerated, this tolerance was both reluctant and fragile. The faiths lived together in a state of perpetual instability and dislike for this minor religion was present as early as the seventh century.

Over the proceeding centuries, cracks in the brittle accord began to expose more and more suppressed hatred towards the Jews and by the thirteenth century, religious acceptance had become just an idea. In 1235, the Council of Arles made the persecution of this religious minority very real, ordering the Jews to wear yellow circles upon their person for all to see; their beliefs made conspicuous as if they were diseased outcasts. The following century saw unrest surge to greater heights with focused attacks on the Jews.

During the *Pastoureaux*, or 'Shepherd Crusade', which began in France and entered Navarre in 1321, second-class citizens were seen as symbols of the sovereigns' wealth and supremacy and were openly attacked. Assassinations took place in Pamplona, then in nearby Estella in 1328, after Franciscan monks preached against the Jewish worshippers and what they saw as their insidious acquisitions of high-profile and finance-based roles throughout the country. The continual displays of antipathy and frustration which – year by year – grew more violent, ensured the establishment of anti-Semitism in Spain. The Jews became scapegoats for rebels and dissenters vexed by a poor economy. They blamed the monetary-minded Jews for cheating them through heavy taxation.

Caballeros – Spanish noblemen – used this common concern to challenge the rule of King Peter the Cruel and violence broke out in Toledo in 1355.

This escalating antagonism peaked with the pogrom of Seville in 1391, which would ultimately see approximately 4,000 Jews massacred throughout Spain. The attacks were instigated by a Dominican archdeacon called Fernando Martinez at the start of the year and by the summer unbridled assaults on Jews were taking place in both Castile and Aragon, specifically in the cities of Zaragoza, Barcelona, Valencia and Gerona leaving the kingdom of Navarre in the north west the sole refuge for the persecuted Jews. And so began the Jewish defence and the creation of the *conversos*. In order to avoid incurring the wrath of Spanish anti-Semites, tens of thousands of Jews converted to Christianity, and it is believed that between 1391 and 1415 more than half of Jewish citizens switched faiths and were baptised.

This conversion under duress acted only as a temporary stay of execution. Orthodox Catholics were not fooled by what was seen as a clear act of self-preservation with Jews swapping religions purely to save their skins. Despite this stubborn contempt the *conversos* were able to climb the political and social ladders of Spain, integrating themselves into important positions of Church and State and mixing with Catholics, guaranteeing Jewish lineage pervaded the blood of true orthodox families. The Jews had dealt with such resolute enmity throughout the centuries that they had developed an ability to assimilate even under such hostile conditions, quickly adapting to whichever was the dominant faith. This well-practised compliance, however, only exacerbated the situation, fuelling the fires of hatred and ensuring bad blood existed between the disparate doctrines.

Throughout the fifteenth century, the converted Jews steadily improved their status, occupying positions of prominence that had been closed off to those who practised Judaism. As the years went by, more and more *conversos* were becoming members of the judiciary, rising to prestigious posts and acquiring titles. Once more rioting broke out among bitter Christians in cities worst hit by an ever-failing economy, such as Toledo in 1467 and Cordoba in 1473. Over the next six years, Ferdinand and Isabella took their respective thrones and in the spring of 1480 the *Cortes*, or Spanish Parliament met in testy Toledo with the Jewish problem high on the political agenda. The sovereigns saw the Jews as a direct threat to Christianity, much as the Cathars and Waldensians were in the twelfth century, bringing about the creation of the Papal Inquisition. The Crown and Cortes concurred that the Jews had become a danger to religious stability, and so several social restrictions were imposed. They were removed from the popular areas of towns and cities and forced to live in ghetto-style quarters, called *juderias*, and the compulsory identification of Jews made a comeback calling for coloured discs to be worn once again. In return for their acquiescence, the new monarchs offered to protect the Jews from further anti-Semitic attacks but this provoked an indignant response from those Jews who had acquired for themselves prestige and status, and who had no intention of relinquishing the associated social and financial benefits. In September 1480, these incensed bureaucrats issued a pamphlet opposing the decrees of the Cortes which forced the monarchy's hand. They reacted strongly, calling for two inquisitors to be appointed in Seville to stifle the unco-operative voices and begin a war on heresy that would last for hundreds of years.

These first investigative agents of the Spanish Inquisition were two Dominicans called Miguel de Morilla and Juan de San Martin. They were appointed on 17 September 1480 to seek out the heretics deemed hazardous to the one true faith and, if they could not be assuaged, the death sentence was to be applied. The inquisitors rode into Seville – the first of so many towns – to apply their strict procedure of interrogation, torture and prosecution. Such a visit would have been commonplace as the Holy Office established itself through the years as a national institution, but what terror must have befallen the city of Seville when these men, dressed austerely in white robes and black hoods, marched for the first time barefoot into the main square. The frightening, foreboding sight of the inquisitors and their entourage, flanked by armed guards, as if preparing for invasion, caused many of the Sevillian citizens to flee, which instantly condemned them as heretics in the eyes of the Spanish Inquisition.

One man who refused to run from the inquisitional incursion was Diego de Susan – a Jew of great wealth – who managed to persuade other prominent figures of Seville to stand firm and eject the unwanted visitors. Their plan may have worked had it not been for de Susan's daughter, Susanna, was known about town as *La Hermosa Hembra* or 'The Beautiful Girl'. She had taken a Catholic lover and foolishly confessed the entire plot to her *inamorato,* which led to the subsequent arrest of all conspirators. Six were found guilty of heresy and given the death penalty.

They were led to the fields of Tablada and burnt at the stake for their combined heresy and rebellion on 6 February 1481.

Such was the beginning of the death and destruction of the nonconformist faiths in Spain. Executions would occur more and more frequently as the Spanish Inquisition discovered seemingly endless suspects to persecute in the name of Christianity. No stone was left unturned. Literally so, as graveyards were plundered for the bodies of the dead who had been posthumously found to be guilty of heresy; their bodies exhumed and chained to the stake to die again in a manner befitting their crime. The fervour and zeal with which the ever-propagating inquisitors sought out the heretical menace created the notorious image of the Spanish Inquisition and caused it to be feared by generation after generation throughout Spain. Judaism which had existed since ancient times was forced underground after a systematic expulsion of its believers saw hundreds of thousands forcibly removed from their homeland. Those that remained followed their unorthodox tenets at their own risk, and would live in permanent fear that their enemy, the Spanish Inquisition, may come to town to hunt for heresy.

THE PROCEDURE

The process by which the Spanish Inquisition would investigate a town for heresy was similar to the methods of the earlier Papal Inquisition. The inquisitor along with his vast entourage of familiars and guards would march into a neighbourhood and instantly impose his authority on the people, stirring up trouble and creating friction between families and friends. An Edict of Grace would be decreed calling for all God-fearing men and women to come forward and confess their sinful ways. However, it was not the voluntary confessions that caused conflict. Better than a self-declaration of guilt was the denunciation of others. The Inquisition demanded that all knowledge of assumed heretical acts be passed on to the Holy See, causing a chain reaction of suspicion and betrayal throughout the town. These perfidious acts ensured a healthy crop for the Inquisition from which to harvest the rotten fruit of heretics. The named and shamed would be arrested by the *alguazils* – the inquisitonial police – but, before they were taken from their homes to a dank, dark prison cell, a notary would make an inventory of all the suspect's assets; the redistribution of wealth clearly in the forefront of their minds even at this early stage.

Incarceration in one of the overcrowded prisons ran exclusively for the Inquisition proceeded in the clandestine manner that was indicative of these heresy hunters. In an attempt to create an air of mystery and subsequent terror around inquisitorial imprisonment, inmates were forbidden to speak of what they had seen or heard during their time behind bars. Everything was shrouded in secrecy, which allowed rumour and invention to breed and ensured the imagined horrors of prison life would encourage good Catholics to inform on their neighbours. Those unfortunate enough to experience the reality of an Inquisition gaol might find themselves detained for weeks or even months on end, isolated from the outside world with the gaoler their only visitor. Once held in captive isolation, the prisoner would be subjected to the inquisitor's examination. This would take place in the company of two supposedly impartial clerics, who would make sure the interrogation followed the correct path. Reluctance to confess or provide names of those believed to be heretical would lead to torture known euphemistically as 'instruction', or 'the question'. The rules that existed for the papal inquisitors still stood in Spain centuries later. They were prohibited from any acts of bloodshed or mutilation upon the prisoner, and had to conduct only one session. As we have seen, there were ways around this law and the torments could be relentlessly pursued by the inquisitors, particularly as the instruction came to an end not when the prosecutor said so, but when the accused begged for the torture to cease. The thinking behind this was if the inquisitor called an end to the suffering, it would suggest that all avenues of pain had been exhausted and the prisoner had succeeded in surviving the torments without denouncing himself or others. However, with the conclusion of the torture decided by the tormentor, it appeared as if the agony was unending; there would always be another nerve to touch, another new device to apply.

After the suffering at the hands of the inquisitor, the suspected heretic would be brought before the judges of the tribunal and bombarded with questions regarding all areas of his or her life in an attempt to prove beyond doubt the defendant's guilt. They were even tested to see if they knew the key Catholic prayers and any slip or hesitation called into question their religious sincerity. However, the conclusion of an inquisitional prosecution came when they had a bona fide acknowledgement of heresy.

There were a range of punishments for heretical behaviour which included exile, fines or confiscation of property, but for those who refused to repent their non-orthodox sins or who had converted to Christianity but had since relapsed, the penalty was death. Just as the inquisitors of the Medieval Office were prevented from passing the death sentence, so were their Spanish equivalents. They were required to hand all unrepentant and reverting heretics over to the secular court to be burned at the stake. It was actually less a handover than an abandonment by the Spanish Inquisition, who believed they had done all they could to save the souls of the unorthodox. The Spanish Inqusition, with their ecclesiastical exemption, were able to burn men and women in their thousands while keeping their hands spotlessly clean.

THE AUTO-DA-FÉ

Before the Spanish Inquisition washed their hands of the heretics they had persecuted inside their private, shrouded prisons, there would take place a religious ceremony in the centre of town called an *auto-da-fé*. Portuguese for 'an act of faith', its purpose was to create an air of reverence and public loyalty towards Catholicism. The condemned would be removed from their cells and paraded past their peers, yet the event was more to do with the crowds that gathered to watch than the prisoners who had already had their verdicts confirmed. The *auto-da-fé* was a lesson to all the attendant faithful that the Spanish Inquisition was all-powerful and all-seeing and woe betide those who failed to toe the Christian line. To ensure the maximum public terror could be inspired, the *autos-da-fé* were held on Sundays and other holy days when large crowds could be assured, although non-attendance on any given day would have been foolhardy as it would have been seen as a sign of unorthodox behaviour. Even the high-ranking officials dared not stay away as, from 1598, the Inquisition decreed such absconders from the *auto-da-fé* would face excommunication. Whether you were pauper or potentate, villager or VIP, such absence, then, risked a personal invitation as one of the attractions!

The proceedings began the day before the *auto-da-fé* when, at two o'clock in the afternoon, the Green Cross procession would take place. The green cross featured on the Inquisition's coat of arms and this emblem of the Holy See would be conveyed to the ceremonial location and placed high on the stage, which was covered in a sombre black cloth. Inquisitional-appointed familiars and armed guards would be entrusted with its protection throughout the night. When these sentinels witnessed the sun hit the inquisitional insignia, the time had come for the prisoners to be removed from their isolation and meet the crowds waiting to show their Christian zeal to the faith's official guardians.

With a long day ahead, the heretics would be gathered outside the prison as early as five o'clock in the morning, with their hands bound and ropes placed around their necks. Such an ungodly hour for such a display of piety was called for as the ceremony often continued well into the afternoon and the more pessimistic of officials wished to complete the formalities before nightfall, as they feared the fervent crowds would – under the cover of darkness – succumb to their sinful urges after a day's persecution and condemnation. In fact, such concern forced many *autos* – such as one in Logrono on 7 November 1610 – to break until the following morning when they ran over time.

The condemned would be forced to wear the uniform of the heretic to further discriminate them from the holy, yet hollering, masses in attendance. This consisted of a cap called a *coraza*, which resembled a bishop's tapered mitre, together with a garment known as a *sanbenito*. This was a loose-fitting, knee-length tunic made of rough, yellow sackcloth upon which was emblazoned various images of hell; supposedly their next destination. The illustrations adorning the front of these tabards were significant in that they denoted both the prisoner's fate and the strength of their resolve under interrogation, for if the design showed flames pointing downwards this revealed that the condemned had been granted a merciful death by the Inquisition having repented his or her heresy. They would not have to bear the pain of the flames alive but would be compassionately strangled before the fire consumed them. However, those who wore *sanbenitos* showing flames pointing upwards, were the persistent prisoners who refused to repent and had stuck fast to their religious beliefs. They would suffer the full force of the Inquisition and would be burnt alive upon their own funeral pyre.

THE PROCESSION

There was still much to be done before the condemned perished at the stake. The procession from the prison to the ceremonial stage would march behind a white cross in strict order. First in line were the clergy dressed in tunics of their own, featuring the green cross motif. Next came the *alguazils* followed by a priest bearing the holy host of the Eucharist, who would initiate the first piece of audience participation. As he passed the crowds that lined the street, with a banner of scarlet and gold held high by assistants above his head, every spectator was to fall to their knees in reverence. Those who failed to comply with this enforced display of loyalty to the Church risked a charge of heresy.

As the people returned to their feet, they would witness arguably the most distressing sight of the *auto-da-fé* ceremony; the parade of the damned. Before the heavily guarded prisoners made their way to the *auto-da-fé* platform, the effigies of those who had been lucky enough to escape the clutches of the Spanish Inquisition were paraded atop green poles before the onlookers. The grotesque faces drawn upon these figures also sporting the uniform of the *coraza* and *sanbenito,* must have added to the carnival atmosphere of this sombre spiritual affair, yet any celebratory feelings must have been quickly dampened when the coffins of those exhumed were carried past. Not even in death could one avoid persecution as those who were posthumously found guilty of heresy caused the crowds to wretch and reel from the rotting stench. Behind the reeking remains finally came, as it were, the living dead, who would have insults and worse thrown at them by the hordes of people keen to show their faith. Each convict would be sandwiched between two Dominican clergymen dressed in white robes and black hoods who would incessantly implore their assigned prisoner to convert. Bringing up the rear were the inquisitors themselves flanked on one side by red silk standards bearing the arms of the people entwined with the arms of the Spanish monarchy. On the other side, the standard bearers carried the arms of the Inquisition – altogether the perfect symbol of a united faith: the monarchy, the monks who served them and the masses.

When the procession reached its destination, usually in front of the cathedral in the town square, the prisoners would be sat on benches dressed in black crêpe placed high for all to see. The inquisitors would take their seats surrounded by the green crosses and incense candles would be burnt to take the edge off the foul odour of death. The crimes of each individual – dead, alive and absent – would be read out before the clerics and other dignitaries and all those who had agreed to repent were called to sign a declaration to that fact. Two sermonic orations to the crowd would then take place either side of Mass, as the Inquisition clearly wished to emphasise the religious tone of the *auto-da-fé* as their final contribution to the lives of the convicted heretics.

After the profuse sermonising and preaching, the Grand Inquisitor would stand and theatrically outstretch his arms before the people. Once more, the onlookers would then have to show their allegiance to the Inquisition and the Church, and drop to their knees, pledging to defend the Holy See against its enemies. In unison, they swore to dedicate their lives to the Spanish Inquisition, agreeing to abide by whatever it asked of them, even if that meant plucking out an eye or cutting off a hand! Yet again, any reluctance to make this histrionic promise would have adverse consequences except, however, if you were the sovereign. Whenever the *auto-da-fé* was honoured by the presence of Ferdinand and Isabella, they would refrain from uttering the vow and it was not until the reign of Philip II during the latter half of the sixteenth century that the crown of Spain participated in this oath.

This public demonstration of faith was almost at an end. The Inquisition had one last act before they passed the condemned men and women over to the secular court for execution, or 'relaxation' – as it was euphemistically known. In a vain show of compassion towards the heretics they had prosecuted on spurious claims and evidence, the Grand Inquisitor would rise one final time and appeal to the attending secular judge to show mercy upon those who had been given the death penalty. Such a melodramatic performance was a fitting end to the farcical *auto-da-fé* as the heretical criminals were removed from the platform and escorted to their own private stake.

THE EXECUTION

The *auto-da-fé* was over. The Spanish Inquisition had prayed for the souls of the heretics and extolled the virtues of the Catholic Church while simultaneously intimidating the townsfolk forced to attend for fear of religious retribution. Now, the secular arm would apply the punishment suggested by the inquisitors, while these heretic hunters sat back and admired their handiwork with crystal-clear consciences. The focus now moved from the spiritual to the corporal as the *alguazils* led the condemned to their place of execution. This was called the *quemadero* – the place of burning – which was commonly an open field or meadow, rife with stakes that had been prepared earlier by the royal justice department. The resolve of the unrepentant and relapsed heretics must have been severely tested on encountering the numerous stakes jutting out from the ground like demonic trees in winter. The realisation that their sentences had long since been decided would have, no doubt, added to their anguish.

Each prisoner would be guided to their own personal post accompanied – even at this late stage - by their devoted pair of persistent Dominicans who continued to wrestle with their souls. These relentless exhortations bombarded the ears of the ill-fated as they were compelled to climb the ladder to their fixing point. They would be perched upon a small seat located some 3.7 metres (12 ft) high, allowing the civil executioner to fasten the human faggot securely to the stake. Once in place, their moral counsel would climb the ladder for a final entreaty and if no contrition was forthcoming, the priests would admit defeat and leave them to accompany the Devil who, they believed, was waiting to take their spirit into the flames of hell. These men and women with heroic levels of resilience were left to be devoured alive by the flames.

The thought of being conscious as the searing heat ravaged their flesh and bone, along with the incessant beseeching of the priests, caused many hitherto steadfast religious rebels to repent and call for strangulation. Screams for absolution would be heard across the *quemadero* by those unwilling to endure the flames alive. So many changes of heart took place, that it began to undermine the power and threat of the Spanish Inquisition. Aware that these last-minute conversions were interrupting the proceedings and making a mockery of the punishment, the inquisitors began to order the tongues of the condemned to be tied to prevent any softening of the sentence. On 30 June 1680, after an *auto-da-fé* in Madrid, six of the prisoners who had received the death penalty converted while bound to the stake – only moments from being consumed by fire. These endemic reversals of faith must surely have had something to do with the gagging of twelve prisoners at a subsequent ceremony later on that year in Madrid.

With the condemned chained to their stakes and their personal decisions as to their demise made, the priests would step clear of the combustibles and allow the executioner to begin his work. Dressed in a long black, sack-like robe with his face hidden behind a black hood with two holes for the eyes, the executioner would be a most frightening final sight for the damned. Before death there would still be time for some last-minute torture. The crowds that had followed the burning party from the *auto-da-fé* to the *quemadero* wished for some sport after the religious-heavy ceremony, so would call for the singeing of the heretics' beards. As a taste of the blazing horrors to come, the executioner would light some dry grass or gorse affixed to the end of a long pole and thrust it into the faces of the condemned. This burning away of the beards was known as 'shaving the new Christians' and as the poor wretches suffered first degree burns to the face, the kindling 3.7 metres (12 ft) below them would be ignited to cries of delight from the bloodthirsty masses. Those with any drop of courage left in their terrorised bodies plunged their hands and feet into the flames that licked away beneath them, reaching out for their fiery finish, reaching out for martyrdom in a final move to frustrate their killers who sat hands folded, despairing at their obstinance.

The executioner then tossed the effigies and exhumed cadavers into the fire as the screams of the living were slowly rendered mute. The tumult of the spectators would no doubt be reduced to a deathly silence as they witnessed the horror of flesh falling from bone, eyeballs popping from skulls, deformed faces contorting into grotesque expressions, before

THE RISE AND FALL

Ferdinand and Isabella, together with the valuable assistance of their trusted inquisitors, had created a strong and resilient organisation fully equipped to expel all religious enemies from Catholic Spain, and methodically maltreat those *conversos* who remained behind. They had nurtured the Holy See through its formative years, but with the death of Isabella in November 1504, Ferdinand was left to develop the Spanish Inquisition alone and defend it against growing opposition. On 23 January 1516, the last of its creators died and Ferdinand and Isabella's son, Charles, became King of Spain. It was hoped that a change in monarch would also bring a change in attitude towards the Spanish Inquisition. Its detractors looked to Charles V to address the excesses and abuses of the religious office which had been rife under the reign of Ferdinand, its unashamed sponsor. Unfortunately for those who regarded the Inquisition to be an excessive monster of the Catholic Church, the persecutory practices were far from curbed by the succeeding son. In fact, the Inquisition was allowed to spread throughout the unified lands of Spain. From Seville to Córdoba and from Villareal to Toledo, Charles V allowed for tribunals to be created to handle the mounting cases of heresy and, by 1538, there were no less than 19 courts condemning unrepentant and relapsing heretics to the secular arm and thus the stake to burn.

With the progress of global exploration, the kingdom of Spain had grown considerably and with the acquisition of lands in South America, its Inquisition had a new stomping ground. The first inquisitional court of these new territories was set up in Lima in 1570, which dealt with all heretical cases throughout Peru. The following year, Spanish-ruled Mexico received its own tribunal, which would continue to investigate unorthodoxy and other threats to Catholicism well into the nineteenth century. It was deeply involved, for instance, in the punishment of those who dared to react against Spanish occupation during the Mexican War of Independence between 1808 and 1815. Miguel Hidalgo – the reactionary priest and leader of the rebels – was eventually captured by the Inquisition and executed by firing squad on 30 July 1811, outside the Government Palace in Chihuahua.

The Spanish Inquisition was clearly developing into a worldwide force but during the latter half of the seventeenth century, its power and authority mirrored that of the Spanish monarch who sat upon the throne. King Charles II was not inclined to ensure the continued rise of the Holy Office. Charles was known as *El Hechizado,* or The Bewitched, owing to his many mental and physical disabilities such as epilepsy, senility and an enlarged tongue which caused unsightly drooling, all of which he blamed on sorcery. Charles did very little to develop either the country or the Inquisition in comparison to his predecessors. The deformed potentate's failings seemingly ran to impotence, as he was also unable to ensure the continuation of the Hapsburg line. This was undoubtedly a blessing as his countless defects were less to do with witchcraft and far more a product of the persistent inbreeding of the family down the years.

While an heir was beyond his capabilities, Charles did manage to create a council known as the *Junta Magna,* which was called upon to investigate and reform the Spanish Inquisition in 1696. The council, which consisted of two officials from all councils from Castile and Aragon to Italy and the Indies, was required to meet once a week where it poured over the endless documents in the Inquisitional archive.

The council's report, known as the *Consulta Magna*, uncovered such damning evidence of abuses and excesses that the Inquisitor General of the time, one Juan Tomás de Rocaberti, convinced the weakling monarch to consign the tell-all tome to the flames.

Charles the Bewitched died on 1 November 1700, bringing to an end the Hapsburg dynasty that had ruled the Spanish territories for almost two centuries. As the Inquisition entered into its fourth century, it had expanded to twenty-two tribunals and was paying the wages of over 20,000 inquisitors, *alguazils* and other familiars doing 'holy work' throughout Spanish-ruled lands. The established supremacy of the Holy Office was undeniable yet, in little over a century, Spain had drastically reduced its population having lost three million inhabitants since 1586. So when Philip of Anjou took over the throne on 16 November 1700, beginning a new dynasty, that of the House of Bourbon, he inherited a Spain in economic decline. The Jews and the Moors had been a huge industrial force in Spain, but now they were gone and had taken their combined skills with them. Philip V was then forced to rule much of his reign struggling for finances, which was in no small part down to the effects of the heretic hunting office. The continual eradication of all unorthodox believers over the centuries not only caused a weakening of the Spanish economy but it also meant the Inquisition had to search harder and harder for enemies. The only threat posed to Catholicism in Spain apart from the Moriscos and Marranos, were newly formed Protestant sects that tried to infiltrate the country in the early sixteenth century, and by the eighteenth century the witch hunting craze had come and gone.

In short, the Inquisition had lost its *raison d'etre* and by the end of Philip V's reign in 1746, it was in steady decline in both wealth and numbers. Without a new religious foe, the end of the Holy Office was inevitable, however its critics would not witness a rapid destruction. Much like the long drawn-out trials and executions of thousands of the heretics they condemned, it would take time to see the end of the Spanish Inquisition.

THE DEMISE OF THE INQUISITION

The outbreak of revolution in France at the end of the seventeenth century became the spark that would eventually erupt into an all-consuming fire to singe and scorch the powerful Inquisition and ultimately bring about its destruction. With Napoleon leading France into battle against many of the European powers, he fell out with Portugal after they refused to adhere to his commercial embargo of Britain and so in 1807, he looked to Spain and the incumbent monarch, Charles IV, to assist with an attack on Portugal. This call for support was refused and so Napoleon invaded Spain with over 12,000 troops. King Charles decided to abdicate in favour of his son Ferdinand, Prince of Asturias, but he was ultimately replaced by Napoleon's brother, Joseph Bonaparte, when Madrid was taken in December 1808. One of his first moves as ruler of Spain was to abolish the Spanish Inquisition and the Suprema was forced to flee the capital to escape a decree calling for the imprisonment of its members. The death knell was sounding for the Holy Office.

Yet the Inquisition exhibited a resilience more associated with the unrepentant heretic. Thanks to relentless guerrilla attacks and continual opposition to the newly devised Constitution of 1812, Joseph Bonaparte's rule was unable to grow roots and it collapsed the following year after defeat at the Battle of Vitoria. This allowed Ferdinand to return from exile in March 1814, informing the *Cortes*, or Courts, that he planned to uphold the new charter supported by the liberals but, once securely back on the throne, Ferdinand sided with the conservatives of which the

Catholic forces were part. He rejected the Constitution on 4 May, arresting its leaders days later. Ferdinand made clear his religious zeal by reinstating the Inquisition on 21 July 1814, much to the dismay of the liberals; the persecutory organisation was back in action but it would not enjoy an uninterrupted revival. In 1820, the liberals were able to restore the Constitution and, once again, suppress the Inquisition. This to-ing and fro-ing between *Cortes* and Crown was not over. Ferdinand managed to regain control and proceeded to rule with severity and rigour. The Inquisition was restored although, in a bid to assuage the religiously tolerant supporters of the Constitution, it performed its work under the banner of Faith Commissions called *juntas-da-fé* which were created in every diocese; their focus being the last remnants of heresy: banned literary works and the freemasons.

The Inquisition had been forced underground, compelled to change its name to continue its existence. The irony must have been thick enough for even the most single-minded inquisitor to see. Just as the Jews and Moors were forced to practise their religious acts in secret while in public pretend to abide by the ecclesiastical law of the land now, in a true taste of their own medicine, so were the officials of the Spanish Inquisition! Burning corpses chained to wooden stakes were no longer filling the air with their speciously heretical stench. In fact, execution at the hands of the Inquisition ended in Spain on 26 July 1826, with the death of Cayetano Ripoll – a schoolteacher from Ruzafa in Valencia – who foolishly declared that Jesus was not the son of God. He was arrested and imprisoned for two years before being officially accused of deism, whereupon he was given the death penalty. Ripoll managed to avoid the agony of being devoured by the flames and was hanged by the neck although, in what amounts to a hollow and soft alternative, his body was placed in a barrel which had flames painted on it before being buried in unconsecrated ground.

After the death of Ferdinand VII, his wife, Maria Cristina, acting as regent to their daughter and future queen, Isabella, passed a decree conclusively bringing the Spanish Inquisition to a close. The reign of terror and persecution was now, finally, at an end. The heresy hunters had condemned tens of thousands of men, women and even children (as in the case of the Toledo *auto-da-fé* of 1659 when two ten-year-old girls were burnt) in their relentless endeavours to cleanse Catholic Spain of religious undesirables. All those residing in Spain holding alternative beliefs must have emitted a unified sigh of relief when, on 6 June

1869, religious tolerance became law in unified Spain, leaving no demand for the Inquisition and no need for fear.

TOMÁS DE TORQUEMADA

The man credited with the rise of the Spanish Inquisition masterminded a revival of the persecutory regime and consigned thousands of convicted heretics to the stake. He instilled fear into the hearts and minds of all in Spain at the end of the fifteenth century. His name has become inextricably linked with the Spanish Inquisition and the horrors it exacted. In fact, if any one man was the physical embodiment of this Holy Office, it was Tomas de Torquemada; the prototype inquisitor. His name struck terror into those that heard it. A true *nom de guerre*, his sinister surname began with the Latin *torque*, meaning twist, and could be compounded with the Spanish *quemada*, meaning burnt, thus providing a perfect soubriquet for the man who subjected many to agonising torture techniques and, to those more unfortunate a heretic's fiery death. In reality, his name originated from his familial hometown, Torre

Cremata, or 'burnt tower'. Even with this true derivation, it seems fire was destined to feature prominently in his life.

THE EARLY YEARS

Tomás de Torquemada was born in 1420 in the Castilian district of Palencia in north-west Spain, a short distance from Valladolid, the resident city of the kings of Castile. Little is known of his parents, Pedro Fernández de Torquemada and Mencia Ortega. However, his uncle, Juan de Torquemada, had achieved considerable renown as a theologian and author, while also retaining both the cardinalship at San Sisto and the archbishopric of Valladolid. From an early age, this ecclesiastical bent was quickly and wholeheartedly appropriated by Tomás, who would go on to outshine his uncle and become the most famous Torquemada of them all. For more than half a century, he would live his life in the shadows, only coming to the fore in the 1470s when he became an influential member of a royal circle. However, before gaining this position, only a handful of facts are known about the life of the most infamous of all inquisitors.

After excelling at school, Tomás completed a bachelor degree in theology and then, still in his teens, chose to join the Dominican order at the priory of San Pablo in Valladolid. The life of a Mendicant friar suited Torquemada's pious and austere nature and he soon took on all the attributes of an ascetic; refusing to eat meat, suffering discomfort with the wearing of a hair shirt underneath his habit while also choosing to walk bare foot. His unabashed and unequivocal godliness made him – what the Church would consider – a model Catholic. He was offered many titles but consistently refused the majority of them, including the archbishopric of Seville. Despite declining such profitable positions, Torquemada was able to amass a great fortune; in contrast to his austerity and Mendicant faith.

One of the few positions he did take was the priorship of Santa Cruz monastery in Segovia around 1455. Some time after this, he chose to become the confessor and spiritual counsel to Cardinal Pedro González de Mendoza, who was also the Archbishop of Seville. This would be ideal training for his future, more illustrious employer: Princess Isabella. Due to the shaky status of the Castilian monarchy, Isabella was not predicted to take the throne when Torquemada agreed to become her confessor. Today, we are left to debate whether or not he would have chosen this high-profile role if he had known his mistress's imminent rise to power. Isabella became Queen of Castile on 13 December 1474 and, approximately five years later, her husband Ferdinand took the throne of Aragon. The royal couple began a new decade with the personal union of two distinctly separate kingdoms of Castile and Aragon, but further changes were on the horizon and they would involve Tomas de Torquemada.

INQUISITOR OF SPAIN

On 11 February 1482, soon after the official coupling of the two territories, events began to move swiftly for Tomás who, now in his 60s, was appointed as an inquisitor by Pope Sixtus IV. Seeing this as a perfect platform from which to impose his austere and severe religious beliefs, Torquemada quickly established himself as one of the leading minds within the organisation and soon put himself in contention for the Inquisition's principal position: Inquisitor General. The seniority of this señor, along with his devout and unwavering faith, meant that there was no one better to take the lofty role and less than two years later, on 2 October 1483, Sixtus IV bestowed upon him the honour and responsibility of Inquisitor General of Castile. Fifteen days later, his sphere of influence expanded to take in Ferdinand's north-western territories of Aragon, Catalonia and Valencia, which had just enjoyed a year's papally authorised suspension of all inquisitorial activities. This freedom would soon be replaced with fear.

With the official backing of the papacy under his belt, Torquemada accompanied Ferdinand to a *Cortes* or parliament assembly at Tarazona in April 1484, to receive the support of the Aragonese. The king wished his territories to follow Castile's lead and assist the new Inquisitor General with his eradication of heretical beliefs. His wish was not shared by the Aragonese officials who refused to accept Torquemada's appointment, not only because they feared the confiscation of their wealth which a hunt for heresy would undoubtedly bring, but also the Inquisitor General was a Castilian, a non-native, and so contravened the *fueros*, or charters, of Aragon. Ferdinand was forced to impose his authority in order to attain the compliance of his parliament calling for the kingdom of Aragon to assist the Inquisition, together with its chief Torquemada, or run the risk of being accused of heresy themselves.

Torquemada then appointed two inquisitors to begin the probe for nonconformity throughout Aragon. The two officials, Pedro Arbués de Epila and Fray Gaspar Juglar, marched through the territory into towns and villages seeking out the heretics which resulted in two *autos-da-fé* taking place in Zaragoza during May and June 1485. The resistance to this

Castilian intrusion became all too clear when Juglar mysteriously died just before the June ceremonial prosecution. The remaining inquisitor grew increasingly nervous, travelling everywhere with a bodyguard, armour worn beneath his habit and a steel cap under his hood. Unfortunately, Arbues' safety measures proved ultimately ineffective against an attack masterminded by Juan Pedro Sánchez, who convened a group of like-minded rebels keen to diminish Torquemada's influence over their kingdom. The group hired assassins to pounce upon Arbués as he knelt in prayer inside the Metropolitan Church of Zaragoza. It took several blows and two days for the poor inquisitor to die, succumbing to his wounds on 17 September 1485.

This strike against the Inquisition failed to effect a quick exit from Aragon. In fact, it produced the opposite reaction. Torquemada sent three replacement inquisitors to Zaragoza taking the heavily -protected Castle of Aljafería as accommodation from which to root out those culpable for the killing. The plotters were rounded up and brought before an *auto-da-fé*. Sánchez, the ringleader, managed to escape the clutches of the Inquisition and fled Spain, so his effigy was burnt at the stake. Those caught would suffer, in person, the most agonising pain as the flames took hold. The man found guilty of striking Arbués' death blow – Juan de Esperandeu – received the worst punishment. The murderer was dragged through the streets of Zaragoza to the cathedral, where his hands were chopped off. He then underwent the torments of being hanged, castrated and quartered before the crowd. Torquemada wished this *auto-da-fé* be a prosecution and a deterrent to those who would stand in the way of his regime. The strength of the Spanish Inquisition under the leadership of Torquemada had been successfully tested and now they were free to pursue and persecute throughout Aragon as well as Castile.

HIS INSTRUCTIONS

As well as seeing off all resistance to the Spanish Inquisition, Torquemada looked within the organisation to improve its efficacy in making heresy a thing of the past in Spain. As soon as he was made Inquisitor General, Tomás began to create the first laws of this Inquisition; regulations that could be implemented and followed not just for the present period but for the future. These rules were known as Torquemada's Instructions, the first set of which was issued on 29th October 1484. Comprising of twenty-eight articles, these Instructions endeavoured to organise the Inquisition. The edict of grace was initiated by Torquemada, giving all those who had fled a town visited by an inquisitor thirty days to return and face their religious interrogation or else be considered a heretic. Such strict, unrelenting doctrine was evident throughout this new Inquisition code. He also called for those who failed to provide true confessions to be immediately passed to the secular courts for burning. Tomas' policy called for the *auto-da-fè* ceremonies to fall on holy days, knowing this would attract a larger crowd and therefore more witnesses to the inescapable fate of a heretic. But perhaps the most significant instruction was article fifteen, which encouraged the use of torture upon prisoners whose heresy proved tricky to substantiate. This authorisation of violence would be keenly implemented by many inquisitors throughout the time of the Spanish Inquisition. Torquemada had excelled in his role as Inquisitor General and, in 1484, was promptly given further papal support when Sixtus IV sent him an appraisal commending him on his ceaseless efforts. Further additions and revisions to the inquisitorial laws followed steadily throughout his reign with sets issued in 1485, 1488 and finally in 1498.

In only a year as the inquisitor of Spain, Tomás de Torquemada had set out his stall as a thorough regulator of this religious establishment, helping the Inquisition to swiftly grow in stature and authority.

Yet more was to come from this most dominant Dominican. As the power of the Spanish Inquisition developed, so did the influence of Torquemada, who would be central to several key decisions in the ever-evolving religious and political climate of Spain.

On 12 August 1484, Pope Sixtus IV, the man behind the official validation of the Spanish Inquisition and Torquemada's elector, died at the age of seventy – only six years older than the Inquisitor General himself. He was succeeded by Innocent VIII. However, any opponent to the Spanish Inquisition hoping for a papal-enforced curtailment of the establishment's power, would be greatly disappointed. It would be a case of the same support and in February 1486 the new occupant of the Holy See issued a bull confirming Torquemada's position as Inquisitor General. In addition to this re-affirmation, Tomás was given the power to appoint further inquisitors rather than have to refer back to Rome for reinforcements. The year got worse for the heretics as Innocent VIII further empowered Torquemada by giving him the right to receive the appeals of those sentenced by the Inquisition. Originally the job of the Archbishop of Seville, this effectively ensured a reduction in the amount of successful appeals now that the Inquisitor General would play prejudiced judge, jury and, indeed, executioner. Tomás de Torquemada's power was clearly growing.

THE EXPULSION OF THE JEWS

It is a widely held belief that before she became queen, Isabella made a solemn promise to her confessor that if she ever took the throne of Castile, she would make the elimination of all counter-Catholic beliefs her main priority. This vow would have pleased Torquemada who, in 1478, wrote a memo to Ferdinand and Isabella from his priory residence in Segovia, detailing the problems he felt they should remedy as the sovereigns of Spain. The main focus of his letter was the Jewish faith. He attacked the Jews and labelled them as the root cause of many of the problems within Spain and Catholicism and called for the revival of old Church laws, introduced back in 1215 at the Fourth Lateran Council to combat the growing Jewish threat. These laws included an enforced separation of the inferior Jewish community from the superior Christian one, as well as a demand for visible identification to be worn by all Jews.

This fervent anti-Semitism demonstrated by the Inquisitor General was not uncommon on the Iberian peninsula. Torquemada sensed a growing concern held by much of Spain, that the Jewish population was becoming a viable threat to Catholicism. Catholic Spain feared an uprising from the hundreds and thousands of non-Christian believers – *conversos* to *moriscos* – who they believed were not only remaining true to their publicly relinquished faith, but were actively converting those 'new Christians' back to their original religion. Now, with the authority of the new Inquisition governed by Torquemada – a man sensitive to their suspicions – the anti-Semitic scaremongers would be able to push for action against the suspected Jewish menace.

As anti-Semites go, Torquemada was an ardent one and he led the charge against the Jews fuelled by a personal, deep seated hatred that stemmed from his own ancestry. Tomás' grandfather, Alvar Fernandez de Torquemada made what could eventually be described as the momentous and far-reaching decision to marry a Jewess back in the fourteenth century. The consequence: Tomas de Torquemada, the man who would become known as the Scourge of the Jews, was in fact part-Jewish himself! In his mind, his blood was tainted and if transfusions had been possible back in those late medieval times, he undoubtedly would have requested one in an attempt to rid himself of his Jewish connection. This, then, casts his persecutory stance in an altogether more intimate light. His desire for the expulsion of the Jews was the closest he could come to driving out the Jewish blood from within him.

Along with the hatred of his Jewish lineage,

Torquemada hated the thought that thousands of Catholics in Spain were practising other religious customs in secret, and pushed for a suitable punishment when Ferdinand and Isabella returned from their successful war against the Moors in the southern territory of Granada. Torquemada made his fury known in no uncertain terms to the Spanish monarchy, resulting in the Alhambra decree which was signed on 31 March 1492. The ruling took less than three months to finalise and was more ruthless than any Jew could have imagined, revealing how adamant Torquemada was in wishing to deal with a supposed Jewish threat. Every Jew in Spain, regardless of age or status, was given two options: convert or leave. Those who wished to remain in Spain would have to be baptised and turn their back on their faith. Those who would not abandon their religion would be forced to leave Spain with what they could carry. Although all gold, silver and currency was to be left behind – no doubt to line the pockets of the inquisitors who invaded their homes. The declaration stated they had four months to decide their fate. After the July deadline, all remaining Jews in Spanish territories would be arrested and handed over to the secular court for burning.

Such a terrible proclamation caused the resident rabbis to seek some way of preventing this enforced exodus and, knowing that the war in Granada had hit the royal coffers hard, sought to buy their way out of trouble by offering them the considerable sum of 30,000 ducats. This attempt by Rabbis Abraham Seneor and Isaac Abravanel to appeal to Ferdinand and Isabella's material side almost worked.

This Jewish pay-off may well have paid off if it had not been for the intervention of Torquemada who, on hearing a possible financial deal was being discussed, exploded into the room holding aloft a crucifix. Ever the preacher, Tomás reminded the sovereigns of Judas Iscariot who sold their saviour for 30 pieces of silver, and the king and queen of Spain quickly steeled their resolve and turned away the Jewish offer. Such was the power of Tomás de Torquemada that even the monarchy of Spain bowed to his holy authority.

Torquemada then dispatched numerous inquisitors into the *juderías*, the Jewish quarters, to implement this decree. With an official stance of conversion not execution, between 50,000 and 70,000 Jews chose to convert to Catholicism to escape expulsion. However, many of these failed to escape the Spanish Inquisition which later hunted and persecuted them into confessing their heresies and burnt them on the stake.

THE FINAL YEARS

By the time the edict of expulsion had been decreed, Tomás de Torquemada was an old man of seventy-two years. His incessant persecution, predominantly focused upon the Jews, was unrelenting even at this ripe old age and it has been estimated that between 1483 and 1498 he was responsible for the deaths of as many as 8,800 heretics throughout the Spanish-controlled territories, with over 90,000 receiving lesser sentences from the elderly Inquisitor General. Tomás not only sent heretics to burn, he also had an abundance of non-Christian literature consigned to the flames. Copies of the Talmud from the Jewish faith, along with many Arabic tomes, were destroyed in an attempt to check the spread of the heretical beliefs. Torquemada was a true trailblazer for Christianity. His energy and drive were unequalled at this time, or by any future inquisitor of Spain. His desire to oppress his nonconformist foes diffused into other areas of his life as well.

The persecution of the heretic was not his sole passion. Torquemada was also a fan of architecture and, with the wealth he was able to accumulate through the confiscation of property, he could afford to fund the construction of various medieval buildings, the most notable of which was the Monastery of

St Thomas Aquinas at Avila. This structure took him ten years to complete and, unsurprisingly, incorporated his hatred of heresy in its design. In the bowels of the magnificent monastery, he had several prison cells built, in which he incarcerated those he suspected of following an unorthodox faith.

Despite this untiring dedication to the cause, Torquemada was not able to efficiently manage his excessive work load as he continued to rack up the years and on 23 June 1494, Alexander VI, the third pope to witness his reign as Inquisitor General, issued a bull appointing assistants to help the forever burning 'Light of Spain', as he became known. Martin Ponce de León, Inigo Manrique de Lara, Francisco Sánchez de la Fuente and Alfonso Suárez de Fuentesalce provided inquisitorial support to the establishment's head, enabling him to continue in his given roles as hammer of the heretics and honour to his order. With this aid in place, Torquemada was able to focus on one of his last triumphs, managing to secure papal permission to have all *conversos* banned from the Dominican priory at Avila. The ruling, which came into effect on 12 November 1496, was sanctioned on the grounds that these converted Jews were impeding the spiritual work of the true Catholics with their lack of Christian faith and hatred of Torquemada's Inquisition.

His fourth and final set of Instructions were composed in May 1498, just four months before his death. These revised laws were generally considered to demonstrate a more temperate attitude to heresy and its management. At long last the ascetic friar from Castile was showing signs of softening, but his legacy would remain strong. In his fifteen-year reign of violence, persecution and terror, his Spanish Inquisition grew from a single court at Seville to a network of more than twenty holy seats of judgement, enabling a more efficient style of Inquisition to the original papal system of the thirteenth century.

Tomás de Torquemada finally stopped fighting on 16 September 1498, dying peacefully in his bed in Avila at the grand old age of seventy-eight. He could afford to rest for he had assisted in the successful expulsion of the Jews from his beloved Spain and had lived long enough to witness the Moors driven out of Granada. His reign as Inquisitor General was the fundamental reason for the ascendancy of the Spanish Inquisition. It should come as no surprise, what with his love of architecture, that Torquemada provided such strong foundations for lasting success as well.

Despite being laid to rest in the chapel of his own monastery in Avila, Torquemada – or at least his remains – endured a restless existence. It began with Philip II of Spain who, holding Torquemada in such

DIEGO DE DEZA

Succeeding the infamous Torquemada in the role of Grand Inquisitor, Diego de Deza endeavoured to surpass the level of terror and torment reached by the original head of the Spanish Inquisition, sending more than 2,500 heretics to the stake. He ensured that the Holy Order continued to instil fear into its enemies as they entered a new century of religious control. Like many of the Grand Inquisitors to succeed him, Diego de Deza came from humble beginnings. Born in the ancient, high-plain town of Toro in North-west Spain to parents Antonio de Deza and Doña Inés de Tavera in 1444, Diego would soon attain his own personal 'high plain', with royal connections and titles galore.

Diego de Merlo, his guardian through childhood and a prominent member of the Crown of Castile, used his contacts to ensure Deza entered the royal circle at an early age, being made *doncel* – a royal page or squire – to Henry the Impotent, King of Castile, on 2 August 1461, aged just seventeen. Throughout his adolescence, Diego showed himself to be both a scholarly and spiritual teen and so would inevitably follow the well-trodden path to the door of the Dominicans, albeit not until the relatively advanced age of twenty-six. In 1470, he returned to his birthplace to join the order at the Convent of San Ildefonso to practise the Mendicant faith and focus on his piety. It was in 1480, however, that Diego de Deza would reveal signs of his future calling as a prosecutor of non-Catholics. His inquisitorial debut began well before his official appointment in 1498, when he was called to sit on an assembled tribunal to discover the heresies of one Pedro de Osma. Osma was, at that time, chief professor of Theology at the Dominican college at Salamanca but thanks, in part, to Deza's examination, he was found guilty and, though not sent to the stake, he was immediately removed from his academic post. Deza had received his first taste of inquisitorial power and quickly stepped into the now-vacant role at the Salamancan college; one of many positions he would acquire over the coming years.

This stint as tribunalist for the Spanish Inquisition brought Deza to the attention of many influential figures, none more so than the Spanish sovereigns themselves, Ferdinand and Isabella. The royal couple brought him further inside the royal circle in 1486, when they entrusted to him the esteemed position of tutor to their only son and heir apparent, Juan, Prince of Asturias. Unfortunately, the prospective king would not make it out of his teens, contracting tuberculosis and succumbing to the illness in October 1497. His death failed to hinder Deza's progress, as Ferdinand of Aragon quickly appointed him as his own personal confessor and spiritual counsel. By this time, Deza had already amassed the bishoprics of Zamora and Salamanca and, in the following year, would acquire a third, becoming the Bishop of Jaen in 1498. However, this would not be his most prominent appointment of that year. He went on to achieve the highest ecclesiastical role in all of Christendom, that of Grand Inquisitor. In a short space of time, Diego de Deza had created a close bond with the Spanish monarchs and had numerous religious titles that brought with them not only authority and responsibility, but considerable wealth as well. As the fifteenth century drew to a close, Diego de Deza was at the head of the world's most feared religious establishment: the Spanish Inquisition.

THE GRAND IMITATOR

Diego de Deza reached the dizzy heights of Grand Inquisitor on 24 November 1498. However, this appointment only allowed him jurisdiction over the lands of Castile, Leon and Granada so he still had one more rung to climb to achieve ultimate control. Typically for Deza, this post was not a long time coming. In less than a year, his sphere of influence was increased to include all the territories under the rule of Ferdinand and Isabella, when on 1 September 1499 the lowly Castilian was made Grand Inquisitor of Spain. Due to his many commissions throughout Castile, it took Deza some time to actually begin his duties as the head of the Spanish Inquisition. Numerous dioceses for which he was responsible demanded his attention but, when he had seen to his sees, he was quick to put into effect his own ideas for strengthening the power of the Inquisition and the Catholic Church and, in turn, his own position.

Deza was not the innovator that Torquemada had been. Instead, this exceptional inquisitor chose to emulate his predecessor in almost all areas in a bid to improve the efficiency of the Inquisition. He built on existing ideas. This allowed Diego de Deza the freedom to be more aggressive than the first Grand Inquisitor of Spain. Similar to Torquemada's four sets of Instructions, Deza developed his own inquisitorial laws and called it his Constitution which comprised of seven articles. They were officially issued on 17 June 1500 in Seville and included an insistence for an examination of all unchecked towns and villages throughout the unified kingdoms as well as a hunt for all unorthodox literature. The new Inquisitor General also called for renewed resolve against all heretical acts, placing the responsibility to inform on all suspicious conduct at the doors of all good Catholics. Those that failed to make known any recognised heresy would risk censure themselves. A further six articles followed later on but, as with the initial seven, there was nothing groundbreaking within these laws though they did reveal the vigorous and merciless manner in which Diego de Deza planned to rule.

Deza shared Torquemada's anti-Semitic stance and was quick to unleash hell upon all Jews who refrained from converting to Christianity. Even the *conversos* who did agree to relinquish their nonconformist faith and be baptised were hated by Deza who believed, as did Torquemada before him, that these religious turncoats were secretly practising their old Jewish ways away from the prying eyes of the Spanish Inquisition. This belief led to a paranoid victimisation of all Jews whether they had switched faiths or not.

At the time of Deza's rule, there was a particular occurrence which infuriated the Grand Inquisitor. A great number of Jews were pouring into the country, homesick for their ancestral land. Those who had been expelled from Spain in 1492 under the reign of Torquemada now wished to come back and, pretending to be new arrivals rather than returning Jews, promised to accept and adapt to Christianity when questioned. Believing that they had no intention of truly converting, Deza wished to curb this mass homecoming and decreed that all Jews entering Catholic Spain should be immediately conveyed to the secular courts to be burnt alive. Many Jews chose to ignore this proclamation, risking their lives to be back in their homeland, and were subsequently sentenced to death or, if they renounced Judaism, hunted as *conversos* by Deza and his inquisitors.

The Jews were not the only faith to feel the wrath of this Inquisitor General. There were still a sufficient number of *mudejares,* or Muslims, in the territory of Castile to concern Deza and, believing they too persisted with their unorthodox faith, praying to Allah and following his word in the Koran, targeted them for persecution. Much as Torquemada had done with the Jews, Diego de Deza forced the conversion of the remaining Muslims in 1502 with those refusing to renounce their heretical beliefs sent to the flames.

Throughout his reign as Grand Inquisitor, Deza continued in his endeavours to emulate and outshine the accomplishments of Torquemada. His victimisation of the Jews and efforts to strengthen the laws of the Spanish Inquisition were not the only similarities between these first inquisitor generals of Spain. Their fanatical fervour and commitment to the cause ran parallel to one another and brought considerable opposition within the Church. Many believed Deza was overly cruel and heavy-handed in the way he managed the Inquisition and this unease began to grow throughout his ecclesiastical rule of Spain.

The hostility towards Deza's overzealous behaviour led to several uprisings against the Inquisition and even brought a charge of heresy against the Grand Inquisitor himself. Deza was accused of the very crime for which he had prosecuted so many – that of secretly practising Judaism. It is doubtful Deza was guilty of following a faith so vehemently hunted under his persecutory regime and this allegation was most likely an attempt to destabilise his powerful position. Efforts such as these seemed to succeed in chipping away at Diego's supremacy at the head of the Spanish Inquisition for, when it came to a rather ugly affair involving one of his inquisitors in 1507, his position was not strong enough to withstand the pressure and Julius II was forced to intervene. He publicly called for a more restrained approach to the duties of the Holy See and clearly felt that Deza was not the man to direct this new, more temperate administration. Deza was forced to resign from the most illustrious of all his posts, bringing to an end a religious reign which, some believe, managed to surpass that of Torquemada in terms of terror.

Despite this fall from grace, Deza did not lose his ability to obtain positions of great wealth and power. In his later years, he was offered yet another bishopric, giving him responsibility over the diocese of Toledo but – in a move possibly without precedent in the title-collecting life of the ex-Grand Inquisitor – he refused to accept the role. Fast approaching his eighties, Diego de Deza had grown too old and unwell to hold office and would soon succumb to his ills on 9 July 1523. Diego de Deza had acquired an assortment of commissions and titles during his lifetime from the chancellorship of Castile to the archbishopric of Seville and was even made executor to Queen Isabella's will when she died in 1504. However, it was his actions while Grand Inquisitor of Spain that would be his legacy.

With the enforced resignation, his period of office lasted a mere nine years, and yet in this short space of time Deza managed to chalk up a surprisingly large amount of victims. The figures are an approximation as no accurate records exist, but it is thought that between 1498 and 1507 Diego de Deza ordered the execution of 2,592 convicted heretics and sent nearly 35,000 to prison. Who knows to what terrible depths he could have reached if he had been allowed to remain in office?

DIEGO RODRÍGUEZ LUCERO

There were many examples of widespread persecution by those holding the highest office within the Spanish Inquisition. However, such religious atrocities were not committed purely by the inquisitor generals. Many common inquisitors appointed throughout the Spanish territories etched their own scars upon society, inflicting terrible pains upon the towns and cities for which they were responsible. One could argue there was not a more reckless and ardent pursuer of the heretic than Diego Rodríguez Lucero who laid siege to the city of Córdoba in the opening years of the sixteenth century. Known to all as *El Tenebroso* – The Darkness – Lucero cast a sinister shadow over an entire city which saw many of its citizens sent to the stake and burnt alive.

Little is known about Diego's childhood. His early years are shrouded in obscurity. However, Lucero's time as an inquisitor was very much in the spotlight. He was sworn into the role on 7 September 1499 after the incumbent inquisitor was found guilty of extortion and was forced to retire. Lucero would surpass these relatively minor crimes committed by his predecessor and the Córdoban authorities would quickly come to regret his appointment.

He exploded onto the scene in such a way as to attract the attention of both supporters and opponents alike. On 11 December 1500, he received a letter of commendation from Ferdinand of Aragon expressing pleasure at the rise in the number of convictions in Córdoba, and the king also called for a sustained push for persecution with a focus on *conversos* who had reverted back to their non-conformist faiths.

Meanwhile, the local authorities endeavoured to obstruct the work of the Inquisition. As early as 1487, the Crown had to intervene, requesting that magistrates refrained from impeding the heresy hunters. Despite this royal appeal, in 1501 the mayor of Córdoba took it upon himself to highlight the Inquisition's unpopularity in his town and attacked the Holy Office's notary responsible for recording the confiscated assets. The inquisitor had the mayor stripped of his office, arrested and cast out of Córdoba as punishment. An example had been made. Lucero would not stand for any further outbursts from the enemies of the Inquisition and zeroed in on the prosperous communities of Córdoba.

Córdoba was an affluent city set on the bank of the Guadalquivir River, deep in the heart of Andalusia in southern Spain. It had once been one of the richest cities in the world under Muslim rule, and was where many wealthy *converso* families resided. These powerful Andalusian nobles would not throw Lucero from his religious obligation. In fact, this inquisitor targeted the rich Córdobans and tore into them, spreading condemnation throughout their ranks. He set his sights on the moneyed members of the city which ensured sustained Crown approval, as the confiscated assets of the accused heretics were redistributed into the royal treasury.

As well as filling up the royal coffers, the prison cells were also packed full with incarcerated heretics. This owed much to the questionable system of investigation under Lucero. He arrested subjects on the merest shred of evidence and used a number of ingenious, though improper, methods to achieve a prosecution. Diego de Algeciras, one of the prison assistants, was often called upon to create evidence with which to convict. He had no qualms lying under oath and often committed perjury in Córdoba and in the neighbouring town of Jaen in order to assist the

Inquisition with their cleansing of Catholic Spain. Lucero also forced *conversos* to teach Jewish prayers to his Christian prisoners so he could spuriously claim that they practised Judaism.

The main prison in Córdoba was the Alcázar de los Reyes Cristianos, which was actually an ancient Moor palace which was taken over by Ferdinand and Isabella and used as their summer residence. However, since 1482 it had been appropriated by the Inquisition as their headquarters and used to incarcerate the unorthodox believers they discovered in Córdoba. Its ancient Arabic baths were used for an altogether more sinister cleansing as they became the torture chambers. The onus was placed on informing on others and the torture techniques administered to the imprisoned persuaded many to betray relatives and loved ones. One such incident tells of a fifteen-year-old girl being stripped and whipped at the behest of Lucero to force her to denounce her own mother. There were clearly no depths to which Lucero would not stoop in order to obtain a confession or accusation and this lack of humanity resulted in the city of Córdoba being ripped apart by this over-zealous inquisitor.

CONSPIRACY THEORY

On 26 November 1504, the impervious partnership of Ferdinand and Isabella was irrevocably broken when the Queen of Castile died in Medina del Campo aged fifty-three. Her death threw Spain into political turmoil as Ferdinand and Philip the Handsome – married to Ferdinand's daughter, Joanna – contested supreme control over Spain. This period of instability caused many to fear for Spain and its loyal Catholic subjects. This included Diego Lucero, who was convinced his beloved country was being secretly undermined by *conversos* plotting to restore Judaism to its former greatness and replace Christianity throughout all of Spain. His obsession with this Jewish conspiracy caused Lucero to double his efforts, resolving to shed light on the secret schemers.

One alleged conspirator was Juan de Córdoba known as the mad *jurado* who, Lucero believed, was a pro-Jewish millenarian activist. These Millenarians believed the end of the world was nigh and so any prosecution from the Inquisition for practising forbidden faiths meant little to them. Lucero ordered the demolition of two buildings, one of which belonged to Juan. He suspected that they were secretly being used as synagogues. He then proceeded to hunt heretics with renewed vigour and went on a frenzy in a bid to seek out more synagogues and prosecute enemies of Christian Spain. Less than a month after the death of Queen Isabella, Inquisitor Lucero ordered an *auto-da-fé* at which he sent 120 heretics to the stake. This was followed by a further twenty-seven *conversos* in May 1505. Diego Rodríguez Lucero was on the rampage against heresy.

Not even international law could stop Lucero's obsessive persecution when two suspected heretics fled to Portugal to escape the threat of the pyre. The inquisitor sent officials after Alfonso Fernández Herrero and Fernando de Córdoba, blatantly flouting international regulations by neglecting to ask for royal permission. Manuel the Fortunate, ruler of Portugal, demanded to hear the legal reasons for such a contravention. Yet again, Lucero was able to rely on the support of Ferdinand who appealed to Manuel not to obstruct the efforts of the Holy Office. This unsubtle threat was enough to clear Lucero of any law-breaking and he was allowed to continue unhindered with his hunt for Córdoban heretics.

By 1505, Lucero was enjoying an unrestrained period of inquisitorial rule in Córdoba. The confidence this must have brought him was illustrated when he focused his attention on the most illustrious of his targets: Hernando de Talavera, the Archbishop of Granada. This much-loved octogenarian, who had been confessor to the late queen, was known for the great work he did to promote Christianity throughout the area and was even respected by the Moors he endeavoured to convert. It was a strange choice indeed. However, Lucero was adamant that this popular high-ranking clergyman was part of the Jewish conspiracy and went about manufacturing evidence to fit his accusation. He turned to a Jewish woman in his custody whom he believed to be a prophetess. This seer had been regularly tortured by Lucero in the past to obtain dubious reports on the guilty of Córdoba and, again, she was used as a condemnatory tool in accusing the archbishop of using his palace residence as a synagogue. Further enforced prophesies resulted in Talavera's entire household being arrested and his relatives tortured to such an extent that they confessed to Talavera's guilt. Fortunately for the archbishop, he was eventually acquitted when Pope Julius II intervened and found the allegations to be false.

Lucero's unfounded allegations against one of the Pope's most holy representatives, together with the unresolved position of the Spanish monarchy, soon saw Lucero on shaky ground. Ferdinand – his most vital ally – was caught up in affairs in Italy, leaving Philip free to take charge. Believed to be a fairer monarch in terms of religious orthodoxy, the *conversos* of Córdoba were hopeful that Philip would restore balance to the city while Ferdinand was out of the country. Lucero must have believed this too, for he called an immediate *auto-da-fé* to sentence to death another 160 prisoners in June 1506. Thankfully, orders from the serving sovereign came through to prevent a mass conviction and Lucero was removed from office. The relief in Córdoba must have been palpable. However, their escape from Lucero's persecution would be fleeting.

LUCERO'S DOWNFALL

The freedom afforded to Córdoba would last only a few months. Unfortunately for the poor Córdobans, Philip I of Castile would fall mysteriously ill and die on 25 September 1506. Rumours of an assassination flourished though it was more likely to have been typhoid fever that took the new king. Philip's sudden death allowed Lucero to return to his role, much to the chagrin of Cordoban society. Like a recurring virus, Lucero came back stronger and more virulent. He hit out at the nobles of the city and the surrounding areas in Andalusia, declaring them all practising Jews, and vowed to systematically prosecute them. Knowing that a renewed campaign from a more ferocious Lucero would be unbearable, the

Marquis de Priego and the Count de Cabra among others, resolved to make a stand against the inquisitor's terrible deeds in early 1507. Priego expected an imminent investigation by Lucero, so had little to lose by fighting back. These Córdoban rebels called for Lucero's arrest and they stormed the Alcazar, effecting a gaol break. As poor men, noblemen and clergy broke out of the thirteenth-century palace-turned-prison, Lucero managed to escape out the back making his getaway on a mule. While the authorities condemned the inquisitor's abuses and excesses, his chief, Grand Inquisitor Diego de Deza, sent his nephew, Pedro Juarez, to prosecute the rebels in Lucero's stead. Inquisitional order was resumed and the freed prisoners were soon returned to their cells. This brave response to the return of Lucero was still not enough to remove him permanently from office. This feat would require the intervention of Ferdinand who had long been Lucero's constant supporter.

Ferdinand returned from Naples, and was able to rule the Spanish territories as regent. With an unhindered position, he quickly took charge of the turbulent situation in Córdoba and, in conjunction with the Pope, removed Deza from the head of the Inquisition replacing him with Francisco Ximénez de Cisneros on 5 June 1507. He then called for Lucero to stand trial for the murderous mayhem he had inflicted upon the Andalusian city and on 17 October of the same year, Lucero was tried and sentenced to imprisonment by a papal-appointed judge. Even with this official judgment passed, Lucero managed to avoid incarceration; such was the resilience and deep-rooted power of the inquisitor. It took almost a year for the Supreme Council to arrest him but finally in May 1508 he was taken in chains to Burgos to face a congregation which would investigate the atrocities that occurred in Córdoba.

With such damning evidence against the fallen inquisitor, Lucero was found guilty of excessive violence and extreme prejudice in July 1508 while, with such a deficit of evidence against his prisoners, hundreds of Córdobans were released. Yet justice was not fully done. The executions at the stake went unpunished. Nearly 150 deaths by fire and yet Lucero's punishment was nothing more than enforced retirement. Diego Rodríguez Lucero stepped out of the spotlight that had been for eight years focused firmly upon him and returned once more to relative obscurity living in the newly acquired town of Almeria where he worked as a teacher to the clergy.

PART THREE

THE WITCH-HUNTERS

WITCH-HUNTING ORIGINS

Belief in witches goes back to ancient times and was widespread throughout many cultures, including those of Mesopotamia and Egypt. During these times, witchcraft had both good and evil connotations. Spell-casting and magic was believed to have restorative powers and could improve even the crop yielded from a year's harvest. However, along with positive associations, witchcraft was also seen as harmful – a black art used for the purposes of evil – and so these early believers sought ways to defend themselves against such malevolent magic.

Owing to the perceived bond between witches and the Devil, it was deemed appropriate that fire – an element of purification – should be used to check the ways of a sinful sorcerer. Fire was synonymous with Satan, so how better to condemn his followers than to set as their standard punishment one of the most brutal forms of execution: that of burning. This idea is said to have originated with Saint Augustine of Hippo who, during the fourth and fifth centuries, was one of the leading theologians whose works helped influence Western Christianity. His beliefs helped establish the idea of a fiery hell as the dwelling place of the Devil he wrote:

... Pagans, Jews and heretics would burn forever in eternal fire with the Devil unless saved by the Catholic church.

References to witches can also be found in the Bible itself. In the first book of Samuel, King Saul consults with the witch of Endor after falling out of favour with God. This clandestine meeting with a necromancer is seen as a forbidden ritual and so would have gone some way to colouring Christian followers' opinions regarding witchcraft. Throughout the Old Testament, witches are tainted as wicked, referred to as women who utter evil curses in order to injure or destroy. The Book of Ezekiel told of Jewish women who could control the souls of others and were able to kill as well as bring the dead back to life. With the advent of Christianity, witchcraft began to lose its positive spin and it became paired with evil as the scripture in chapter 18 of Deuteronomy clearly states:

There shall not be found among you any one that ... useth divination, or an observer of times, or an enchanter, or a witch ... for all those that do these things are an abomination unto the Lord.

With the fall of the Roman Empire, Germanic people soon spread throughout Europe and this helped spread the fear of witchcraft throughout the Western World. Even those tribes that furiously resisted Christianity had their own thoughts and beliefs concerning witches. For example, the Saxons, with their pagan practices, trusted in their demon gods such as Thor, Wotan and Loki, and believed in their most witch-like of women, the Valkyries; supernatural battle maidens who rode the skies upon winged steeds. It is from the Anglo-Saxon word *wicca* – meaning sorcerer or prophet – that we actually get the word: 'witch'.

Order gradually assumed control over a wild and uncivilised Europe and laws were created prohibiting witchcraft. Alfred the Great, King of the Anglo-Saxons in Britain through the latter part of the ninth century, imposed the death penalty for those who used magic to kill. But rather than opposition from the monarchs of Europe and their associated governments, it was hostility from religious circles that helped enforce the negative profile of witches. Pope Zachary issued a rare ban on all wizardry and spell casting in AD 747. The *Canon Episcopi*, written around AD 906, stated that all witchcraft was, in fact, superstition and fantasy. The idea that the existence of magic was nothing but a figment of delusional imaginations created a dearth of judicial attacks on the papacy over the proceeding centuries. However, by the thirteenth century, records show that popes in office were beginning to proclaim once more the existence of witchcraft, and these papal interventions would slowly and surely sound the death knell for all satanists and sorcerers throughout Christendom.

From the thirteenth to the fifteenth centuries there was rarely a pope who did not issue a bull – a papal charter or law named after the *bulla*, or lead seal, used to endorse it – against some aspect of witchcraft. Pope Alexander IV issued two in 1258 and 1260 calling for a distinction to be made between witchcraft and heresy. In 1437 and 1445, Eugene IV called for the Inquisition to purge Christendom of witches. The first pope to call for the re-classification of witchcraft as an improper religion and, therefore, making any 'follower' guilty of heresy, was Sixtus IV, with three bulls in 1473, 1478 and 1483. These paved the way for the witch-hunters who could legitimately accuse their victims of blasphemous acts.

Despite these papal attempts to alter thinking in reference to witchcraft, it was not until a bull was issued on 5 December 1484 that the persecution of witches was allowed to take place. At this time, God's appointed man in the Vatican was Innocent VIII, whose name fully contradicted his most severe and violent behaviour. Not only was he the author of this eliminative edict, but he fathered numerous illegitimate children and, during his final dying months, took to sucking milk from women's breasts and transfused blood from young boys – causing the deaths of three – in a vain attempt to survive.

In full opposition to the *Canon Episcopi*, the bull, called *Summis desiderantes affectibus*, concerned itself with those who deviated from the Catholic faith, preferring a life of devils, spells and incantations, as well as the lack of support his dutiful witch-finders were receiving among the Christian townships. The Pope called for the removal of all obstacles from the path of his inquisitors, and effectively sanctioned the persecution of all those they found guilty. The bull's efficacy stemmed not solely from its groundbreaking contents but also because of the uniquely comprehensive circulation it secured in being appended to the front of the most essential published work on witchcraft: the *Malleus Maleficarum*, which translates as 'The Hammer of Witches'. With the advent of Gutenberg's printing press in the middle of the fifteenth century, this all-out attack on witchcraft, backed by the head of the Catholic Church, was able to reach districts and dioceses that had previously remained untouched.

This well-distributed *Witch-hunters' Bible* was written in 1486 by two Dominican priests called Heinrich Kramer and Jacob Sprenger, who were also pope-appointed inquisitors. Divided into three parts, the authors detail the power of the Devil channelled through these witches – his earthly accomplices – and thus the need for their destruction. In the last section, they provide a step-by-step guide on how to prosecute a discovered witch, from the initial accusation through an interrogation-induced confession to a successful conviction at trial. The tone of the piece was indicative of their dedication to the downfall of witchcraft, often departing from logic and reason to justify the proposed actions. For example, the two priests went as far as to suggest that the failure to shed a tear at one's trial was a true sign that the accused was a witch!

Such was the demand for Kramer and Sprenger's book that it had been reprinted up to twenty times by 1520 and a further sixteen editions were printed between 1574 and 1669. It was translated into French, English, Italian and German and, therefore, became the primary source of stimulation for the witch-hunting craze that swept right across Europe. And sweep it so fervently did. Like wildfire, the relentless search for sorcerers spread far and wide. What had been a relatively rare practice preceding the publication, with as few as thirty-eight witch trials reported in England, eighty in Germany and ninety-five in France during the fourteenth century, accelerated, causing hundreds of thousands of unfortunate victims to lose their lives. The declaration of the Carolina Code in 1532 went some way to boost the beliefs so vehemently expressed in the *Malleus Maleficarum* adding fuel to the fire. The code, adopted by the vast Holy Roman Empire made up of approximately 200 independent states, legalised torture and the death penalty as punishments for witchcraft. It seemed, legally, the witch had no place to run.

From 1550 to 1650, the witch-hunting craze was reaching its murderous peak. Witches all across Europe found themselves bound and burnt at the stake, rooted out by inquisitors and witch-hunters and convicted by God-fearing judges. This century-long period of persecution is often referred to as 'The Burning Times', and is attributed by many to the incessant fighting between Catholics and Protestants that was also at its height. The emergence of Protestantism in the first half of the sixteenth century ensured their followers would come to blows with the Catholics over religious supremacy and this struggle for power over the Holy

Roman Empire's many self-governing states came to a head in what would be forever remembered as the Thirty Years War, taking place between 1618 and 1648. The preoccupation with religion during this time was responsible for the overwhelming shift from focus upon the unwanted pagan rituals prevalent throughout early medieval Europe.

CEREMONY

The execution of a witch was predominantly a secular responsibility despite it being a religious matter. It was often the case that the Inquisition or the witch-finder would establish the guilt of the accused and then hand over the confirmed witch to the state which would decide on the degree of punishment. This judgement was handled not with sombre sobriety but with fanfare and flourish. The execution became a show, an event to both entertain and instil fear into the audience – a display of terror to fill the hearts of those who flocked to see such a deadly drama with fear, and to provide a worthy and thorough punishment for the culpable witch. Schools were closed on execution days and pupils would receive what amounted to extra-curricular religious studies educating them on the demise of those who favoured the Devil.

During its French ownership, the now Swiss canton Neuchatel was often the scene for witch executions. The pomp and circumstance surrounding these began with a formal procession from their cells in the prison tower to the twelfth century Chateau, both of which still remain today. The chatelain, or commander, of the castle was charged with opening the ceremony before the bells – often covered in wet cloth to intensify the melancholia of the peals – were tolled. The witch was made to kneel before the ogling spectators and forced to recite a resume of his or her trial. The mayor would publicly rebuke the prisoner and if they failed to heed this vocal dressing-down, the victim would be dragged back to the prison for further torments. A priest delivered a sermon followed by a formal reading of the sentence by a scribe. With these formalities completed, the prisoner would then be presented to the final link in the chain: the executioner. Once the oft-masked man had seen to the completion of the sentence, a banquet was held for those involved in the successful extermination of yet another satanic sorcerer. The chatelain, mayor and various court officials would gorge themselves on food and drink to celebrate the execution, none of whom would be required to put their hands in their pockets as the feast was paid for by the victim!

Similar ceremonial events took place in the divided German states responsible for the main bulk of witch executions. So many took place in just one year that it was reported the execution site resembled a small wood, such was the abundance of stakes protruding from the earth. With at least 100,000 death sentences carried out against alleged witches in these loosely unified territories efficiency was crucial.

History tells us that ovens came into practice in order to speed up the process – a development scarily portentious of the events of the holocaust. In Neisse, Silesia, forty-two females were oven-roasted for witchcraft during 1651, and over a period of nine years as many as 1,000 were cooked to death, including some children as young as two. There is evidence of an oven being used by Heinrich Kramer, the co-author of the *Malleus Maleficarum*, who started a Tyrolian witch hunt in the 1480's, although its use was far more indirect. Kramer was experiencing considerable opposition in this area and so required damning evidence against certain members of the community with which to kick-start his purge. He managed to convince a woman to hide in an oven and pretend the devil resided there. From within, she denounced various names providing Kramer with sufficient, yet dubious, evidence to administer severe interrogation. This bamboozlement of the Austrians eventually ensured Kramer was arrested and expelled from the region by the Bishop of Bixel. If there had only been more instances of ecclesiastical intervention, perhaps the gross number of sorcerers sentenced to death would have been reduced. Instead, entire villages were wiped out in the purge. Two villages disappeared outside Treves or Trier – an ancient German city sought after by the French during the Thirty Years War – when 368 witches were burnt, and a further two villages were left with only two remaining women alive in 1586.

As in France, the execution itself, was transformed into a drama in order to leave an indelible mark on the minds of spectators. The people were summoned by the fanfare of trumpets and the tolling of bells to the killing zone where the judge – holding his staff of office – would call upon the court officials to testify that the trial had been conducted lawfully. One by one the accused would be brought before the judge where they would be asked for their own admission of guilt. The judge would then ceremoniously break his staff and call for the executioner to carry out his orders, although not before those present were given the opportunity to point an accusatory finger and thus ensure that the slaughter continued.

In the Duchy of Prussia, a Protestant German area centred around Berlin, they had their own formal executions of those deemed in league with the Devil. A ceremony was recorded in 1687 at Arendsee where the amtmann, or magistrate, publicly asked the prisoners if they were accountable for witchcraft. This was purely procedure, for if they failed to admit their guilt they would be tortured until a confession came forth. The notary would then read the sentence and the prisoner would be passed to the executioner. The breaking of the magistrate's staff would take place as in other areas of Germany along with a ritual up-turning of the tables and chairs. A procession led the witches, bound by ropes and surrounded by armed guards, to the pyre and on this final journey psalms would be sung and prayers given for the souls of the condemned. This would continue well after the head had been separated from the body providing a most solemn soundtrack as the bodies were pulled by chains onto the flammable faggots and burnt to ashes.

With the exception of England, all countries that took part in the witch-hunting executed their con-demned satanists by burning. As with the ceremony that preceded an execution, there existed both similarities and differences between the executions themselves. While burning was standard, there were different ways of administering this punishment. Those witches in Spain often found themselves sus-pended above a heap of faggots by chains and irons; their final agonising moments of life on show for all to see. Alternatively, others were tied to a stake and had the combustibles heaped around them hiding their suffering from sight. A third method which was often used in the Germany consisted of a ladder upon which the prisoner was bound. With the top of this apparatus tied to a frame, the prisoner would then find themselves swung down onto the fire.

It would have been preferable to die as a witch in Germany and France than in the Latin countries of Italy and Spain, for those caught in the latter would have been burnt alive upon the pyre and would have missed out on the mercy of the Germans and the French who strangled the condemned before the flames took hold. This version was common after Scottish trials, too, although it was dependent on the co-operation of the condemned. In 1643, Janet Reid was taken by her executioner, or lockman, as he was known, and bound by the hands to her tinder-stacked bonfire. Here, she was strangled at the stake before being reduced to ashes. If she had revoked her confession, she would have foregone the strangulation and be forced to endure the unbearable heat. Further modifications to the pyre could have been made to increase the torture. It was common for the executioner to stack slow-burning green wood around the stake if the witch remained obstinate thus prolonging the agony.

THE END OF THE CRAZE

As with any fire, the flames of witch hunting slowly petered out, doused by a mounting wave of opposition. The rapid decline of the persecution was as swift as its onset in the fifteenth century. The arrival of the eighteenth century brought with it the Age of Enlightenment and advocation of reason over all things, the supernatural world of witchcraft had no place. Witch trials were still in existence but the number of those condemned to death dwindled. This was down to a diminished reliance on spectral evidence used to convict accused witches. In the past, it was sufficient to claim the prisoner had used spectres or apparitions of themselves to torment and bewitch their victims. Now, with considerable scepticism surrounding such paranormal phenomena, higher standards of evidence were required by the courts.

As with any major change in collective thinking, there were those who still pushed for the purge to continue. John Wesley, a staunch methodist in England, believed that the failure to accept the power of witchcraft was effectively denying the power of the Bible. Delivered in 1768, Wesley's view had come much too late for England was comparatively quick to bring an end to witch executions. In 1682, Temperance Lloyd, Mary Trembles and Susannah Edwards were tried and executed in the port town of Bideford near Devon and are considered to be the last English witches put to death, though others suggest Alice Molland is the unfortunate recipient of this title. She was sentenced to die on the Exeter gallows in 1684. Those north of the border required a little more time to follow suit, ending their reign of persecution in 1722 with Janet Horne, who was burnt at the stake in the Highland county of Sutherland.

This cessation of the death sentence swept across Europe beginning with France in 1745 with the execution of Father Louis Debaraz at Lyons and then to Germany thirty years later. Germany's last victim was Anna Maria Schwagel, a single servant girl in her mid-thirties, who, after being seduced by a coachman and tricked by a friar, found herself in the care of a mental asylum in Laneggen. There, a nurse attempted to force her to admit to sleeping with the Devil, and when she refused she found herself moved to a gaol cell where she spent the two weeks before her trial in Kempten, Bavaria. Before the judge, she freely confessed that she had made a pact with Satan and was beheaded on 11 April 1775.

Many historians state that the final execution of a witch in Europe occurred in Switzerland on 17 June 1782 against one Anna Goeldi. Switzerland was central to the witch-hunting cause but it has also been documented that the last trial and death sentence dished out to a Devil-worshipping necromancer took place in Poland ten or eleven years later with the burning of two nameless old crones.

The fact that these two debated execution dates are a decade apart shows the European witch-hunt was now becoming a thing of the past, a blot on religious history, a dark time that humanity would wish to forget. Depending on which figures you choose to believe, between 30,000 and 200,000 convicted witches lost their lives upon the flames or on the gallows throughout a Europe smothered in superstition.

MATTHEW HOPKINS
– WITCH-FINDER
GENERAL

Between the years 1645 and 1647, this self-titled 'Witch-finder General' dressed in the fashionable Puritan tunic, cloak and hat, marched through numerous towns in Eastern England, confirming the suspicions of townspeople who believed that one of their own was in league with the Devil. In only fourteen months, Hopkins the witch-hunter passed his own dubious judgement on almost 200 suspected witches, almost surpassing the number of all his fellow witch-finders combined.

Matthew Hopkins's success was, for the most part, down to timing. By 1650, the country was embroiled in civil war, creating an unsettled atmosphere particularly in the eastern counties where there was a considerable amount of support for the republican Roundheads. Owing to these uneasy times of

Parliament versus Crown, the regular assizes were suspended and in their place, special commissioners were ordered to dispense rough justice. In the east of England, these commissioners would be parliamentarians with a tendency towards the puritanical and a hatred of Catholicism. Unable to vent out their frustrations on the Catholics, the republicans needed scapegoats for their built-up anxiety. It was, therefore, the perfect time for someone to provide the people with a focus. Enter: Matthew Hopkins.

Matthew was brought up under the influence of his father, James Hopkins, a Puritan minister in Wenham, Suffolk, who ensured that Protestantism coursed through his veins. Rather than following in his father's footsteps, Matthew chose to study law, and eventually moved to Ipswich to practise. This was far from successful so Hopkins was forced to pursue other avenues. And pursue he did, hunting witches throughout the eastern counties and preying on the insecurities and paranoia of the people during this troubled time.

Hopkins would tell us later in his published work, *The Discovery of Witches,* how he began the chase to rid towns and villages of these unwanted Satan worshippers. In March 1644, in his home town of Manningtree in the north of Essex, he watched seven or eight witches meet every sixth Friday with others of their kind from neighbouring towns and villages, where they would make sacrifices to the Devil. In an attempt to further instil fear in anyone who'd listen, Hopkins went on to claim that four of these sorceresses sent a bear 40 kilometres (25 miles) to kill him in his garden. Clearly, this example of sorcery was not potent enough to succeed and Hopkins went on to make formal accusations against these alleged witches, of which nineteen were hanged. A further four died during their incarceration. And so Hopkins' career as a witch-finder began. The training needed to become a witch-finder cannot have been as extensive as the books and tomes required for his law training. At that time only three publications were widely available to teach Hopkins the way of the witch and how to spot them.

King James I, a known believer in witchcraft, published his own work in 1597 before he came to the English throne, entitled *Daemonologie, in Forme of a Dialogue. The Trial of the Lancashire Witches* was documented by the clerk of the court, Thomas Potts, in 1612 and twenty-five years later Richard Bernard, a Calvinist Puritan, wrote his *Guide To Jurymen,* which dealt with protocol involved in bringing charges against those suspected of witchcraft. With the education of such texts, Hopkins was prepared to go among the unenlightened and ill-informed and make use of his training. The majority of the illiterate villagers he came across were easily swayed by the all-knowing witch-finder, and regarding those that did not trust his word he appealed to their religious convictions and directed them to Exodus 22:18 in the King James Bible wherein it stated that, '*thou shalt not suffer a witch to live*'.

THE DISCOVERY – THE HUNT

Matthew Hopkins used many irrational and puzzling methods to divine a witch from an innocent, though often the people needed little persuading. In their minds the subject was already guilty and all that was required was confirmation. Such proof was ultimately achieved through confession. This is where Hopkins and his team came in. Suspects would very rarely admit to their collusion with the Devil without a degree of coercion. Hopkins expertly ensured that the suspect would come out the shadows and admit their true status as well the crimes they had committed.

Witch-finding began with the search for the Devil's mark. This required the subject to be shaved to ensure all areas of the body could be thoroughly inspected. The reference books on witchcraft studied by Hopkins and others like him all state this mark to be a true confirmatory sign that the subject is a witch. This visible symbol upon the skin would often take the form of a teat or nipple which was believed to be used to suckle supernatural imps known as familiars; low-ranking demons given to the witch by the Devil. These came in the shape of domestic animals which were commonly found in the homes of the suspects. If a supposed witch was found not to own a cat or dog, Hopkins and his people would attest that an insect such as a bee or fly discovered in the home was the witch's familiar!

Even when the poor victim passed this examination and no visible marks could be found on the body, the witch-finders administered a technique known as 'pricking' to discover invisible marks. These unseen marks were unique in that they were resistant to the pricking made by a bodkin – a sharp, pointed dagger – which was stuck into the skin. If the witch felt no pain and blood failed to exit the wound, this was confirmation that the undesirable had the sign of Satan upon her. Hopkins carried his own special bodkin to prove to the cynic that such invisible marks existed. After stabbing the skin, the knife was withdrawn and lo and behold no mark would appear. Little did the witnesses know that Hopkins' bodkin was a fake. The blade would retract into the handle, therefore inflicting no pain and drawing no blood.

One way or another, Hopkins was determined to find some sign that the subject was a slave to Satan, bringing further interrogation in order to extract the damning confession. As torture was illegal, Hopkins had to be creative with his techniques and developed alternative methods to acquire the admission; methods that would fail to leave any marks on the body. Some victims would experience sleep deprivation for days on end. Others would be forced to pace up and down without respite or sit cross-legged on a table for twenty-four hours, destroying any last trace of resolve. When put through such anguish, the suspect would admit to almost anything in order to stop the torment and Hopkins and his fellow hunters would accept the faintest of grunts and groans as answers to questions or admissions of guilt.

There was another common practice that reached its peak at the time of Matthew Hopkins. In the eyes of the witch-hunters, witnesses and even the alleged witches themselves – it could clear up any doubt and confirm innocence or guilt. This was known as 'swimming' and saw the accused submerged in a nearby lake or pond by her tormentors. The witch was bent double with their arms crossed between their legs and their right thumb tied to their left toe. Another rope was then fixed around their torso and held by a man on either side of the pond. The logic behind this 'dunking' came from the Christian act of baptism. Being in league with the Devil, all witches immersed in this way would be rejected by the sacred water and so float to the surface. Those who were pure of faith and innocent of witchcraft would sink and unfortunately drown. Such was the price for absolution. Very few achieved such exoneration, because the men holding the rope were in control and often ensured the submerged suspect would rise from the water, sealing their fate – to be condemned as a witch before their accusers.

Hopkins would then move on to the next town beseeching him to deliver them from the evil residing in their humble neighbourhood. With the tricks of the trade he had developed it was relatively simple to prove to the next village that they had a witch among them. This witch would usually be the weakest, poorest soul in the village; one that the community deemed undesirable. All that was needed was the smallest doubt or hint at some strange activity. In such an unenlightened time, almost anything slightly askew could be pounced upon and reviled.

THE HUNTED: ELIZABETH CLARKE

His first find was a one-legged woman called Elizabeth Clarke. Her mother had been hanged as a witch before her, so the suspicions and rumours had always surrounded her. This was an easy start for

Hopkins. He quickly approached a local justice of the peace and swore that Clarke was an enchantress. These accusations saw her arrested and thrown into prison. Behind bars and away from the public eye, Hopkins, and his assistant John Stearne had her stripped, whereupon she was found to possess the devil's mark in triplicate upon her body. Three 'teats' (probably moles) were found, prompting the acquisition of an order to have her watched. Clarke was starved of food and sleep for three consecutive nights, and on the fourth she capitulated, confessing her sins to Hopkins and Stearne. In order to bring an end to the suffering she promised to call one of her familiars – a white imp – and play with it on her lap as proof of her supernatural powers. Her request was refused and soon after she admitted that she regularly slept with the Devil. She told Hopkins that he would take the form of a gentleman and appear several times a week at her bedside demanding sexual relations. The accused confessed she never rejected these advances.

Along with this carnal confession, Elizabeth continued to disclose further bewitching acts she had committed in the past. She told of how she was instructed by Satan to kill a pig belonging to a Manningtree local, and the horse of one Robert Tayler. She revealed that the white imp was just one of five familiars she kept. This menagery included a white kitten called Holt, Newes the polecat, a black rabbit called Sack-and-Sugar, Jarmara the spaniel and Vinegar Tom, a long-legged greyhound with the head of an ox. These familiars were surely just misunderstood pets of the one-legged woman but were apparently seen by others, including Hopkins, who on 25 March 1645 during the trial perjured himself in court by swearing under oath that he had seen four of Clarke's imps appear before inexplicably vanishing into thin air.

Clarke went further still, implicating other supposed witches in the area. Anne and Rebecca West, Anne Leech, Helen Clarke and Elizabeth Gooding were all given up by Clarke and, when questioned, these women surrendered yet more names. In all thirty-two people were indicted, revealing that there clearly was no honour among witches! The trials of these accused slaves of the Devil began in Chelmsford on 29 July 1645. The presiding judge was one Robert Rich, the Earl of Warwick who, after hearing the prosecution from Hopkins, found twenty-nine guilty of witchcraft. Ten of these were hanged in Chelmsford, the others were executed in the surrounding villages. Their specific crimes varied though the most common was bewitching to death. The deaths of many unfortunate townsfolk residing in a community that harboured witches were considered to be the work of satanists. Blame was placed not at the doors of poor sanitation and disease but at those of strange old women. Such was the illogical, irrational behaviour of seventeenth century England.

News of the Chelmsford trials spread quickly throughout the South East and Matthew Hopkins was soon called upon to provide his skilled witch-finding techniques in other towns and villages that believed they too had an infestation. The demand for his services was so great that he had to expand is team. Along with his assistant John Stearne, Hopkins employed Mary 'Goody' Phillips a midwife skilled in finding devil's marks and Edward Parsley and Frances Mills soon followed.

THE HUNTED: LOWES

On 15 August 1645, the people of Great Yarmouth agreed to send for him and in the same month Hopkins and his band of witch-finding employees arrived in Bury St Edmunds where they performed fifteen examinations of possible witches. After the routine search for marks of the devil, four confessions were given freely to the Witch-finder General. Then came the careful invisible torturing or 'watching'. Confessions from the remaining prisoners came soon after. Two after one day of watching, four after two days and five after three days; the maximum period allowed to achieve a declaration of guilt.

His next find was John Lowes, the vicar of nearby Brandeston, proving that Hopkin's prey were not always women. Despite being instituted to the vicarage back in 1596 and with more than fifty years of service, his parishioners turned on him. It has been chronicled that he was a 'painful preacher' from whom the townsfolk were keen to liberate themselves. No doubt the fact that the old clergyman was now well into his eighties and so fitted the profile of the unpopular old crone helped suspicions to grow among the anxious and afraid of Brandeston. He was forced to undergo the 'swimming' in the castle ditch of Framlingham, and on being rejected by the water he was kept awake for three days and nights and then made to walk without rest until his feet blistered from constant running back and forth. After this painful and energy-sapping torture, his confessions came thick and fast. He admitted to making a pact with the Devil and sealing it with his own blood, to receiving three familiars which he suckled upon three teats found by the searchers; one on the crown of his head and two under his tongue. He even owned up to causing a ship to sink at Landguard Fort near Harwich, sending out his yellow imp to scupper the vessel, killing fourteen aboard. His confession of this evil act ensured the fate of the minister while also showing how much faith the authorities placed in it, for it is believed that nobody made the necessary effort to find out if a ship had actually foundered that day!

Lowes was found guilty of many acts of witchcraft and condemned to death. Despite Lowes's admission that he owned a charm given to him by the Devil, which would prevent him being hanged, the convicted witch was executed by rope on 27 August 1645, but only after reciting his own burial service as an illustration of his innocence.

FOUND OUT:
THE END OF HOPKINS'S REIGN

By the close of 1645, Hopkins had almost 200 suspected witches locked up awaiting trial in Suffolk. The Witch-finder General's prolific pursuit and prosecution of these poor unfortunates was now infamous. However, along with those who fervently sought his hunting skills, there were those who had begun to doubt his 'talent' for sorcerer spotting. In April 1646, Hopkins abilities were openly challenged. On arriving with his team in Huntingdonshire, he met with opposition from the vicar of Great Staughton, John Gaule, who spoke out against the actions of witch-finders in his services. On discovering this resistance, Hopkins reacted by writing to one of the parishioners, accusing Gaule of ignorance and threatening that he would soon be forced to recant his rants from the pulpit. A battle of words ensued, provoking Gaule into publishing his *Select Cases of Conscience Touching Witches and Witchcraft*. The book exposed Hopkins as a torturer of the innocent.

His livelihood under threat, Hopkins retaliated with a published work of his own entitled *Discovery of Witches*. This was effectively a defence of his role written in question and answer form. It listed fourteen frequently asked questions. In it, he refuted the claim that he was purely out to fleece his countrymen of their money, stating that he never went where he had not been called. This seems to have been the case. As well as finding witches, Hopkins found a steady flow of income worth an estimated total of £1,000. He was invited all over East Anglia visiting Bury St Edmunds, Ipswich, King's Lynn and Stowmarket, where the authorities even imposed a special tax on its parishioners to pay the rate of £28.3d for witch-finding services. This was a huge amount of money considering the average monthly wage at that time was only sixpence.

The remainder of 1646 saw Hopkins continue offering his services to the towns and villages in the eastern counties. On 26 July 1646, Hopkins saw to the demise of 20 Norfolk witches and in his home county of Suffolk, he is thought to have been responsible for the arrest of 124 supposed witches of whom 68 were executed. After this time, however, the call for his witch-hunting prowess grew quiet. Had he successfully rid East Anglia of all witches? Had the desire to attack undesirables died? Or was the faith of these towns in the abilities of Matthew Hopkins lost? It is known that Hopkins retired to Manningtree in Essex, while his second in command, John Stearne, chose to move away to Bury St Edmunds, fearing he would stir up public hostility if he remained close to his 'General'. Stearne went on to write his own work called *A Confirmation and Discovery of Witch-Craft* in 1648, the year following Hopkins' death, which is often used to contest the myths that surround Hopkins' demise. The legend has it that Hopkins was forced to taste his own medicine following an accusation that he was himself a witch. The fairy tale ending has him ducked under the water to prove his innocence. Stearne wrote that in fact Hopkins died peacefully after suffering from consumption – another term for tuberculosis – and was buried in the nearby village of Mistley on 12 August 1647.

While Hopkins's ability to discover witches is doubtful, his skill as a spin doctor is inarguable. He was able to heighten awareness of witchcraft as a

These unfortunate coincidences were seen as the work of the Devil, such was their reaction to anything that could not be easily explained. This belief in the evil acts of Satan was perpetuated by the theocracy that governed the state. A strict and stern Puritan faith focused on good and evil and taught predestination, accepting that the fate of one's soul was already decided at birth. The people felt constant need to seek out signs confirming an evil heart. Anything out of the ordinary was seen as a potential symbol of Satan and anyone not conforming to the norm upheld by the close-knit, church-going community, was seen to be in league with Satan and, therefore, deemed a witch.

The events in Salem were not without precedent. In 1688, the children of John Goodwin across the state in Boston began behaving strangely when Mary 'Goody' Glover, their Irish laundry woman, was accused of stealing linen by thirteen year-old Martha Goodwin. The fits thrown by Martha and her younger brother of two were so violent that they were often seemingly struck deaf, dumb and blind, leading the townsfolk to only one conclusion: the washerwoman had bewitched the children. Her inability to recite the *Lord's Prayer* added to the evidence against her, the authorities never taking into consideration the fact that she could not speak English! Unsurprisingly, she was found guilty by the court and condemned to death for witchcraft. The whole affair was published by Cotton Mather in his book, *Memorable Providences Relating To Witchcrafts and Possessions,* that year, so the young girls at Salem would have been privy to the powerful effects of the Goodwins' performance.

In November 1689, Samuel Parris moved from Boston and was installed as the new minister of Salem, where he was met with considerable opposition. His over-zealous preachings did little to endear him to his congregation. By October of 1691, many were keen to drive Parris out of Salem, and they refused to contribute to his salary. If only they had made good their threats, many of Salem village would have avoided severe persecution.

TROUBLED TEENAGERS

The trouble started when a group of impressionable young girls began to regularly visit the house of Samuel Parris to listen to Tituba – Parris' Caribbean Indian slave – tell unsettling tales of voodoo and other West Indian folklore. This prompted a keenness to experiment in the occult and they became obsessed with fortune-telling. The girls endeavoured to predict, among other things, their future social standing. Elizabeth Parris, the minister's nine-year-old daughter and her cousin, Abigail William aged eleven, were the youngest of the girls, and they would become so excited by the gatherings that they would begin to convulse, complaining of being pricked or cut. These fits were not confined to story-telling sessions. Elizabeth Parris was reported to have thrown a Bible across a room and Abigail made a scene during a day of fasting, disrupting prayers. The girls' behaviour got steadily worse. They covered their ears during Parris's sermons and barked like dogs when scolded. Even worse was to come. Soon the other older girls began exhibiting similar lawless behaviour, no doubt seeking the same attention that the youngest were attracting. This contagion affected Ann Putnam, Mary Walcott, Mary Warren, Mercy Lewis among others – all girls between the ages of twelve and twenty.

By February these public displays of petulance had grown to such a level that something had to be done. The village physician, Doctor William Griggs, was unable to provide a true medical diagnosis and so, in keeping with their puritanical belief in the un-explained, witchcraft was seen to be the only other possibility. This prompted Mary Sibley, the aunt of Mary Walcott, to call for a witch cake to be made; the unsavoury ingredients of which were rye meal mixed with the urine from the teenage girls. This creation was then fed to a dog and if the dog fell ill it would show the girls were not truly bewitched. However, if they had truly been afflicted, the dog would then identify the guilty witch. While the result of the spell remains unknown, the outcome prompted the townsfolk to pressure Elizabeth into revealing who caused her demonic convulsions. These subsequent accusations would unleash chaos throughout Salem and make it impossible for the girls to play it off as a teenage prank or a bid for attention. There was no turning back now. These 'witch bitches' – a term used by Old George Jacobs of the town – were about to become witch snitches.

WITCH SNITCHES

These troubled teenagers moved their theatrics on to a brand new and disturbing level, burning all bridges when they were pressed to name names. They blamed the obvious scapegoats of the town, first turning on the story-telling slave, Tituba who, after several days of interrogation, confessed to bewitching the girls before receiving a reduced sentence of imprisonment. Next the collective finger of blame singled out two more women vulnerable by their peculiarities. Sarah Good was a poverty-stricken, angry old woman who was often seen muttering under her breath as well as smoking a pipe, while

Sarah Osborne was a thrice-married cripple. None of these three were church-going folk; the clearest sign that they were in cahoots with the Devil.

The fourth victim of these witch snitches was to be more of a surprise and would increase the panic already prevalent in the town of Salem. The treatment of the first three suspected witches received opposition from Martha Corey, a member of the Church, and the girls' reaction was to label her a witch. She was excommunicated and condemned to death and on being cut down from her rope was buried in a shallow, unmarked grave. This strengthened the position of the Salem witch spotters for now it was clear: any opposition to the girls' accusations would be seen as a sign of guilt. Nobody was safe from the condemnations of these convulsing teens.

John Willard, a farmer and deputy constable, had been involved in the arrest of the first suspects but, on realising that the true criminals were the teenagers, he vocalised his suspicions and was forced to flee the town. He was picked up ten days later and brought before the girls, who promptly found him to be a witch. John Willard was hanged on 19 August. He was not the only official who bore the wrath of these young wenches. In Andover, Justice Dudley Bradstreet issued forty arrest warrants but when he refused to sign any more, his lack of co-operation was seen as sympathy for the sorcerers. With the indictment of nine murders over his head, he fled for his life and, unlike Willard, he managed to keep it.

Not even the accusers themselves were safe. Twenty-year-old Sarah Churchill was a servant to George Jacobs and when he was apprehended and examined, she refused to continue with the charade. Her Salem sisters immediately accused her of being a witch so, fearing for her own life, she quickly rejoined the fold. The other teenage turncoat was Mary Warren. When her employers, the Proctors, were accused of witchcraft, she could not bring herself to testify. Knowing that a public plea for their innocence would bring accusations upon herself, she secretly spoke with the other girls in the hope that their lives could be spared. It made no difference. Mary Warren was hounded by her friends until she confessed that John Proctor's spectre afflicted her. Save these two exceptions, at no time was any regret or remorse shown on the part of the girls. As the verdicts were read out in court and as the condemned were made to swing by their necks, the girls remained steadfast.

The Salem girls, now unable to show any signs of culpability, went on a widespread trail of denuncia-tion, their techniques improving with experience and leaving no doubt in the minds of the town magis-trates. When the girls failed to synchronise their spasms they found other ways of confirming bewitchment. The examination of William Hobbs is the perfect example. In a far from subtle manner, Abigail Williams forecast who he was tormenting, at which point the chosen girl would fall into fits and complain of biting and pricking.

When neighbouring towns began to suspect that they, too, were harbouring witches, the girls were sent for. In the villages of Topsfield and Andover, they were forced to adapt their technique to get round the fact that they did not know the names of the people they wished to censure. It was then that they created the touch test, which involved Ann Putnam and Mary Walcott going into spasms while the suspects were lined up before them. In turn, they were asked to touch the convulsing girls. If the girls became quiet the toucher was guilty of witchcraft. Two alleged witches who failed this test were Ann Pudeator and Mary Parker, who were eventually hanged on 22 September 1692.

THE EXECUTIONS

Some of those who confessed to dabbling in sourcery during the Salem trials never found their neck in the noose. A confession and a promise that no further afflictions would be made was enough to produce a reprieve. Those twenty who were executed in 1692 were those stubborn ones who denied all charges of witchcraft and collusion with the Devil, but were unfortunate enough to have an accusatory teenage finger pointed at them.

The first to be sentenced to death was Bridget Bishop. She was known in the village as possessing a dubious moral character. The pervasive Puritan values of the community frowned upon her colourful attire and late night partying, making her an easy target for fanatics hellbent on eradicating the town of riff-raff and undesirables. When they were brought into the courthouse these malicious sisters of Salem began to writhe in agony despite never having met Bridget before. This was sufficient proof that Bishop was guilty and in just eight days she was tried, sentenced and executed upon Gallows Hill, where she continued to profess her innocence.

Bishop was the only 'witch' to be hanged alone. There followed a short recess during which time the authorities sought advice from Cotton Mather, the head of the Boston clergy, on whether this drastic course of action was correct. The reply was an affirmation of their actions and so what followed were three hanging days over the next three months. Five were executed on 19 July, a further five met their maker a month later on 19 August and eight more were hanged on 22 September.

As with all crazes, this trend was short-lived. The urge to purge their communities of witches was soon out of vogue. In October, the town of Gloucester sent for the female band of witch-finders. During this visit they discovered only four, and on being summoned the following month, they were met with a rather frosty reception resulting in no arrests. Clearly, the flames of fanaticism were no longer raging as they once had, and the girls' testimonies were not wholly believed. At this time, in the nearby town of Ipswich, the girls went into one of their performances on seeing an old woman and they were promptly ignored, such was the apathy surrounding the witch-hunters by the end of 1692.

In May 1693 an amnesty was granted and all those in gaol were set free. Finally, the crazed stupor was beginning to wear off and there were clear signs that the people of Salem were returning to their senses. Only one of the girls ever apologised for her actions. This came in the form of a written apology in 1706 from Ann Putnam. She claimed that she had never acted maliciously during that wild witch-seeking year but, in fact, had been deluded by the Devil into denouncing the innocent. Over the coming years, a petition was created listing the names of all those that had been falsely accused of witchcraft and in 1711 compensation was granted to twenty-two of those listed, the authorities acknowledging the huge mistake they had made. It was not until the fitting date of 31 October – Halloween – 2001 that Governor Jane Swift finally proclaimed the innocence of all those accused in Salem and its surrounding towns more than 300 years ago.

THE WITCH-
HUNTERS: FRANCE

JEAN BODIN

Born in 1529, 320 kilometres (200 miles) south-west
of Paris in the town of Angers, Jean Bodin was to
become one of the most ardent of witch-hunters in all
of France. Like many of his fellow persecutors, Bodin
was a well-educated man attending both the local
university in his home town and, after a brief period
as a Carmelite monk, the University of Toulouse,
where he later became the professor of Roman Law.
In 1561, Bodin moved to Paris to serve King Charles
IX and began writing his successful though controversial publications on philosophy, politics and
sovereignty – the latter subject was extensively
covered in his *Les Six livres de la République* (The Six
Books on the State), completed in 1576. That same
year he married the daughter of a King's prosecutor
at Laon and established himself as a provincial lawyer.

Later he became a public prosecutor, which brought him face to face with many suspected witches. Attending these trials helped him to form his major work on witchcraft entitled *De la Demonomanie des Sorciers* (Of the Punishments deserved by Witches), which revealed his brutal point of view. It covered ways in which judges could battle the witch problem and legally defined a witch as, 'one who knowing God's law tries to bring about some act through an agreement with the Devil'.

Bodin took the witch infestation very seriously and this was reflected in the punishments he advocated in the third part of the book. Torture during interrogation was essential to unmask the suspect and reveal his or her true identity, and Bodin often went all out, using hot irons to cauterise inflicted wounds in order to extract a confession. No punishment was too cruel for a witch in his eyes, and not even the young and old escaped his wrath – he was known to torture children and the elderly. An agonising execution upon the flaming pyre was not enough for Bodin, who considered burning to be too good for witches as even the slowest fires would last only half an hour.

His hatred was directed not solely towards those who – under duress – confessed to witchery. Judges who failed to give the maximum sentence to a sorcerer were themselves condemned to death. Those who failed to believe in the influence of Satan through witchcraft were also heavily rebuked by Bodin. Dealing with the Devil required relentless verve, leaving no room for half measures or scepticism. It was imperative that the full force of the law should be administered for the security of the state and to assuage God's vengeance. He insisted upon the disclosure of accomplices and even called for children to testify against their parents if witchcraft was suspected. Such suspicion, without prior evidence, was grounds for torture followed by condemnation from which they could never be acquitted. For Bodin, this was not man's inhumanity to man but the Lord's work. Such belief was illustrated in 1566 when a woman from Vermandol near Saint Quentin was mistakenly burnt alive after the executioner overlooked the customary strangulation. Bodin was far from apologetic. He passed off this miscarriage of justice as the judgement of God. Presumably, it was also God's handiwork when Bodin contracted the plague and died in 1596.

NICHOLAS REMY

Our second Gallic demonologist and executor of witches hailed from Charmes in the Lorraine region of France. Nicholas was born around the year 1530 into a renowned and noble family, a branch of the ancient house of *Saint Remigio de Câlons-sur-Marne*. They were a family of lawyers. His father, Gerard Remy, was Provost of Charmes and his uncle was Lieutenant-General of Vosges. It was unsurprising, then, that Nicholas followed suit. He studied law at the University of Toulouse before taking over the Lieutenant-General post on his uncle's retirement. The titles were bestowed upon Nicholas with continued regularity, being made a Privy Councillor to the Duke Charles III of Lorraine in 1575 and six years later he became the State Attorney of Lorraine and Sheriff of the Court of Nancy. It was at this point that his hatred for witches revealed itself in the cruellest of ways.

As State Attorney and Sheriff, Nicholas quickly established himself as a fervent detester of devil-worshipping witches, and the torturous acts he performed upon his suspects earned him the moniker, the 'Torquemada of Lorraine'. He was known to punish children as young as six or seven and torment their minds by having them parade around their parents as they burnt at the stake. This passion for persecution began at an impressionable age when, as a child, he often frequented the trials of suspected sorcerers. Yet it was an incident in 1582 that would truly give birth to his widespread extermination of so many unfortunate French men and women.

Nicholas Remy was approached by an old beggar woman and, not knowing his attitude towards such vagrants, she was promptly snubbed by him. A few days later, Remy's eldest son was taken ill. Doctors were unable to restore his health and he died. A livid Nicholas demanded vengeance and, with his witch-hating beliefs fuelled by grief, he hunted down the elderly transient and had her prosecuted for bewitching his son and causing his death. An accusal from someone so respected in the community was enough to condemn such a good-for-nothing hobo and instead of alms she was given something far more life-changing: a death sentence.

From this moment on, Remy went on a crusade against those he believed were in league with the Devil, and took every case of sourcery as personally as that which had seemingly befallen his son. Rather than roaming the district of Lorraine wildly looking for signs of witchcraft, Remy used his background in law to rationally justify his accusations. This above-board approach ensured that his prosecution success rate soared above those of his witch-hunting contemporaries. On his retirement to the country in 1592, he wrote his book *Demonolatreiae*, in which he revealed the extent of his witch-hunting exploits. To lend further weight to its contents, printed on the title page of this work was the self-congratulatory revelation that he had condemned 900 witches in only fifteen years, naming 128 of them. This work went on to be reprinted many times after its initial publication in 1595, and even substituted the *Malleus Maleficarum* as the accepted handbook for witch-hunters.

Those who were consigned to the flames for witchcraft and association with the Devil stood no chance of acquittal after being charged by Nicholas Remy. On his death in April 1612, he could boast such titles as the Attorney General of Lorraine and *Seigneur de Rosieres-en-Blois et du Breuil*; the latter raising him to the level of aristocracy. Yet it was the title of witch-hunter that would brought arguably his grandest boast of all: that he sent around 2,500 suspected witches to their deaths during his career.

PIERRE DE LANCRE

Another witch-hunting aristocrat was to make an name for himself during the early years of the seventeenth century, purging provincial towns and villages of supposed satanic evildoers. His name was Pierre de Rostegny. Born in Bordeaux into a prosperous wine-growing family, de Rostegny went on to pursue a career in law before turning his attention to the pursuit of witches. Attaining a doctorate in 1579 after extensive study in Turin and Bohemia, he was soon practising law for none other than the parliament of Bordeaux. During this time he chose to adopt the noble name of *de Lancre*; a name that would soon become synonymous with the hunting and severe persecution of so many witches.

His unerring belief in the existence of witches was given significant credence during a stalled pilgrimage to the Holy Land in 1599. His journey came to a halt in Naples and, while still in Italy, he witnessed Satan himself transform a young girl into a boy. This delusion spurred the Lord of de Lancre on to greater impassioned discoveries of the Devil's work, prompting him to write three books on witchcraft. Despite possessing a well-educated, well-travelled mind, the beliefs documented in these works were steeped in irrational fear and reveal a mind full of religious neuroses. He believed that, while sex with the Devil existed, Satan favoured married women over singletons as this would effect a sinful act of adultery. He also believed that demonic children were being created through incestuous acts between mothers and sons all over France.

These documented revelations prompted King Henry IV of France to direct de Lancre to Labourd in 1608 to look into the possibility of witchcraft occurring within this Basque province. The unwavering zeal of this noble witch-hunter was renowned and so

Henry IV's government suggested its president, D'Espagnet, should join him to ensure the investigation did not become a bloodbath. Unfortunately, this wise move was scuppered with the submission of D'Espagnet's resignation on 5 June 1609, leaving de Lancre free to persecute the unfortunate inhabitants of Labourd.

De Lancre stayed in the village of Saint-Pée-sur-Nivelle during this purge, occupying the castle of Amou, and soon discovered that the entire population – reported to have been approximately 30,000 – had been touched by the Devil in some way. According to the witch-hunter, Labourd had become a sanctuary for the pagan ritualists, or *sorginak* as they were known who had been forced to flee the Orient after the arrival of Christian missionaries. He was provided with reports that 100,000-strong sabbats were regularly taking place, and there were confessions from the witches themselves telling of their dates with the Devil.

Sixteen year-old Marie de Naguille and her mother told how Satan himself had invited them to a sabbat ritual. Marie de Marigene and her friends confessed to riding on the Devil in donkey form to nearby Biarritz and seventeen-year-old Marie Dindarte spoke of how the Devil had hidden an ointment that allowed her to fly. Confessions were extracted in abundance by de Lancre, allowing him to burn at the stake 600 predominantly female witches in the area. This wholesale slaughter of sorcerers came to a sudden halt when the husbands and fathers of the executed returned from their summer fishing off Newfoundland. As many as 5,000 Basque fishermen discovered they had lost their loved ones in the massive witch-hunt and they went in search of the man responsible. Fearing he would become the victim of a new hunt, de Lancre was forced to take flight, leaving what he believed to be tens of thousands of witches unpunished.

In 1616, Pierre de Lancre gave up his pursuit of witches altogether, retiring to Loubeur-sur-Garonne in the Bordeaux region of France where he continued to write works on witchcraft. In 1622, he published his *L'incredulité et mescreance du sortilège plainement convaincue,* which warned against the erroneous belief that magic performed by these witches was some sleight of hand or illusion. Until his death in 1631, aged seventy-three, Lord de Lancre was adamant that witchcraft existed and felt considerable pride that he was able to rid his beloved France of so many of these spell-casting satanists.

THE WITCH-HUNTERS: GERMANY

BENEDICT CARPZOV

As we have seen, the prominent witch-hunters in France were noted for their elevated social standing and ancestral association with law and its practices. Their witch-finding counterparts across the border in Germany were no different. In 1595, Benedict Carpzov Junior was born into a family of eminent jurists and statesmen in the south-eastern district of Saxony. His father was a renowned law professor at the University of Wittenberg, known for one of its most famous alumni: the Protestant theologian Martin Luther. With a background such as this, it is unsurprising that Benedict Carpzov developed into a committed Protestant and high-principled judge, known throughout the country as the Lawgiver of Saxony for his relentless pursuit and prosecution of more than 20,000 German witches.

Carpzov attained various prominent positions which soon ensured a level of power. As well as being a professor at the University of Leipzig, he was also a member of the Leipzig Supreme Court. This enabled him to influence verdicts throughout all of Saxony. His belief in the power of witchcraft ensured no leniency was given when it came to sentencing suspected witches. It was the combination of his knowledge of law and religious conviction that saw him send so many devil worshippers to the stake. He was known to attend church without fail each Sunday, take Holy Communion almost as regularly and even claimed that he had read the Bible an astonishing fifty-three times. Such was the extent of his religious zeal.

This extreme piety never manifested itself through acts of mercy when witches were concerned. The Protestant faith to which Carpzov belonged advocated as vehement a hatred of witchcraft as Catholicism, and it was thanks to Lutherans such as Carpzov that witches were beset on all sides by righteous crusaders seeking to cleanse their communities of heretical heathens. The Lawgiver of Saxony assisted in the offensive when, in 1635, he published his *Practica rerum Criminalum*, in which he sought to systemise the legal persecution of those guilty of sorcery. In this publication, which soon became the Protestant version of the *Malleus Maleficarum*, he insisted that local judges should be given the freedom to mete out the severest of penalties to witches and not be constrained by judicial minutiae. This included torture, which he believed was called for within his oft-read Bible.

Carpzov listed as many as seventeen varied techniques for acquiring a confession, such as the placing of candles underneath an alleged heretic, allowing for an agonising slow burn. He also refers to driving wooden wedges under the nails to obtain 'the truth' from a prisoner, and if this failed to obtain an admission, then the wedges would be set alight to increase the pain.

Carpzov was not concerned with a fair trial for, in his eyes, there was only one true outcome where a witch was involved. To ensure this foregone conclusion was reached in the shortest time, Carpzov believed that witches should be prevented from questioning any witnesses called to the stand, and so they were unable to prove their innocence before the court. He suggested that allowing these sorcerers to cross-examine would give them the chance to use their satanic powers to bewitch and befuddle their accusers, reducing the validity of their testimonies and even leading to a not-guilty verdict. Removing this legal right shows the lengths to which Carpzov was prepared to go to ensure the suspected witch became a dead one.

Even after successful execution, Carpzov's oppression continued. He forbade the burial of any witch because this was a Christian custom and should not be extended to those guilty of heresy. Instead, he called for their bodies to remain above ground to rot and become carrion for the birds – this posthumous punishment acting as a deterrent to all witches in hiding.

By the time of his death in 1666, Benedict Carpzov had become the most prominent German figure in the pursuit and eradication of witchcraft. His pen worked overtime signing death warrants and sealing the fates of so many so-called witches. Yet it was his published beliefs that secured this position of distinction. Rather than bringing to light new thoughts and beliefs regarding the persecution of witchcraft, Carpzov reappropriated old Saxon laws from the previous century, and made certain the topic of witchcraft was in the forefront of many German minds. His success is revealed with the example of Anna Maria Rosenthal who, in 1728, was sentenced to death for witchcraft in Winterberg after the prosecutor quoted Carpzov's published words. Over sixty years after his death, his power to persecute was still strong.

scrupulous behaviour knew no bounds, leaving no one safe from his merciless authority. He even turned on his own staff when, during a visit to the river town of Siegburg, he discovered that his own executioner was guilty of witchcraft. Familiarity bred contempt in the worst possible way when Buirmann promptly had his employee burnt at the stake.

It is unsurprising, then, that Buirmann was faced with opposition wherever he went. A known frequenter of bars, Buirmann was reported to have been attacked outside one such tavern, suffering a broken arm at the hands of the relatives of a witch he had executed. By the time Franz Buirmann was done with the town of Rheinbach, he had tortured and burned alive 150 convicted witches out of 300 households, leaving an entire community broken.

PART FOUR

IMPALEMENT

IMPALEMENT

DRIVING HOME A POINT

Impalement is a method of execution whereby the prisoner is pierced with a long (usually wooden) stake. Penetration can occur through the sides, the rectum, the vagina or the mouth. The stake, which is planted in the ground acts as a plug, preventing severe blood loss and, thereby, prolonging the victim's suffering. Death by impalement is extremely painful and can take up to three days to kill. For this reason, one might be forgiven for thinking that it was reserved for serious criminals who were themselves guilty of unspeakable acts of violence and depravity. Unfortunately, this is not the case. Many victims of impalement were wholly innocent of any real crime – they just happened to be in the wrong place at the wrong time.

THE METHOD

Methods of impalement have differed depending on the whims of various tyrants throughout the ages.

Sometimes the stake was sharpened to cause ripping of the vital organs and agonising pain, and on other occasions the stake was left blunt and simply greased with animal fat at the inserted end, which had the effect of pushing and squeezing the organs aside. This method was also extremely painful, especially when organs burst under pressure, but prolonged the victim's suffering even further.

THE UNFORTUNATE PAPPENHEIMERS

The story of the unfortunate Pappenheimers demonstrates just how easily innocent people found themselves on the receiving end of an impaler's spike. The Pappenheimers were a vagrant family from Bavaria in the late 1500s. They took seasonal employment as privy cleaners and beggars. Duke Maximilian of Bavaria needed a show trial to teach the community that 'crime does not pay'. He rounded up the Pappenheimer family and had them charged with as many unsolved crimes as he could think of, including murder, and he roped in other criminals to perjure themselves in order to help prosecute them.

One night while they were sleeping, the Pappenheimer's lodgings were raided and the inhabitants (including their children) arrested. They were kept in the custody of a man named Alexander Von Haslung, who was initially put in charge of their torture and ultimate destruction. He decided that the Pappenheimers were in league with Satan, and accused them of witchcraft. Haslung was not particularly interested in the Pappernheimers' case and thought this would get them taken out of his custody. He was correct and the Pappenheimers were transported to Falcon Tower in Munich.

Once installed in the tower, the Pappernheimer family were tortured using methods such as *strappado* (the pendulum), *squassation* (weights attached to the body during the process of strappado), rope burns and torch burns, among others. At first they insisted upon their innocence, but as the torture sessions drew on, becoming more intense, they eventually changed their plea. Between them they ended up confessing to almost every major and minor unsolved crime committed in Bavaria during the previous decade and implicated at least 400 other people, some of whom did not even exist.

The head of the family, Paulus, confessed to have crippled or slain a total of 100 infants, forty-four adults and ten elderly people. He also apparently stole alcohol from the cellars of innkeepers, robbed churches and set fire to houses and barns. His wife admitted killing 100 children and nineteen elderly people through sourcery, as well as causing four gales and hailstorms, poisoning crops and cattle.

When this bout of torture was finally over, the family were taken to the place of execution. Commissioner Wrangereck forced the Pappenheimer's youngest son, ten-year-old Hansel, to stay and watch the ordeal, as if this would somehow transform the young boy into a model citizen. First the executioner took hot pincers to Paulus and his eldest son, ripping wounds in their tired torsos.

His wife, Anna, had her breasts cut off and these were used to torture and degrade her and the two men further. Next, as if this was not enough, the prisoners were taken to a cross to pray and drink some wine (as was the custom in this part of Bavaria). Christoph Neuchinger, the official in charge of proceedings, made the following official statement, giving his approval to the executioner. It was common at this time for executions to generate such hysteria that executioners were sometimes lynched by the spectating crowd. Neuchinger's words gave him passage to proceed in safety.

I order the executioner to carry out his duty, and I warrant him peace and safe conduct, whatever may befall him.

The executioner had been instructed to draw out the deaths as much as possible, and so was careful not to kill them too quickly, but after being broken on the wheel, Anna was eventually burnt alive and Paulus was impaled, as described here in the German manual 'Punishment in Life and Limb':

This (impalement) was one of the most revolting punishments ever devised by human imagination and even in those days it was hardly ever used. The penal code of Charles V did not make provision for it. In barbaric regions, particularly the Algiers, Tunis, Tripoli and Salee where inveterate pirates dwell, if a man is thought guilty of treason he is impaled. This is done by inserting a sharply pointed stake into his posterior, which then is forced through his body, emerging through the head, sometimes through the throat. The stake is then inverted and planted in the ground, so that the wretched victims, as well we can imagine, live on in agony for some days before expiring ... It is said that nowadays not so much trouble is taken with impalement as once the case, but such criminals simply have a short spit thrust into their anus and are left to crawl thus upon the earth until they die.

This was poor Paulus's fate, skewered like a hog for no reason at all other than to provide an example to his fellow citizens.

Duke Maximillian was certainly not the first, and he would not be the last person to inflict this punishment on his fellow man. The ancient Egyptians, the Persians, the ancient Indians and the Romans all practised some form of impalement. As did the Zulus, the Polish-Lithuanians and the Swedes. There are a few historical figures in particular who made impalement their trademark, and in some cases even their *raison d'etre*. Their names were Ali Pasha and Vlad the Impaler.

VLAD THE IMPALER

Vlad the Impaler, also known as Vlad III Dracula, or Vlad Tepes, was born in Sighisoara, Transylvania, late in 1431. He was the second son of Vlad II or Dracul, a military governor and an esteemed member of the Order of the Dragon, a secret brotherhood whose membership comprised Slavic rulers and warlords sworn to defend Christendom from the Turkish infidel.

The word 'Dracul' has two meanings, the most common translation is 'dragon' but it can also be used to mean 'Devil'. As a young man Vlad added an 'a' to Dracul meaning 'son of', so the translation of his full name would have been something similar to 'Vlad Son of the Dragon' or 'Son of the Devil'– not a name to forget in a hurry, and one that the young man would certainly grow into.

VLAD: THE EARLY YEARS

In order to begin to understand the life and actions of Vlad the Impaler, it is important to understand a little about the world he inhabited. Romania during the

Middle Ages was nestled between two powerful forces: the Hungarians and the Turks. During this time of widespread political and social unrest, paranoia was rife within the ranks of the aristocracy. Life was cheap – even the life of a Romanian aristocrat. Infighting, inbreeding and frequently shifting alliances meant that anyone in a position of wealth or influence was in danger of being betrayed and killed by a member of their own family, and the House of Basarab, the royal family of Wallachia, were no different.

Vlad II and his brood lived an opulent lifestyle during Vlad III's early life. In 1436, his father assassinated Alexandru I – a Danesti prince – and rose to the throne of Wallachia. He and his family took up residence in the palace of Tirgoviste.

Vlad Senior had been playing a dangerous game, remaining apparently faithful to the Order of the Dragon while simultaneously paying tribute to the Turkish sultan. Following the Hungarian invasion of the area, he betrayed the order of the Dragon, pledging alliegance to the Turks in order to secure his position on the throne of Wallachia. He committed his two sons Vlad III and Radu the handsome to the Turks as 'insurance'. Vlad senior sent them as hostages to Adrianople, where Vlad III would remain until 1448. It was here that he would have learnt about the

Turkish culture, and the extremely violent ways they dispatched with their prisoners – impalement was widely used by the Ottoman forces at this time. On the death of his father at the hands of the Huns, at just seventeen years of age, Vlad III was installed on the throne of Wallachia – and then – just when it seemed that Romanian history could get no bloodier – the real carnage began.

BLOODIER AND BLOODIER

Most of us know Vlad the Impaler as the inspiration for Bram Stoker's novel *Dracula*, published in 1897. Compared with Stoker's work of fiction the true story of the man himself is far more horrifying. The young Vlad III grew up to become one of the most brutal and depraved tyrants the world has ever known. In 1456, during his second reign as king of Wallachia (this time supported by the Huns instead of the Turks), Vlad began building Poenari Castle in the mountains near the Arges River. The very construction of the castle was a bloody affair, as anyone too old or weak to work could expect to be swiftly executed, and many of the slaves forced to build it expired due to injury or exhaustion in the course of the project. Vlad had already made his name as a particularly ruthless tyrant who was not to be trifled with, but worse was still to come.

THE METHOD

Impalement is one of the slowest and most painful, not to mention gory, ways a human being can die. Vlad's chosen method meant a horse was attached to each of the prisoner's legs, and a stake was slowly driven into the body, usually through the buttocks, though sometimes through the abdomen, the chest or another bodily orifice. There is some evidence to suggest that infants were sometimes impaled on the same stakes forced through their mother's chests, and ocasionally victims were impaled upside-down on the stake. Presumably, in these instances the stake entered the body through the mouth and existed at the other end – it's difficult to guess which would be more painful! The stake itself was made of wood and oiled at the top, its length indicated the rank of the victim. Care was taken to make sure that the point was not too sharp so that the condemned died slowly in agony, rather than quickly from shock or ruptured vital organs.

Vlad III was particularly concerned with matters of female chastity, so an unmarried woman who entered into a sexual relationship, an adulterous wife or a promiscuous widow could expect to endure an incredibly agonising death. Her genitals would be removed and her breasts sliced off, then she was skinned alive and impaled through what was left of her vagina on a red hot stake. Given this threat it is difficult to believe that any woman would consent to intercourse with any man outside of the marital bed! The likelihood is that these so called 'adulterous' women were actually victims of rape to begin with and innocent of the charge against them, but that didn't seem to matter to Vlad. He killed them anyway.

Most societies who utilised impalement as a form of capital punishment tended to reserve it for special cases – those of high treason or mass murder. Vlad, however, did not descriminate, using any excuse he could find. He murdered peasants and noblemen, men, women and children – anyone he considered superfluous to his master plan, or an unnecessary waste of resources. The sick, the lame, the poor and the destitute all met with this punishment. Many of the people he murdered were boyars – or members of the upper class, merchants and civil servants, who he considered deceitful. He recruited their replacements from the loyal working class in order to further secure his position on the throne. It was the boyars who were responsible for the betrayal and assassination of Vlad's father and his elder brother Mircea, who was buried alive after his eyes were gouged out, following defeat at the battle of Varna. Vlad hated the boyars with a passion, and it seems he attempted to wipe them off the face of the earth, sometimes destroying entire families.

Vlad impaled his victims in their hundreds and even thousands. The stakes were often arranged in geometric patterns, most commonly in a ring of concentric circles around a city's outskirts. The decaying corpses were often left to rot for months on end – the sight and smell of such a spectacle must have been overwhelming and the potential for disease and parasites would have weakened the surviving population still further.

THE FOREST OF THE IMPALED

In 1462, the Turkish army were growing stronger under the leadership of Sultan Mehmed II, and they invaded Wallachia with the intention of transforming it into a Turkish province. He came with an army three times larger than Dracula's, possibly because Vlad had systematically brought his own country to its knees and murdered many of the people who would otherwise have fought in his army. Not having any allies he could call on, he was forced to retreat. He made for the capital Tirgoviste, burning his own villages and poisoning the wells on his way so that the Turkish armies would have nothing to eat or drink in persuit of him. When the sultan and his armies reached Tirgoviste, hungry and exhausted, they were confronted with a horrifying sight. The rotting carcasses of some 20,000 Turkish prisoners impaled on stakes were there to greet them at the entrance to the city. The incident came to be known as 'The Forest of the Impaled'. The exhausted Turkish army fled in terror.

Perhaps Dracula's sole reason for these mass culls was to scare prospective invaders into believing that a sadistic madman ruled Wallachia, a man so depraved he would torture and kill his own subjects in their droves, poison their wells and burn their villages just to thwart his enemies. After all, if he did this to his own people – what would he do to his *real* enemies?

Historians differ in their analysis of Vlad the Impaler's motives. Some believe he, like Dracula of the novel, was actually involved in satanic rituals and enjoyed drinking the blood of his victims, believing it made him more powerful. Others think his actions were committed as an act of revenge against a society he hated for betraying his father, Vlad II. It is also possible that he committed these atrocities as a genuine attempt to enforce a stern moral code. However, few historians doubt that Vlad the Impaler derived some kind of perverted sexual pleasure from these cruel, painful and degrading executions.

As an example of an executioner Vlad the Impaler is quite unusual. Most people who kill on behalf of the state are fairly level-headed members of society who believe they are working for the moral good, and confess a sense of discomfort at the prospect of dispatching people who are essentially innocent of any serious crime. Vlad relished administering pain and suffering to anyone – even young children. He made no known attempt to justify his actions and did not confess any feelings of remorse, putting him in much the same league as psycopathic serial killers such as Elizabeth Balthory or John Wayne Gacy. Indeed, later in his life, as a prisoner in Russia, it is recorded that Vlad tortured and executed the birds and animals that were unfortunate enough find themselves in his cell. He routinely impaled them on tiny spikes, perhaps proving that, far from killing his victims out of commitment to a strict moral code or as part of some convoluted home-defence strategy, he enjoyed it immensely – and found the thrill of the kill both personally and perhaps sexually fulfilling.

ALI PASHA

Ali Pasha, or the 'Lion of Yannina' as he came to be
known, is generally remembered as something of an
enigma. He was regarded by many as an important
political figure in Albanian public life. Ali Pasha was
born in 1744 in the village of Hormove, near the
Albanian town of Tepelene. His contemporaries regarded him as the promising son of a powerful clan
and an energetic, quick-witted, sharp and determined
young man with a bright future ahead of him. He was
apparently extraordinarily skilled, democratic, non-
religious and surprisingly modern in his general outlook.

THE ROMANTIC 'HERO'

Later in his life, European authors, men of letters and
emminent scholars visited his camp, and consulates
from the four major world powers of England,
France, Russia and Austria existed in Ioannina under
his rule. It is easy to see why a formidable figure like

Ali Pasha would have excited and intrigued western romantic writers and thinkers such as Lord George Gordon Byron, who remarked in his work *Childe Harold* that 'his highness is a remorseless tyrant, guilty of the most horrible cruelties, very brave, so good a general that they call him the Mahometan Bonaparte . . . but as barbarous as he is successful, roasting rebels etc, etc.'

And there's the rub. Ali Pasha was not as civilised or as forward thinking as he seemed on the surface, and he certainly was not without a troubled past. In 1758, when his father Veli, the governor of Tepelene was murdered, the young Ali escaped to the mountains with his mother Hamko, joining the bandits who infested the region at this time. Ali's natural mental tenacity, coupled with the position of his birth, meant he quickly rose to power among the bandits. It was during this period that Ali Pasha honed his leadership skills and developed the violent, vengeful temper and bloodthirsty lust for power that would see him go down in legend as an oppressive tyrant who was hellbent on attaining and holding on to power by whatever means necessary.

When the government, recognising his talent for leadership, installed Ali Pasha as the governor of Rumelia, he quickly became dissatisfied and seized power of Ionnina. It would become his base for the next three decades. He then exploited the weakness of the Ottoman government to expand his territory still further, gradually gaining control over most of Albania, western Greece and the Peloponnese.

As a ruler, Ali Pasha was both strict and unforgiving. He punished his many prisoners and enemies using the most barbaric practices, burning, roasting and drowning among them (he once had a rival publicly executed by sledgehammer – breaking every bone in the man's body) but the gory, excrutiatingly painful and visually spectacular process of impalement was his favourite method of punishment, and he engaged in it as often as possible.

ALI THE IMPALER

In Ali Pasha's favoured method, the victim was made to lie down with his legs spreadeagled and his hands tied behind his back. So as not to distract the executioner from his work, the victim was rendered motionless by the executioner's assistant who sat on a saddle placed on the victim's back while the executioner prepared the stake. He smeared the shaped end of the stake with lard and then grasped it with both hands and forced it into the anus of the victim as deeply as possible. Presumably this would have required quite a lot of energy on the part of the executioner – perhaps even a small run-up! Then he picked up a mallet and pounded the end of the stake so that it penetrated another 38-50 centimetres (15-20 inches). The victim was then hoisted upright and the stake implanted firmly into the ground. The victim's feet were left dangling in the air so that the weight of his struggling body forced him down still further on to the stake. Relatives of the condemned may have attempted to pull downwards on the lower half of their loved one, forcing the stake further on it's journey, thus hastening death.

As with the Romanian method adopted by Vlad the Impaler some 300 years earlier, the end of the stake was left blunt so that it squeezed aside the vital organs rather than punctured them. Victims could expect to survive in agony for up to three days, depending on where the stake left the body. Friends and relatives hoped that the stake took a quick exit through the left side of the body, causing cardiac arrest. If it took a right and pierced the armpit, the shoulder or the chest, the victims agony would be prolonged and death would finally come through gradual blood loss or exposure. If a roasting was in order, the family of the impaled prisoner would be forced to turn the spit on which they sizzled, or face the same hideous fate.

PART FIVE

NEWGATE PRISON

NEWGATE GAOL

The first prison in London became the final home for many condemned to death. Newgate was where the majority of convicted criminals were sent to await execution, but the inside of this prison proved just as deadly as the executioner himself.

Newgate was one of the seven main gates into the capital set in the surrounding Roman wall. During the twelfth century a prison was built on the banks of the Fleet River, which ran parallel to this rough, ragstone boundary. It started life as a royal prison incarcerating those deemed dangerous to the Crown, that is until the reign of Henry IV, when it no longer discriminated, taking any common criminal from London and Middlesex. The structure of Newgate changed many times over the centuries, usually out of necessity. Along with the countless volatile characters that dwelled within its walls, Newgate was visited regularly by fire, ensuring constant renovation. Not only was it badly damaged during the Great Fire of 1666, but fire returned in 1762, then in 1780 as a consequence of the Gordon riots and yet again in 1877. These incendiary incidents must have gone some way to perpetuating the belief that those who resided in the cells dwelled in the depths of hell.

THE KEEPERS OF THE GAOL

One of the reasons why Newgate was always in such bad shape comes down to those responsible for its upkeep. These were the keepers of the gaol who had been appointed by the sheriff to run the day-to-day administration as well as the maintainance of the building. On the whole, those that applied for such a role were not the most discerning and particular of men, and so it is unsurprising then that the prison was forever in a state of disrepair.

Indeed, these turnkeys were often contemptible characters, extorting money from all inmates and inflicting vile tortures upon their person. They would lead a new prisoner into the darkest, most squalid chamber of the gaol and place as many irons – each weighing as much as 3.6 kilograms (8 pounds) – upon his legs as they could manage, then offer the unfortunate prisoner the chance to pay his way out. The wealth of a Newgate victim would be systematically stripped by these gaolers, who squeezed every penny from the condemned in order to line their own filthy pockets, and would often leave destitute those lucky enough to leave free men. These fees were known as 'garnish' and helped the keepers turn a profit. If a prisoner failed to pay the going rate, their lives were made yet more miserable. The meagre menu would be forbidden to those who did not pay and they would be given no water. They would be placed in heavier restraints and iron collars, then bound by chains fixed to the wall or sometimes to the dirty parasite-ridden floor. The payment of these fees persisted until the nineteenth century despite various acts outlawing the custom. The keepers continued with their racketeering even after 1734, when they were eventually paid a wage of £200 a year, and it was not until 1823 when these illicit payments were effectively abolished after it was discovered that many of those incarcerated had been detained for up to thirteen years for minor debts.

THE INMATES

Those that had been sentenced to death at the Old Bailey were taken to the prison to await their fate. These could well be considered the lucky ones, for they at least could see an end to the foul and fetid conditions to which they were subjected. These prisoners would be escorted into the Lodge and then into the Condemned Hold, often called Limbo, from which we get the term, 'in limbo'. They were not trapped inside the rotten cells of Newgate for long, especially if their crime was murder. After 1752, such a conviction ensured their death would come within two days of sentencing. The only exception was if the sessions took place on a Sunday, in which case the prisoner was executed the next day. On the whole, sentencing took place on a Friday, allowing the condemned the weekend to come to terms with their fate. The majority who had not killed but had been given the death penalty for lesser crimes could face a more lengthy stay; anything between two weeks and four months languishing within the confines of an overcrowded, unventilated chamber.

This protracted wait gave these prisoners time to hope for a reprieve. The more optimistic inmates crossed their fingers that the recorder's report suggested they should have their sentences commuted. This report was submitted to the king and the Privy Council after the Sessions at the Old Bailey had ended, and it detailed those the court felt should be executed and those that should be granted a reprieve. The king and council would then meet in what was called the Hanging Cabinet, where they would ultimately decide the fate of each individual listed in the report.

If no reprieve was forthcoming, then there existed only two other ways to dodge the drop. It was fairly common for prisoners to escape their cells. The poor condition of the walls seems to have made it relatively easy to break out of Newgate. In fact, its history is littered with many successful escapes. In 1275, there was a mass breakout when nineteen prisoners successfully found their way to freedom. There are instances in 1758 and 1763 of further mass breakouts where the prisoners attempted to saw through the bars, and in 1679 seven convicts escaped by picking the stone from the walls. Some prisoners found it so easy that they repeatedly escaped, such as condemned robber Daniel Malden who escaped twice in 1736 and 1737, not forgetting the most infamous Newgate escape artist, Jack Sheppard, who did the same more than ten years earlier.

Before making a mockery of London's first prison, Sheppard made a name for himself by escaping from St Giles' Round House and New Prison in Clerkenwell. He was given the death penalty on 12 August 1724 and sent to Newgate which only managed to hold him for nineteen days. On Monday 31 August he broke out through loosened bars and is thought to have dressed in women's clothes to effect his escape. Despite being proficient at prison breaks, he clearly was not as talented at evading capture, for he was arrested again on the 9 September and returned to Newgate. After two further foiled attempts that month, his gaolers transferred him to a fortified room known as the Castle, fixing him in leg irons and chaining him to the floor. Even these measures could not hold him as he took a delight in showing his keepers how he could pick the locks with a small nail.

Stories of this defiant scoundrel brought many curious visitors to his cell before his second breakout. This was quite an accomplishment. He scaled a chimney, broke through six barred doors and lowered himself down from the prison roof using a blanket, all the while bound by leg irons. Predictably, Jack Sheppard was soon caught yet again and found himself back at Newgate from where he was unable to escape a third time.

The remaining self-made reprieve was for women only and existed as early as 1387. If they were unfortunate enough to fail in receiving a commuted sentence, then many would confess to being pregnant. This was called 'pleading the belly' and proved a successful method of escape, as those who were found to be with child by the appointed matrons were often later reprieved. Pregnancy must have been easy to achieve for without any segregation of the sexes, there were always plenty of men with whom to fraternise, including the gaolers who, for a price, would have turned 'child-getter' as it was known. It is documented that between 1674 and 1830, 268 women sentenced to death declared they were pregnant, so the authorities soon decreed that no woman could claim a second time, ensuring female convicts could not continually exploit this rule. This practice was only rendered legally invalid by the Sentence of Death Act of 1931.

A RASH OF EXECUTIONS

Newgate was in such a state that even free men and women who passed the prison walls on the outside were inclined to hold their noses at the awful stench emanating from within. For those inmates who were not able to vacate the area and were manacled inside, they would run the risk of a sickness known as 'gaol fever'. It was such a problem that by the early 1700s for every person who died at Tyburn, four perished in Newgate from this highly infectious disease. For the inmates trapped in these overcrowded, un-sanitary quarters, it was not the masked hangman upon the scaffold that they feared but this faceless executioner residing with them in their cells. Gaol fever was easily spread by the rat-riding fleas and lice so rife that the floor crunched under the feet of prisoners and guards.

In June 1419, Ludgate prison was closed and its prisoners transferred to Newgate, however, after four months this move had to be reversed after sixty-four inmates as well as the keepers from both prisons died from the fever. The contagion – effectively typhus fever – manifested itself through a rash of red or purple spots and a high delerium-inducing temperature. The Mayor of London at that time was Richard 'Dick' Whittington who, on his death four years later, left sufficient funds to rebuild Ludgate prison which would gain the nickname of Whit's College – a place where many graduated with dishonour. Even this philanthropic gesture failed to stop the spread of the disease. In 1750, more than sixty people died from the fever including jurors, barristers and past and present mayors. The prison walls were washed down with vinegar in an attempt to protect the prison from further outbreak. Records show that this failed as between 1758 and 1765, eighty-three more prisoners perished from the contagion – sixteen in one month.

The welcome addition of a windmill built on the roof of the gatehouse to improve the air flow brought a brief respite from the fever until it seized up, no doubt from the lack of maintenance by the keepers. The illness was allowed to continue in its role as in-house executioner, condemning men and women to death not by noose nor axe but infection.

ST SEPULCHRE'S CHURCH

For those that were lucky enough to survive the fever, but were unlucky not to receive a reprieve, the execution day drew inescapably closer. When they reached their final night on earth, at the stroke of midnight they heard the tolling of a bell across the road at St Sepulchre's Church. This tradition began in 1605 when London merchant, Robert Dow, left an annuity of fifty pounds to pay for a bell ringer to toll three times the night before a hanging. This was traditional night music for the condemned for almost a further 300 years and along with the bells the bellman would sing out the following:-

All you that in the condemned hole do lie,
Prepare you for tomorrow you shall die;
Watch all and pray: the hour is drawing near
That you before the Almighty must appear;
Examine well yourselves in time repent,
That you may not to eternal flames be sent.
And when St Sepulchre's Bell in the morning tolls
The Lord above have mercy on your soul.

The last inmate to hear this ominous lullaby was Mary Pearcey on 23 December 1890, when a guest staying at the Viaduct Hotel near the church was taken ill. So as to not concern the sufferer unnecessarily, the vicar of St Sepulchre's called for the ringing of the bell to stop as hearing such words would not help improve the guest's health! The bell tolled no more and the prison itself lasted only another twelve years. In August 1902, it was pulled down to make way for the Central Criminal Court – known as the Old Bailey – which still stands today.

PEINE FORTE ET DURE

Many never made the feted trip to Tyburn to receive their slice of fame. Some were subjected to a torturous practice which often resulted in death. This method of execution was known as 'pressing' or *peine forte et dure*, meaning hard and strong punishment. This punishment soon became a capital one administered not by the celebrated and notorious hangmen of the time before bloodthirsty London crowds but by unknown executioners hidden from public view behind the thick walls of Newgate gaol and other prisons around the country.

The reason for this most private of executions stems from a loophole in the law. Criminal justice in medieval times was not as comprehensive as it is today. The courts only involved themselves in prosecution once a charged prisoner had voluntarily submitted themselves to trial. A plea of either guilty or not guilty was required to sentence an arrested individual and without this the courts would be – dare one say – hard-pressed to convict the defendant! If the prisoner stayed silent, or stood mute as it was called, then the case could not proceed. Such a glaring technicality must have been fully exploited by countless suspected criminals. The authorities found it necessary to create a deterrent.

Coercion was needed to make this silent minority speak up and so in 1275, during the reign of Edward Longshanks, the First Statute of Westminster decreed that those who refused to be tried by the Law of the Realm were to be put in a hard and strong prison; a term known as *prison forte et dure*. Basic incarceration had, by 1406, developed into the *peine forte et dure*, a more torturous tradition that often became a death sentence. Here, Lord Chief Justice Gascoigne condemned two robbers who had held their tongue in order to delay their death. He sentenced them to receive, '... as great a weight of iron as they can bear and more ... and so lie until death'.

SILENT MOTIVE

Several reasons have been cited as to why these arrested individuals chose to remain mute rather than plead their innocence. The main reason must have been a financial one. It was customary at the time that if a prisoner was found guilty of the crime with which he had been charged, all his possessions and estates would be forfeited to the king. Refusing to plead ensured that one could not be found culpable and, therefore, any wealth would pass to relatives and loved ones rather than disappearing into the Crown's swollen coffers. This was illustrated with the pressing to death of Walter Calverley at York Castle in August 1605. He had slaughtered two of his sons and attempted to kill his wife at Calverley Hall before pursuing another son, Henry, with murder on his mind. Thankfully, he failed to get close to his remaining son and was arrested. In a complete turnaround, overcome with such remorse, Calverley refused to plead in order that his substantial estates found their way to Henry, the son he had tried to kill.

Further familial grounds for choosing not to plead was to spare one's relations the pain and suffering that would occur from a public execution. To be executed behind closed doors saved the prisoner's nearest and dearest the anguish of seeing a loved one put through the theatrical rigmarole of a public execution as well as help them avoid any undue attention from the crowd themselves.

Many have said that another motive for choosing the *peine forte et dure* could well have been the desire to preserve a reputation. It must have been easier to bear a private death sentence than a public one. The avoidance of an actual sentence would ensure an air of mystery surrounded a man who went to his grave by way of pressing.

PRESSING ENGAGEMENTS

On failing to plead either way, the prisoner would return to the gaol and be placed in a more fitting cell for punishment; dank, dirty and dark. The room would have been one of the lowest as the prisoner would soon have no occasion to stand. The gaol keeper would then strip the prisoner down and lay him naked on his back save a piece of ragged cloth to cover his nether regions. A board would then be placed upon his chest upon which various slabs of stone and iron would be balanced and the weight would be incrementally increased the longer the man or woman remained mute. As the severe load pressed the chest, ribs broke in the process. The silent sufferer would be given a diet of three morsels of barley bread on the first day of the punishment. The second day they would receive no food but were given only water brought not from any fresh source but from the inside of the prison. This alternating diet would continue until the prisoner uttered his last painful breath.

How long the prisoner survived was dependent on the amount of weights placed on the body as well as the individual's own pain threshold. Some would quite literally crack under pressure and plead, while others remained silent to the very end such as Henry Jones, who in 1672 perished under torture after forty-eight hours. While two days seems a long time to suffer such pressure, it was considered that anything beyond five or six days in such a state would demand superhuman strength, which makes Cecilia Ridgeway's case even more extraordinary. It is believed she survived a pressing of forty days without food or water in 1359 and was subsequently pardoned by Edward III, duly acknowledging this superwoman's staying power.

In addition to the obvious chest pains and asphyxia that such weight would cause, there were other unexpected results. In 1722, a highwayman named Spigot was being pressed in the usual fashion when he turned to the chaplain at his side complaining of a painful weight on his face. The chaplain told the prisoner that there was nothing but a thin veil of cloth there, revealing that Spigot's veins were being so violently squashed beneath the load that the blood was being forced up into his head. The pain must have been so unbearable for he soon agreed to break his silence and plead. He was eventually found guilty of his crimes and executed at Tyburn the following year.

These in-house executioners made further

developments in order to force the accused felon to plead. Sharp stones and jagged pieces of wood were often placed underneath the victim. These would dig into the back and undoubtedly pierce the flesh. This additional atrocity happened to Margaret Clitherow on 25 March 1586 when she had a fist-sized stone placed under her during her imprisonment in York. A 363 kilograms (800 pounds) load was piled on top of her, she died within fifteen minutes.

If death was not forthcoming, these crushing killers had one final move to bring about either their plea or passing. If all else failed, the gaoler – surely not the sveltest of men – would add his own considerable weight by standing on top of the slabs of iron and stone. This took place in 1735 when John Weekes received the *peine forte et dure* after refusing to plead at the Lewes assizes. Pressure from three 45-kilogram (100-pound) weights bore down on Weekes after which the gaoler added two 23-kilogram (50-pound) weights to the load. With the prisoner still alive after withstanding 181 kilograms (400 pounds), the gaoler turned executioner and placed himself on top, killing Weekes in an instant.

The gaoler was not always the executioner, however. Major Strangeways found himself imprisoned in 1676 after killing a man called Fussell, who was his sister's lover and lawyer. He invited his friends to the low cell where he instructed them to dress him in white along with a mourning cloak and, in some sort of euthanasic ceremony, he called for his friends to promptly pile the heavy stone and iron mass upon his chest in the corner of the press yard to end his life. Unfortunately, this burden was not enough to kill him so they added their own weight by standing on him. This finally brought death to Strangeways who, rather than keeping his death from his loved ones, allowed his friends to play executioner and have a major part in it.

The last known occurrence of this pressing torture and execution took place in Cambridge in 1741. Little is known of the victim and whether or not his silence or his chest broke under the load. However, it would be another thirty-one years until this coercive method was stamped out, ending 366 years of crushing pain. This abolition brought both good news and bad. From 1772, any prisoner who took a vow of silence would not escape conviction as his plea would automatically be recorded as guilty! No more were alleged criminals able to prevent their wealth from passing from their willed nominees to their God-appointed monarch. This lawful injustice was soon corrected when in 1827 an Act was passed that called for the court to enter a plea of not guilty whenever a prisoner remained mute.

Lord George Gordon, led a protest calling for the repeal of the 1780 Roman Catholic Relief Act. The purpose of the act was to repeal the severely anti-Catholic laws which were introduced in Britain during the 1600s. The Protestant Association wanted these laws reinstated, and they marched on the Houses of Parliament brandishing the legendary slogan 'No Popery'. The protest quickly got out of hand and a violent mob began to attack Catholic churches and chapels, including the Sardinian Chapel, near Lincoln's Inn Fields and the Bavarian Chapel in Warwick Street. Later, the angry rioters turned their attention to the homes and business practices of Catholic Londoners, as well as institutional buildings such as the Bank of England, the King's Bench Prison, Newgate, Fleet and Marchelsea Prison. Legend has it that by the evening of the following Wednesday, one could see no less than thirty-six separate properties alight from Tower Bridge.

Fortunately, weather conditions meant that the flames were well-contained, but the king had had enough and ordered the army to close down the riot at whatever cost. In the battle that ensued between rebels and the soldiers, 285 people were killed, 173 wounded and thirty-nine arrested. Most of the casualties were rioters themselves, who didn't stand much chance against the might of the British army.

The hangman Edward Dennis was one of those arrested and brought to face the judge. In court, he claimed that he was passing through Holborn when a group of marauding rioters recognised him as the famous hangman Ned Dennis, and threatened to kill him there and then if he didn't participate in the destruction of a house belonging to a man named Edmund Boggis. In fear of his life, he assisted them.

The likelihood that anyone would threaten a man like Ned Dennis is a matter for debate. Executioners were generally seen as people to be feared and avoided under all circumstances. The judge did not believe Dennis's story – and sentenced him to death. Aware of the poverty awaiting his family on the occasion of his execution, Ned begged the court that his son may be able to take on the job of executioner, claiming that he was '*a youth of sobriety and ability, who would be a credit to the profession*'. This appeal was rejected on the grounds that such a move would mean the son was forced to execute the father.

Dennis eventually received a reprieve, the judge was wise enough to recognise the urgent need for an experienced executioner during this time of political and social unrest. He was, therefore, free to execute those who had not been so fortunate. Thirty-five people were sentenced to death. During this time the judge had the power to order that the execution take place near to the scene of the crime. It is likely that he chose to utilise this power in order to send out the message loud and clear that anyone convicted of breaching the peace could expect to be hung in the streets. Gallows were especially constructed all over London for the purpose of punishing the rioters. We have no way of knowing how Dennis felt as he operated the drop and sent these particular men and women to meet their maker. Perhaps he saw them as martyrs for the cause who would receive a bountiful reward in heaven; on the other hand perhaps he just forgot about politics and went ahead regardless. The experience can't have changed his view of the job that significantly, because he continued to act as public executioner for a further six years.

WILLIAM BRUNSKILL

William Brunskill took over from Edward Dennis as chief executioner on 21 November 1786, following the death of his former boss. During his long and prolific career Brunskill executed a staggering 537 people outside Newgate Gaol, and a further sixty-eight at Horsemonger Lane Gaol in Surrey, from its opening in 1800 to 1814.

The gallows he preferred to use were the 'New Drop' gallows, the same as those on which he had trained under Ned Dennis. It had two parallel beams from which a maximum of twelve people could be hung at once. Sometimes the executions were performed in batches. The platform measured 3 metres (10 feet) long and 2.4 metres (8 feet) wide, and was released by a pin acting on a drawbar underneath the trapdoor. The prisoners were afforded a drop of 30 to 60 centimetres (1 to 2 feet), so death was often a long and agonising process. The sight of twelve men and women struggling desperately for breath, simultaneously choking to death, must have been a strange and obscene spectacle indeed. One wonders whether congregating spectators ever placed bets on which poor wretch would be the first to expire. Occasionally the pin contraption failed, the platform did not release properly and a simple beam and cart method would be used instead, like the one that was used to execute Ann Hurle.

William Brunskill is probably most famous for conducting the last ever burning of a woman in England. The unfortunate woman in question was Catherine (or Christian) Murphy, who on 18 March 1798 was executed for coining (regarded as high treason at the time). Her four co-defendants, including her husband, were executed by hanging at the same time, but being a woman she was singled out for the flames.

Officially women were burnt rather than hung for reasons of decency. It is hard for us to understand how this brutal punishment was any more 'decent' than a trip to the gallows. It is true that hanging allowed spectators to peer up the skirts of female prisoners, but when a woman was hung and then burnt, as in the case of Catherine Murphy, this argument becomes defunct. Perhaps the main reason for burning was to provide extra drama for the blood-thirsty audiences and, therefore, a more severe deter-rent from indulging in crime. It is also possible that the chief intention was to destroy the body by flame, thus removing it permanently from the reaches of body snatchers and other unsavoury characters who may otherwise pillage or abuse it.

Catherine's life was relatively uneventful and little is known about it. Her death, however, has gone down in history as a significant watershed point in the history of the British legal system. At the time of her execution the rules regarding capital punishment in Britain were beginning to change and so were society's views surrounding it. In 1787, two years before Catherine's state-sponsored death, transportation to Australia was introduced as an alternative to incar-ceration and the gallows. Those criminals convicted of their first offence (except for those found guilty of the three most serious crimes: murder, high treason or petty treason) could expect to be transported to Australia rather than dance the Tyburn jig. Within a few years this practice meant the number of criminals being hanged had dramatically decreased. Great news for the criminal fraternity, but Brunskill would have been worried for his job, afterall an executioner is only employed as long as there are plenty of criminals to execute! A new era beckoned, one of rehabilitation over retribution, but luckily for Brunskill and his successors it would be almost 180 years before capital punishment was abolished in Britain for good.

The method used to kill Catherine Murphy on that spring day at Newgate was really more like a modified form of hanging than a traditional stake burning. Murphy was mounted on a small platform in front of the large wooden stake. The noose, which was suspended from an iron bracket projecting from the stake, was placed around the prisoner's neck and tightened. Then Brunskill removed the platform, leaving Catherine suspended by her neck. After thirty minutes, presuming that the noose had done its job, Brunskill placed the faggots around the stake and set light to them.

Ann Hurle was only twenty-two years of age when she was hung by Brunskill for forgery on 14 January 1804. For reasons unknown the 'New Drop' method was not used, but instead a simple gallows was erected near to St Sepulchres Church. Despite her youth, Ann was highly educated and had devised a cunning plan to defraud the bank of England of the sum of £500 – a massive amount of money at the time and the equivalent of about £250,000 today.

Ann met and befriended a stockbroker named George Francillon, and persuaded him to obtain a power of attorney to allow her to sell some Bank of England stock on behalf of an elderly gentleman named Benjemin Allin. George had known Anne for sometime and, therefore, was not overly suspicious of her intentions. She claimed that Mr Allin had promised her the shares in return for her aunt's ongoing help and compassion as his long-term housekeeper. Mr Francillon granted her request and she told him that she would take the document away and get it signed by Mr Allin.

Ann returned with the papers signed (purportedly by Mr Allin) and witnessed by Thomas Noulden and Peter Verney, who both owned businesses in Greenwich. Mr Francillon took the document to be verified, and Anne set off to sell the shares. The verification department noticed that the signature on the form bore little resemblance to the sample signature held by the bank. Anne replied that Mr Allin was nearly ninety and did not often write, which would explain why the signature differed. She even offered to take out another power of attorney and obtain another signature from the wealthy gentlemen.

Nevertheless, the seed of doubt had been sewn, and Mr Francillon began to question Miss Hurle's story. He deferred his next meeting with Anne and investigated the matter a little further – making a visit to Mr Allin. Ann realised then that the game was up and tried to make a break for it, but it was too late. She was charged with attempted forgery.

Both Benjimen Allin and George Francillon were principle witnesses for the prosecution – Allin testified that he had never seen or signed the document in question. Mr Verney and Mr Noulden also testified against her. Ann simply didn't stand a chance.

On the day of her execution Miss Hurle was brought out of the debtor's door at Newgate Prison at 8.00 am. She was placed in a cart and drawn to the widest part of the Old Bailey, where she mounted the platform. She showed considerable remorse, begged forgiveness and prayed silently, fainting more than once. When Brunskill placed the noose around her neck she attempted to speak, but was unable. As with many who faced this destiny before her, her strength had well and truly failed her. Ann's youthful, girlish appearance, that same quality that had most likely appealed to George Francillon, also appealed to the crowd. They began to feel sorry for her and became so clamorous that the sherrif was forced to intervene, shouting at the spectators to calm down. Brunskill then pulled the cap down over Anne's face and the cart was drawn away. Anne gave a faint scream as she was lurched upwards, and for a couple of minutes she appeared to be in great pain and distress, struggling and waving her arms about wildly.

JOHN LANGLEY

John Langley took over from William Brunskill in 1814 as executioner of Newgate Gaol. He executed thirty-seven men and three women in three years as chief executioner. One of the few females he executed was Eliza Fenning in 1815.

Eliza was just twenty years old when she went to the gallows. Very attractive girls often find themselves in trouble of one kind or another. They tend to excite the unwelcome passions of men and the passionate jealousy of their wives. This, some say, is what happened to Eliza Fenning.

She was employed as a cook in the house of Robert and Charlotte Turner, a respectable family who lived with their servants in Chancery Lane, London. On 21 March 1815, Eliza prepared a lunch of rump steak and potatos with gravy and dumplings. Soon after eating the meal, the whole family (including Eliza and an apprentice in the household) went down with chronic stomach pains and violent vomiting. The doctor was sent for immediately and everyone was able to make a full recovery. Whoever attempted to dispatch the Turner family that afternoon, they hadn't done a particularly good job. This error is the first clue to the identity of the would-be killer. The murderer obviously had no idea how much poison would kill the family, and one could conclude that they were not even that determined, considering that they only put enough in to give them all a nasty stomach ache, not nearly enough to kill anyone.

Soon after the incident Mr Turner expressed suspicions that the family had been poisoned with arsenic, because a packet of the poision he kept in his office had recently disappeared. Arsenic was widely available at the time and often used for treating vermin infestations. The Turners had a problem with mice – they also had a problem with murderous servants – or so they believed. The police were called, and an investigation began.

The missing packet of arsenic was never found, but its contents were detected in the dumpling pan on the day following the alleged poisoning. The only person who had a part in cooking the lunch was Eliza, and although the dumplings had been burnt and heavy instead of light and pale coloured (she can't have been a particularly good cook), no one else from the household had been near them.

The apparent motive was revenge, at Eliza's trial Mrs Turner testified that Miss Fenning had recently been discovered scantily clad in a bedroom shared by two of the male servants. Eliza had been severely reprimanded and threatened with the sack if she did not mend her ways. The young woman was actually engaged to be married, so it is odd that she should be frolicking with the hired help, but her prosecutors ignored this. In the following days and weeks, she had been unusually surly and unco-operative with her master and her mistress. Would a serious ticking off such as this drive a young woman to try and murder an entire household? The jury must have thought so, because despite her pleas of innocence on all grounds (the accused wouldn't have had a defence council at that time, and had to rely on his or her own wits to provide a defence), Eliza was sentenced to hang by the neck. And the following July, the responsibility for ending her life fell to John Langley.

On the morning of her death, Eliza Fenning was made ready outside debtor's door at Newgate. It was supposed to be her wedding day, and she was wearing her intended outfit – a white muslin gown and white cap with pretty lilac lace-up boots. But instead of a marriage band, she'd be accepting a very different gift – the hangman's noose. Eliza was to be accompanied in her fate by two more convicted criminals – fifty-one-year-old Abraham Adams who'd been convicted of sodomy, and twenty-four-year-old William Oldfield, who had been convicted of the rape of a nine-year-old girl. Oldfield asked specifically to be hung at Eliza's side.

The crowds were already gathering. Reverend Horace Cotton was present to see to Miss Fenning's spiritual needs, and he asked Eliza if she had anything she wanted to say. She made a short statement of her innocence:

Before the just and almighty God, and by the faith of the holy sacrament I have taken, I am wholly innocent of the offence with which I am charged.

The crowd fell silent and Eliza stood calmly and stoically while John Langley positioned the noose around her pretty young neck. Then things began to go wrong.

He tried to pull the traditional white night-cap down over the young lady's head, but it didn't fit because she was wearing a bonnet style cap containing her long tresses, he then tried to blindfold her with a white muslin cloth, but it, too, was too small. There was only one option remaining for Langley. He drew out of his pocket his own, filthy pocket hankerchief – hardly the most sophisticated piece of equipment in a hangman's arsenal, but infinitely useful in a situation such as this. At this point, Eliza – who had been so brave up to this point – frankly lost it. She begged the reverend not to let the hangman blind her with his filthy rag, but she had no choice. It would be a scandal if she were not blindfolded. On the rare occasions when a prisoner's face had not been covered up, the gruesome grimaces and contortions expressed by the prisoner as he or she writhed and choked had so upset the spectators that violence and hysteria broke out among them. Langley went ahead and tied the hankerchief over Eliza's eyes. At approximately 8.30 a.m. Langley operated the drop, but not before Eliza had once again proclaimed her innocence to the reverend. Eliza died quickly, almost without writhing.

Many male executioners mention in their writings that not only is it much harder for them to execute a woman, both emotionally and practically, but it is even more difficult when the prisoner continues to plead innocence. One wonders how Langley would have coped if he suspected that he'd executed an innocent young woman.

A large number of others certainly suspected that Eliza was indeed innocent of attempted murder, and two more investigations of the case were conducted to try and satisfy all concerned, including the Lord

Chancellor himself, that Eliza was guilty and deserved to hang. No evidence could be found to prove her innocence, so hang she did. In the years following Eliza's death there have been lots of theories about the mysterious matter of the arsenic in the dumpling pan. The most salacious being that Mr Turner had fallen in love with Eliza, and Mrs Turner had 'cooked up' a plot to frame her for murder. Another theory sees Mr Turner as the culprit, who driven mad with lust and jelousy by Mrs Turner's story of Eliza's frolicking with the household servants, decided to use his own arsenic to spike the dumplings and punish the entire household, including Eliza.

JAMES (JEMMY) BOTTING

*A pitiful object who shuffled about in the street,
shunned and disliked by his fellow townsmen*
ANONYMOUS BRIGHTON RESIDENT

At the end of the eighteenth century, the Bottings were a large and established Sussex family who had been resident in the county since Saxon times. Even today the memory of James Botting is considered by his descendants to represent something of a blemish on an otherwise respectable family name. James Botting's story illustrates perfectly just how isolated executioners often were from the rest of society, and how unfavourably the profession was looked upon by most 'normal' people – even members of the executioner's own family. Having said that, it does seem as if James, or Jemmy as he was known, did not do a great deal to help himself.

James Botting lived in West Street, Brighton. He owned a house there that came to be known as 'Botting's Rookery'. The house was often frequented by Brighton's lower class of vagrant, many of whom had few options but to lodge under the same roof as Jemmy Botting, who even they regarded as an 'unsavoury' character. Whether he accepted lodgers for the sake of company or to supplement his executioner's income is unclear, but he was certainly not a man who made friends easily.

Botting was first employed as an executioner at Horsham Gaol at the turn of the nineteenth century and, having trained as an assistant under Langley, he worked his way up to become chief executioner at Newgate Gaol between 1817 and 1820. At the end of his career, Botting often boasted that he had executed a total of 175 people. This number is probably accurate, and it is known that in one week alone he hung a total of thirteen people. For multiple hangings Botting used a gantry-type rope gallows with two parallel beams, similar to the 'new drop' gallows used by his predecessors Brunskill and Langley. Botting is perhaps best known for executing the Cato Street Five, who attempted to overthrow the British government, but failed dismally and paid with their heads.

THE CATO STREET FIVE

During the first part of the nineteenth century, England was suffering from great social, economic and political upheaval, made worse by the effects of England's long war with France. The problems collectively became known as the 'Condition of England Question', and many talented political minds were dedicated to the task of sorting out the mess.

The members of the Cato Street Conspiracy were veterans of the Spencean Philanthropist society, which was named after the radical speaker Thomas Spence. They were essentially a hard-line socialist group that advocated common ownership of land and the destruction of the royal family as well as the English aristocracy. The Spenceans had grown more and more angered by what they saw as the elitist government's mismanagement of English resources, as well as the actions of the army during the events of the Peterloo Massacre in Manchester, when the calvalry charged on a crowd of protesters, killing eleven people and injuring a further 500. These angry Spenceans formed a splinter group who believed in bringing about an English revolution, similar to the French Revolution which had gone before. That splinter group has become known as the Cato Street gang.

Some of the members of the Cato Street conspiracy (including Arthur Thistlewood, the man who would emerge as their leader) had been involved in the spa fields riots of 1816, and so were already considered enemies of the state. Police spies described Arthur Thistlewood as a 'dangerous character' who believed passionately in violent revolution. The name, 'Cato Street', comes from the location of their meeting place near Edgeware Road, London – a premises rented by member John Harrison – from which terrorist operations could be planned and executed.

The death of King George III on 29 January 1820, destablised the government still further and, during the fallout, the Cato Street gang were mobilising. The gang planned to invade a cabinet dinner, hosted by Lord Harrowby, the lord president of the council at his house in Grosvenor Square. Having stormed the building they would then assassinate the entire cabinet, as well as the prime minister, Lord Liverpool.

At his trial, conspirator James Ings, a butcher by trade, claimed he intended to decapitate the cabinet ministers and display two of their heads on Westminster Bridge as a symbol of their victory. It remains unclear which particular two heads he was referring to.

Thistlewood sent Jamaican-born William Davidson, a former employee of Lord Harrowby, to gather information about the dinner. Harrowby's servant told Davidson that his master wouldn't even be in London on the night the dinner was due to take place. This information could have saved the conspirators lives, but Thistlewood would not listen and ordered the operation to proceed as planned.

Little did Thistlewood know that one member of his group, George Edwards, was in fact a government spy who had been recruited by the home office to infiltrate the Cato Street gang and sabotage their revolutionary mission. A few of the other gang members suspected the truth and voiced their concerns, but again Thistlewood ignored them, making Edwards his aide-de-camp. It was a very bad move. Edwards had himself suggested the idea of invading the dinner, which was infact a home-office trap. The home office then placed a fake advert for the dinner in *The New Times* in order to create a convincing background for their sting. The Cado Street gang had been set up.

On February 23, the night of Lord Harrowby's dinner, the members of the Cato Street gang gathered in the hayloft of their headquarters. They were armed with an assortment of weapons: pistols, grenades, knives and swords. Meanwhile two police officers, along with twelve members of the Bow Street Runners were waiting in the public house opposite the gang's headquarters for reinforcements to arrive from the Coldstream Guards. At 7.30 p.m., the Bow Street Runners decided that they could wait no longer and charged into the house. In the resulting brawl, Thistlewood killed Richard Smithers, a police officer, using a sword. Some of the gang surrendered peacefully while others fought for their lives. William Davidson fought desperately but failed to win his freedom, Thistlewood, Robert Adams, John Brunt and John Harrison escaped from the scene via a back window, only to be captured a few days later. On 1 May 1820, the five ringleaders: Arthur Thistlewood, James Ings, Richard Tidd, John Brunt and William Davidson were executed at Newgate by Jemmy Botting.

It is interesting to note that, had the Cato Street gang succeeded in bringing about a bloody revolution, Jemmy Botting could have stood to play a central part. We do not know what his personal politics were, if indeed he had any, but as chief executioner he would have been extremely useful for desposing of aristocrats and landowners – and could even have found himself executing the king himself! As it happened, Thistlewood and his gang of would-be revolutionaries proved no match for the British government, and Jemmy Botting died a poor man's death on the streets of his home town.

The Cato Street five were the last people in England to be hung, drawn and quartered. The sentence was delivered thus:

That you, each of you be taken hence to the gaol from whence you came, and from there that you be drawn on a hurdle to a place of execution, and there be hanged until you are dead; and that afterward your heads shall be severed from your bodies, and your bodies be divided into four quarters to be disposed of as his magesty sees fit. And may God in his infinite goodness have mercy upon your souls.

The execution day itself was a high-profile event and up to 100,000 people were expected to flock to Newgate. The sheriff for the City of London, Mr Rothwell, was put in charge of making the necessary arrangements. He decided, because of traffic constraints, that transporting the condemned men to Newgate on a hurdle was out of the question. Additional barricades were set up in order to accommodate large numbers of spectators and an additional platform was added to the Newgate gallows in anticipation of the execution day. The preparations went on for an entire weekend. Additional security were employed to prevent rioting, sawdust was liberally scattered over the platform in readiness for the spillage of blood, and the condemned men's coffins were placed near to the gallows.

On the morning of 1 May, the prisoners were brought to the scaffold. James Ings and Richard Tidd took time to inspect Botting's work. Ings is known to have addressed Jemmy directly, saying: '*Now, old gentleman, finish me tidily: pull the rope tighter; it may slip*'. His comrade, Tidd, asked Botting to make sure that the knot was placed under his right ear instead of his left. Their concern achieved little but a few minutes distraction from the dismal reality of their situation. Prisoners had very little control over how quickly or how painlessly death came to them. It is true that Botting would have had some degree of control over how carefully he positioned the noose and how accurately he planned the drop, but it was by no means the exact science it became in the twentieth century. At eight o'clock, when the drop fell, Ings and Tidd both struggled and choked for up to five minutes before death finally claimed them. The five men were left hanging for the full half hour in order to make sure they were dead, then each body was cut from the scaffold and lifted back on to the platform, where they were laid in their coffins with their nooses still tightly tied around their necks. Then, in turn, their heads were positioned on a small block at one end of the coffin. A masked man, probably a surgeon or perhaps a butcher, was charged with the responsibility of decapitating each man. Then Botting held the heads up to the crowd proclaiming loudly: '*This is the head of a traitor*'.

It is not clear from historical record whether the men's bodies were actually quartered in public or not. One imagines that this would have been a difficult procedure to carry out on a scaffold, but since the main point of this was deterrent as opposed to further punishment, it seems likely that the full sentence was carried out in full public view.

Sometime after executing the Cato Street gang, Botting became paralysed and had to retire on a five shillings a week state pension. He relied on free drinks from Brighton barmen in exchange for gruesome stories he told about his bloody past. He could only get around using an old seat on wheels as both a crutch and resting place. Local rumour has it that his fellow Brightonians avoided him to such an extent that one day when he fell from his wheelchair at the corner of Codrington Place and Montpelier Road, nobody would stop to help. Jemmy Botting perished alone in the street like a stray animal. It is ironic that although the criminals Botting executed died, as he did, in full public view, at least they were the centre of attention for a large crowd of avid spectators. Botting, on the other hand, was totally ignored by the world and died as a result.

According to local ghost stories, on the occasional dark and windy night, Botting's rickety wheeled chair can be heard dragging past his local – the Half Moon Pub in Brighton's Boyces Street.

PART SIX

TYBURN

TYBURN

THE EARLY YEARS

Tyburn has become synonymous with the ultimate criminal punishment – death by hanging. However, back in twelfth century, the area that would see an estimated 40,000 to 60,000 convicted criminals killed was just 250 acres of rough fields. Through the middle of this untended expanse of countryside ran the River Tybourne. Its name originated from the fact that the bourne – another term for brook – branched off at two major points, and 'ty' means two. This river used to run south into the Thames near today's Vauxhall Bridge. The banks of the River Tyburn were lined with elm trees, one of which which the conquering Normans termed the 'Tree of Justice'.

The first recorded hanging at Tyburn was in 1196. William Fitz Osbert had been found guilty of plundering from the rich. He sought sanctuary at St Mary-le-Bow Church but was soon smoked out by the pursuant authorities and dragged to the terrible location where he was strung up by the neck. The events of his capture and subsequent hanging sound more like that of a lynching than an organised execution, especially as there existed no man-made gallows at Tyburn at this point in time. Instead, Fitz Osbert was brought before a rope swung over a branch belonging to the Tree of Justice.

It was not until 1220 that a gallows was constructed to deal with capital punishment. This was possibly due to an escalating crime rate. A far cry from the structures that would grace Tyburn in future centuries, this primitive design consisted of two uprights and a cross-beam capable of taking the weight of ten prisoners. The procedure was simple. The unfortunate ten were forced to climb a ladder to elevate their position, whereupon the appointed executioner twisted the ladder away, leaving the condemned with only air beneath their feet as the rope went taut. The victims struggled against asphyxia for several minutes after being 'turned off', as this final act was known. One might imagine that any would-be criminals among the gathered voyeurs would be turned off in a different manner at such a sight.

This was certainly the intention of the authorities. Tyburn was in a perfect position to act as a deterrent to all prospective lawbreakers entering the city from the North. Unfortunately, while this was their aim, it is unlikely that it worked. The number of death penalties issued by the Old Bailey increased enough to warrant continued improvements to the structure at Tyburn.

THE TRIPLE TREE

In 1571, the basic gallows made way for a larger, more elaborate structure that became known as the Triple Tree owing to its triangular shape. It possessed three legs like a tripod each between 3.7 and 5.5 metres (12 and 18 feet) high and was fixed in place by crossbeams at the top. This formation allowed as many as twenty-four victims to be hung from the gallows at once, with eight executions on each crossbeam, and was first used to hang the martyr John Storey on 1 June 1571. Clearly, by this stage, there was demand for the new enlarged structure but records show the first instance of it being used to full capacity was not until 23 June 1649, when twenty-three men and one woman guilty of burglary and robbery were conveyed in eight carts and hung upon the wooden tripod. This 'Triple Tree', or 'Deadly Nevergreen', continued to end the lives of criminals for almost 200 years, when further developments were deemed necessary. The last execution upon this triangular gallows came on Monday 18 June 1759, when a cart containing the convicted highway robber Catherine Knowland was backed up underneath its beams. This coincided with a drop in the number of hangings as the permanent fixture made way for a portable version, referred to as the Moving Gallows by one chronicler of the time. The first recorded execution to use this new mobile style, dragged into position at Tyburn by horses, came on 3 October later that year when four men were hanged at once.

Another change in the design of the Tyburn gallows arrived in 1760. This consisted of a hatch elevated approximately 46 centimetres (18 inches) above the level of the scaffold boards, replacing the need for a horse and cart. Earl Ferrers was the first to test the new design on 5 May 1760, revealing further improvements were necessary. When the signal was given to activate the hatch, the rope and the neck of Ferrers stretched so much that the aristocrat was able to touch the boards with his toes! Thomas Turlis, the appointed hangman, was forced to pull on his legs to put an end to the nobleman's misery. It would be another twenty-three years until it would be officially adopted as the city's official method of dispatch.

THE TYBURN THEATRE

The display of death at Tyburn quickly developed into a spectator sport. The Hanging Match, as it was commonly known, attracted thousands to Tyburn, and when hanging days were decreed public holidays by the government they drew even greater numbers, creating a real carnival atmosphere throughout the city as well as about the gallows.

With the rabble that packed the streets came the vendors and hawkers keen to take advantage of the onlookers. Refreshments as well as mementos were sold. Writings purporting to be the last speeches of the dying could be purchased well before the 'dying' had the chance to make one! The sale of alcohol was also permitted around the gallows and copious amounts of gin and beer were consumed throughout the day. It was inevitable that fighting broke out, and these bouts of violence no doubt added to the theatrics of the day, serving as unofficial support acts to the main event.

It was not solely official vendors that did a roaring trade on hanging days. Pickpockets and thieves operated with reckless abandon during the Paddington Fair, ensuring that money and valuables were taken by more nefarious means as well. While all eyes were on those due to be dropped, many pockets were being lifted. The irony here is clear. Many condemned to death for theft became accessories to yet more larceny by providing fellow criminals with an opportunity to commit crime. This could be considered adequate evidence that these events were more of an incitement than a deterrent for some.

Collective eagerness to see people dance the Tyburn jig grew to such an extent that in the early eighteenth century stands were constructed at Tyburn alongside the gallows. These were similar to the grandstands found at racecourses and were open galleries in which seats could be hired out to those who could afford the high prices. These were called Mother Proctor's Pews, after a cowkeeper's widow who used to sell seats on Hanging Day at two shillings each during the early 1700s. These seat-sellers were able to bump up the price when a particularly popular figure was due to be hanged. One Mammy Douglas, a fellow grandstand vendor, chose to increase the rate to two shillings and sixpence when it was the turn of Dr Henesey to be executed for treason in 1758. The punters reluctantly paid the exorbitant fees and sat down to watch the doctor hang, but before the deed could be done a rare last minute reprieve arrived. While relief must have enveloped the fortunate Henesey, those that had come to see him die were overcome with anger and rioting promptly broke out in the handsomely priced grandstands. They had paid to see a neck in the noose and it is reported that Mammy Douglas bore the brunt of their rage: she nearly paid the ultimate price when the mob tried to hang her!

For those who could not, or would not pay the inflated prices, there were other ways of ensuring one had an uninterrupted view of the proceedings. One could hire a ladder to see over the crowds or if you were particularly fortunate, there were the perfectly positioned houses surrounding Tyburn that provided a fantastic view. One of these houses was used by the sheriff and under sheriff of Middlesex and their respective guests. It must have been akin to a modern-day royal box at the theatre. As for the friends and family of the condemned, they would often force their way to the front and stand at the foot of the gallows while those behind would prepare to shout, 'Hats Off!' when the procession pulled in. Far from a mark of respect, this ensured that one got a clear view of the execution and those that failed to heed the call would often have their headwear knocked off and thrown about the crowds. Inane games such as these helped to pass the time while they waited for the paraded prisoners to arrive.

THE MAIN EVENT

Depending on the level of 'traffic' that hindered their progress, the procession of carts carrying the doomed surrounded by mounted javelin men reached their final destination at about midday. The gallows were now in plain sight. Fuelled by numerous ales consumed along the journey, the stars of the show endeavoured to steel themselves on seeing the giant contraption that would publicly and eternally silence them. The convoy of carts trundled over the uneven cobbles; the gallows getting closer and looming larger with every passing second. On reaching the scaffold, the team of executioners would go straight into their preparatory routine backing the carts up underneath the relevant crossbeam while the assistant executioner earned his fee in scaling the 5.5 metres (18 foot) high structure and perching precariously upon the top strut to receive the noose-less ends of the rope that had been coiled about the prisoners' bodies. These were thrown up to him to ensure there was little or no slack afforded to the condemned once they cleared the crossbeam.

The ordinary or prison chaplain who had travelled with the prisoners in the cart would then pray for their souls, reciting the 51st Psalm, which was commonly known as the Neck Verse. In the Middle Ages, it was customary to commute the sentence of those who could repeat the first verse of this psalm as literacy was a rare attribute of that time. As levels of education improved it became necessary to amend this ruling and many of the severe crimes were excluded from absolution.

Up to this point the stars of the show – the

condemned – milked the attention for all it was worth with clever witticisms and parting words or violent acts. Either way it added to the spectacle. The crowd who flocked to Tyburn on the 4 May 1763 witnessed one of the more vicious acts performed at this morbid theatre, when Hannah Dagoe was escorted to the gallows. On reaching the scaffold, this wild Irish woman managed to free herself from her restraints and launched herself at her executioner, Thomas Turlis, striking him on his chest with such force that it almost knocked him down. She dared the hangman to do his job and when he failed to speedily dispatch the harridan, she finished off the final act by throwing herself out of the cart, resulting in an instant but gratifying death for the crowd. One would have expected a far deeper sense of grief and shock from the likes of Dagoe and the countless others condemned to wear the Hempen collar, but it is clear that many were certainly up to treading the boards of the gallows theatre and entertaining the masses with one last performance.

Once the final bow had been taken, it was time for the hangman to take centre stage, often to a volley of insults and missiles thrown from the crowd. The executioner pulled the white night cap over the face of the condemned in order to hide the ghastly contortions they would soon be making as they struggled at the end of the rope. The carts were then whipped away by the execution team, removing the ground from beneath the prisoners. The fall was just enough to cause a slow and agonising death by strangulation and there is every reason to believe that the pain felt was of the very worst, as this short drop method did nothing to affect the sensory pathways but simply caused the rope to press upon the jugular vein and carotid arteries. This pain was widely known, as even the friends and relatives of the dying would often turn executioner and advance on the gallows to pull down on the legs of their loved ones, quickening their passing.

If the twisting, contorting bodies continued to dance without any sign of assistance, then the executioner added his considerable weight by hanging from the legs of his victim. The victims themselves did what they could to prevent a time-consuming death. On Wednesday 3 October 1750, gentleman highwayman James Maclean endeavoured to provide himself with a quick death by kicking off his shoes and jumping into the air with his knees to his chest, effecting a sudden jerk of the rope in order to quickly snap his neck. It worked, and for the last time Maclean robbed the people – this time of a long drawn-out death.

THE AFTER SHOW PARTY

Once the prisoner had been allowed to hang for the proper amount of time (normally no less than half an hour) and an official pronouncement of death had been issued, there would often be a fierce scramble for the deceased. This fervent throng surrounding the just-dead would more than likely include the executioner, who did his best to make sure he acquired what was legally his. One of the rare perks of the hangman's job was his right to the dead man's attire. This often prompted the condemned man or woman to dress in their worst clothing so as to not provide their executioner with anything valuable to sell. (Hannah Dagoe actually stripped and threw her clothes to the crowd!) The more astute dressed in their best clothes in an attempt to appease the man who was responsible for their deaths. Earl Ferrers, the first nobleman to be hanged at Tyburn, took to the gallows dressed in the suit he was married in.

The execution team speedily cut down the corpse and stripped the body before the scaffold area was stormed. The man who executed Reverend James Hackman knew how sharp he had to be to ensure his property did not disappear into the wrong pocket. On 19 April 1779, the clergyman released his handkerchief as a sign for the cart to be whisked away, but instead of whipping the horse, the hangman jumped across and snatched up the discarded fabric, preventing it from being pinched by the crowd.

In keeping with the disturbingly licentious atmosphere that existed among the baying horde at a Tyburn hanging, many fought to the foot of the gallows to make contact with the dead. In these unenlightened times, it was believed a dead body, as well as the acoutrements which accompanied it, held curative powers. The sick lurched forward to wipe their sores with the death sweat from the executed. Touching the still warm skin was thought to heal disease. Those sufferers who could not get to the sick-swarmed body often made for the gallows themselves, as even a strip of wood from the structure was thought to be equally powerful in restoring health.

Headaches were considered no match for the hanging rope or 'anodyne necklace' as it was nick-named. This was the property of the executioner who sold sections of it to believers. The reasoning behind such beliefs finds as much solid ground as the floundering legs of the hanged, it appears that the only true way of curing a headache by the halter was to be hanged by it! Thankfully, faith in such macabre methods dwindled and the only lasting tribute to survive is the phrase: 'money for old rope' that was coined from this practice.

THE DECEASED

Not all those at the front row of executions were there for entertainment reasons. As we have seen already, the friends and family of the condemned would flock to the fore to provide a mercy killing if death was not instantaneous, but they also had another reason for their close proximity. While the hangman would strip the corpse of its clothes, relations would take possession of the body and whisk it away for proper burial.

This seizing of the body became all the more important for the families midway through the eighteenth century with the passing of the ominously titled Murder Act of 1752. Among its clauses it permitted ten corpses a year hanged at Tyburn to make their way to Surgeon's Hall for dissection, the first being seventeen-year-old Thomas Woolford on 22 June of that year.

The doctors sent out messengers to claim the bodies freshly cut down from their ropes, and would have to fight for the cadavers with the relatives who, the majority of them God-fearing, believed that only an undamaged body could be resurrected into the afterlife. There were, however, many unconcerned by such religious convictions. It was not a rare occurrence for the more poverty stricken to help out the surgeons with their annual quota of corpses by selling their dead loved ones to them for anatomisation.

THE CURTAIN FALLS

By the second half of the eighteenth century, the reign of the Tyburn gallows was coming to an end. The riotous and unruly crowds that packed the streets on 'hanging day' had taken their toll on the area and the voices of its detractors were becoming louder. The ever-present, ever-passionate mob brought severe traffic congestion, as well as real danger of violence to Tyburn and the surrounding wards, which were now fast-becoming fashionable places to live. The residents of the district clearly had enough clout behind their complaints and soon managed to force the once permanent fixture out of this newly trendy neighbourhood. On the 7 November 1783, the last execution at Tyburn took place. The highwayman John Austin was disected in the same manner as the gallows. Austin by way of Surgeon's Hall, and the gallows by a carpenter who dismantled the structure to make stands for the beer butts in the cellars beneath The Carpenter's Arms pub.

Having been ousted by the elitist residents, the official execution site for London moved to a more fitting location: that of Newgate Gaol. This brought an end to the celebrated tradition of the 4-kilometre (2½-mile) journey, including the courage-providing pub stops as the prisoners were kept no more than a stone's throw from their eventual place of death. The gallows were built directly outside the debtor's door in a funnel-shaped street the authorities hoped would help minimise the size of the crowds. While this location was indeed a smaller space than at Tyburn, it did not always prevent the masses from congregating. In 1807, the hangings of popular criminals Haggerty and Holloway attracted more than 40,000 citizens of London – a number too great for the area outside the gaol. Many onlookers hoping to catch the sight of a public execution were themselves crushed and trampled to death. Yet from its inauguration on the 9 December 1783, it was considered a success and public executions continued outside Newgate until 1868, when a report by the Capital Punishment Commission proposed private death penalties and a bill quickly became law on 29 May of that year. All further executions would take place behind prison walls. Since its departure from Tyburn in 1783 to the eventual closure of Newgate prison in 1902, a total of 1,118 men and forty-nine women were hanged on the gallows. The last unfortunate 'star' publicly executed was Fenian revolutionary Michael Barrett for his part in the bombing of the Coldbath Fields Prison at Clerkenwell, which killed a dozen and severely injured many others in an attempted prison break.

The remains of Michael Barrett lay undisturbed for thirty-five years in a lime grave inside the walls of Newgate prison. However, when the prison was demolished in 1903, his grave was moved to the City of London cemetery where it has remained undisturbed. Today the grave is a place of Irish pilgrimage and is marked by a small plaque.

THE JOURNEY TO TYBURN

The last day of a condemned prisoner's life was often a celebrated one. Pomp and ceremony surrounded those on their journey from their place of incarceration at Newgate Gaol to the fatal Tyburn gibbet. This 4-kilometre (2½-mile) trip down the capital's narrow cobbled streets took anything up to three hours to complete, as their passage was hindered by thousands of eager voyeurs seeking to catch a momentary glimpse of the convicts destined to die. The day was a happy one for law-abiding citizens for the hanging day was deemed a holiday, and incurred much merriment and frivolity.

For the unlucky stars of the show, the fateful day began bright and early in the morning after what must have been, at best, a fitful night's sleep. At around seven o'clock the prisoner was escorted from his cell to the Press Yard, still manacled at the wrists and ankles. In this room at Newgate the blacksmith removed these unwanted accessories and the executioner of the day, known as the Yeoman of the Halter, bound the prisoner's hands in front of him to allow him or her the opportunity to pray at any point during the remaining hours. At this stage, the rope – this primitive weapon of mass destruction – was placed around the prisoner's neck and the excess was coiled around the body like a deadly snake. Once the rope was in place, the condemned was ready to be placed in whichever mode of transport was provided for the terrible trip to the scaffold.

TAXI TO TYBURN

The manner in which the prisoners made their journey developed over the years. In the beginning, the condemned were unceremoniously dragged by horse across the hard cobblestones and through the filth and feculence of the street. However, this technique was soon scrapped because many never made it to their destination.

This harsh treatment was soon replaced with the less extreme ox-hide or hurdle, which was akin to a sledge fixed behind a horse. Murderess Catherine Hayes endured this means of transport on Monday, 9 May 1726. Such an apparatus must have still ensured the prisoner's last trip would be a bumpy one but at least they did not die en route!

The hurdle made way for a horse-drawn cart, which came with several advantages for all concerned. Aside from affording a more comfortable ride, the cart also allowed for more prisoners (along with their respective coffins) to be transported to the gallows in a shorter space of time, thus speeding up the process. While this may not have been popular with the bloodthirsty crowd, the cart did make the prisoner more visible to the hordes, providing the condemned with an improved mobile stage from which to be seen. The captivated crowds on 16 September 1771 would have witnessed shoplifter Mary Jones in the cart – with her young baby along for the ride!

There was one other mode of transport that was available to these convicted travellers. This was the mourning coach, the eighteenth-century version of the modern funeral car. A black horse would draw this carriage shrouded in black cloth to the scaffold but it was not a free ride. As well as paying the ultimate price for their crimes, if they wished for the seclusion and shelter of such a vehicle then they had to pay further. Those rich enough to cover the cost of the coach opted for this means of transport to protect them from the more vitriolic crowds and also as a boost to their image, much as many modern-day stars use blacked-out limousines. One such celebrity criminal was Jenny Diver. Her real name was Mary Young, but she had been given this sobriquet by her gang on account of her pickpocketing skills. On Wednesday 18 March 1741, she made the journey to Tyburn in a mourning coach dressed all in black with the Newgate ordinary, or prison chaplain, Reverend Boughton, for company. It was to him that Jenny, overcome with remorse and faced with the reality of her fate, confessed the sins of her forty years inside this private coach.

THE PROCESSION

As well as the ordinary, the prisoners were accompanied by other players in their downfall. This procession was led by the city marshall and included the hangman himself along with his aides and a troop of mounted guards equipped with javelins that surrounded the prisoner to prevent escape and to protect them from the masses. The convoy left Newgate and stopped outside the nearby St Sepulchre's Church, where a bell rang to sound the fate of the condemned. It continued until the deed had been done. The minister chanted the following in order to appeal to any piety within both the prisoners and the crowd:

You that are condemned to die
Repent with lamentable tears.
Ask mercy of the Lord for salvation of your souls.
All good people, pray heartily to God
For these poor sinners who now go to their deaths
For whom the great bell tolls.

People outside the church offered the condemned nosegays (small posies of flowers) for the rest of their journey. While this must have been welcomed by many, those chosen to die that day were probably looking forward to something a little stronger.

PUB CRAWL

After passing by St Sepulchre's, the spectacle would then head down Snow Hill and over the Fleet Ditch by way of a stone bridge before ascending the incline at High Holborn. It would then find itself on St Giles High Street, upon which stood St Giles-in-the-fields Hospital – originally a chapel linked to a twelfth-century infirmary charged with the care of lepers. Thanks to Queen Matilda, the wife of Henry I, a charitable gift was granted to the prisoners. They were provided with a 'parting cup' of ale. This bequest soon became a tradition and the records state that it was rare for the condemned to refrain from partaking of a swift pint. One recorded exception of abstention is steeped in irony. Turning down the offer, this Tyburn-bound teetotaller was promptly taken to the gallows and executed where, minutes later, a reprieve arrived for him. If he had drunk that one free pint, his neck would have remained intact!

The free drink at St Giles-in-the-Fields Hospital was eventually discontinued in 1750, but was soon provided by the Bowl Tavern, which stood between St Giles' High Street and Hog Lane. This was not the only place that offered the gift of alcohol to the condemned. Another stop was frequently made at the Mason's Arms in Seymour Place, and in its cellars the prisoners were shackled to chains on the walls. There are some instances of further stops along this route. It must have ensured many prisoners arrived at their destination well and truly intoxicated. This would often have included the executioner himself, knowing the shortcomings of many that held the post. This convention helped to guarantee the mood remained upbeat. Jokes were made by the condemned regarding their state of affairs and it was common for many merry miscreants to offer to pay for their drinks on the return journey! This is reflected in Jonathan Swift's poem of 1727 about one Tom Clinch, who, '... *stopt at the George for a bottle of sack, and promis'd to pay for it when he'd come back'.*

An unfortunate few were unfairly prohibited from taking part in the custom, one being Lord Ferrers who, on reaching Drury Lane, announced he wished to quench his thirst with a glass of wine. He was prevented from doing so by the sheriff on account of the lively crowd that had assembled to see him drop. Rather than cause a fuss, the Earl – the first aristocrat to hang at Tyburn – agreed with the authorities and he swung from the noose dry.

The legend of this final drink lives on through language. It has left us with two terms that hark back to those pub stops on the way to the main event at Tyburn. The phrase 'one for the road' evidently describes the last pint before departing for a less salubrious locale. In addition, the term 'on the wagon' is believed to derive from the custom, although there seems to be some conflict as to how it relates. Many believe it came from the fact that the prisoners who returned to the wagon would certainly never get the chance to drink again while others think it refers to the guards who were forced to remain with the wagon while the condemned enjoyed a drink.

Whatever the derivation, the drunken party would soon leave the last watering hole and make the now short trip down Tyburn Road (now Oxford Street) to the gallows which awaited the condemned. Along with the structure that would see to their deaths, crowds of tens of thousands who had waited all through the night gathered to watch the prisoners pay for their crimes. Not dissimilar to a present day football stand, there was a gallery full of people desperate to see the main event of the day – the hangings. Those who wanted to guarantee the best seat in the house, booked a place in 'Mother Proctor's' pews, because from there you could hear the prisoners' last speeches and also their cries and screams in their final death throes.

The journey of the condemned was at an end and the main event, along with the final curtain, was now close at hand. Mind you, it wasn't the end for their bodies – anatomists stood close by considering which of the prisoners would be best for dissection later. Occasionally fights broke out as the anatomists struggled with friends and family for possession of the deceased's body. It was believed that the body had to be totally intact when buried to ensure that it could receive life after death.

PART SEVEN

THE GUILLOTINE

BEFORE THE GUILLOTINE

The guillotine may have been the brainchild of Dr Joseph Guillotin in 1789, but the idea of decapitation by means of a machine existed hundreds if not thousands of years before. In fact, some believe the origins of the guillotine go back as far as Biblical times with the death of tax collector turned apostle, Matthew. The instrument of his demise may actually have been something similar to a halberd – a long spiked pole with an axe head. If an appliance existed in ancient times, it would have been of rudimentary construction, possibly something akin to that used by tenth-century Persians, which required an executioner to wield a mallet, striking the blade downwards onto the neck of the condemned. However, this is some considerable way from the mechanism used in France to such notorious effect from the 1790s.

The first clear indication that there existed a pre-guillotine mechanism appeared in Holinshed's chronicles published in 1577, which revealed pictorial evidence in the form of a woodcut entitled, 'The Execution of Murcod Ballagh near Merton in Ireland 1307'. The depicted Celtic device bears a striking resemblance to the Gallic machine. The woodcut shows an executioner holding a rope which is attached to the top part. The blade is raised and his assistant is holding Ballagh's head in place below it. The Germans also had their own machine around this time. According to records, five men were executed using this method in Zittau in 1300. No formal name was given to this machine (it may well have been called the Diele) and there exists barely any information on this German version.

Evidence is murky regarding many of these contraptions, ensuring that the question of who invented the first guillotine will be argued over ad infinitum. We may never know who was responsible, but it is known that mechanised instruments for decapitation did exist well before the creation of the guillotine. There are three devices that help to establish the ancestry of the guillotine.

THE MANNAIA

The Italians had their own decapitation device. This was called the mannaia and it was reserved for the nobility, or as one chronicler puts it, 'gentlemen and ecclesiastics'. The mannaia allowed the condemned to avoid being tainted by the hands of the hangman and to be dispatched with superior efficiency, rather than risking numerous swings of the axe – a fate afforded to those lacking in wealth and title. The first record of its use was upon Conradin Hohenstaufen of Swabia in 1268, after his failed attempt to retake the island of Sicily. He was arrested and handed over to Charles of Anjou who had him thrown into the prison of Castel dell' Oro in Naples. He was tried as a traitor and beheaded by the mannaia on 29 October, bringing the Hohenstaufen line to an end.

A comprehensive account of its construction comes from a Dominican priest, Father Jean-Baptiste Labat in his *Voyage en Espagne et en Italie* written in 1730. He tells of a scaffold 1.2–1.5 metres (4–5 feet) high comprising of two uprights joined together by three transversal cross-pieces containing a large sharp blade which was 23–25 centimetres (9–10 inches) long and 15 centimetres (6 inches) across and weighing in at 27–36 kilograms (60–80 pounds). With this substantial blade raised, the captain of the guard gave the signal for the executioner to cut the attached cord, allowing the blade to drop, thus severing the victim's head.

The mannaia is mentioned even before this. There exists an eyewitness account concerning the contraption from 13 May 1507, with the execution of Demetrius Giustiniani. It is also thought to have been used to execute Beatrice Cenci, a young Italian noblewoman who was found guilty of murdering her incestuous father. In the early hours of 11 September 1599, a veiled Beatrice was escorted to the local piazza where, along with her mother Lucrezia, she was executed by the mannaia.

THE SCOTTISH MAIDEN

The Scottish maiden achieved considerable notoriety and took over 120 heads in as many years during the sixteenth and seventeenth centuries. Its existence is attributable to just one man – James Douglas, the fourth Earl of Morton. In 1563, he was appointed lord chancellor of Scotland and it is believed that during this time he visited West Yorkshire, where he witnessed an execution by the Halifax gibbet. So enamoured was he with the swiftness and efficiency of the device that he decided to develop a Scottish version to be used in Edinburgh.

By 1564, the Earl of Morton's commissioned model was complete; its appearance being described as, 'in the form of a painter's easel'. It was made of oak and comprised of a single 1.52-metre (5-foot) beam into which were set two vertical posts standing

3.4 metres (10 feet) high. These were capped by a cross-piece 60 centimetres (2 feet) in length and 8 centimetres (3¼ inches) thick. A hinged iron cross-bar was used to keep the felon's head in place during the procedure – something that was lacking on the gibbet but would later be a distinctive characteristic of the guillotine. The blade itself was made of iron and steel and measured 33 centimetres (13 inches) long and 26.6 centimetres (10½ inches) wide and on its upper side 34 kilograms (75 pounds) worth of lead weights were attached to allow for an extremely potent and forceful drop. This weighty blade was able to slide in grooves cut on the inner edges of the vertical posts which were lined with copper to give a clean line. Attached to the axe was a peg upon which a rope was fastened. The line was cut by the designated executioner, causing the downfall of the blade and subsequently its victim.

It was christened 'the maiden' not, as many believed, because it took so long to be used after its creation. It owes its name to the Celtic word 'moddrun', pertaining to a place where justice was administered. Having said that, the maiden's official debut did not come until 1566. Those unlucky recipients of the new punishment were those accused of assassinating David Rizzio, an Italian courtier and private secretary to Mary Queen of Scots. Thomas

Scott and others were found guilty of stabbing the royal confidante an alleged fifty-seven times at Holyrood Palace on the 9 March 1566 in front of the Scottish monarch in what was considered an Elizabethan-funded murder to unsettle the rival sovereign.

The next major execution by the maiden came fifteen years later and its victim was a shocking one – none other than its architect, the Earl of Morton. In a cruel twist of fate, the Lord Chancellor and Regent in Scotland faced his own invention after being accused of involvement in the murder of Mary Queen of Scot's husband, Lord Darnley. The earl was immediately arrested and received an initial sentence of hanging, drawing and quartering. However, the punishment was soon commuted to decapitation, and on the 2 June 1581, Morton was led to the City Cross in Edinburgh's High Street and beheaded upon the maiden. His head was placed upon a spike on the nearby Tolbooth – the town's council building – where it stayed for six months. His body was allowed to remain with his creation for a further day after execution, before being removed for burial in a common grave.

The maiden had not finished dispensing its swift justice. There were many more executions, although none more surprising than that of the Earl of Morton. Benefiting from the civil unrest that existed in the middle of the seventeenth century, the maiden took many a noble head, including Sir John Gordon, the first Baronet of Haddo. A renowned royalist, he had been granted the title by King Charles I in 1642, only to lose it as well as his head two years later on 19 July 1644. Sir Robert Spottiswoode suffered the same end for supporting the king not long after he was royally appointed secretary of state for Scotland. He was captured at Philiphaugh whilst marching his army south and a maiden was brought from Dundee to the Cross of St Andrews for his execution on the 17 January 1646.

Nearly fifteen years later it proved advantageous to favour the sovereign when Archibald Campbell, the first marquis of Argyll, was arrested for collaborating with Cromwell's Parliamentarians and specifically for the part he played in the death of Charles I. He was sent to Edinburgh to stand trial for high treason. An acquittal seemed on the cards due to the lack of evidence – that is until a collection of letters written by Argyll were found, providing conclusive proof of his guilt. He knelt before the maiden on 27 May 1661. The executioner clearly wished for a head start, as it has been alleged that, at the time of his decapitation, the marquis' death warrant had not yet been signed by the king.

The final victim to be touched by the maiden was Archibald Campbell, the ninth Earl of Argyll, who took to the scaffold on Monday 30 June 1685. He was accused and found guilty of complicity in the Rye House Plot of 1683 – a failed assassination attempt to kill both King Charles II and his brother, James, the Duke of York. He also led an unsuccessful Highland rebellion against the monarchy two years later. He was captured and sent to meet his maker via the Scottish machine. On coming face to face with it, Argyll is said to have placed his head on the block, stating that it was the sweetest maiden he had ever kissed.

The device could have made a surprise return if Simon Fraser, the eleventh Lord Lovat, had got his way. Condemned to death for supporting the Jacobite rebellion in 1745, he is believed to have asked for the maiden, but this request was declined and he fell not by the machine but by the hand-held axe of executioner John Thrift on 9 April 1747. His appeal goes some way to attesting the proficiency of this device. The main reason why Lord Lovat was not allowed to be 'kissed' by the maiden must have been due to the fact that the device had not been in operation for forty years, having been withdrawn from use in 1708. The maiden remains the only forerunner of the guillotine to survive to this day. It has been preserved and can be seen at the National Museum of Scotland in Edinburgh.

THE HALIFAX GIBBET

This device is not to be confused with the gibbets used to hang the bodies of criminals that were common during the eighteenth century. The Halifax gibbet was, in fact, the most famous precursor to the guillotine. Its location is evident from its title although it is believed the Halifax model was just one of many similar contraptions used in England at the time, all with designs peculiar to their region.

The lack of hard evidence makes it impossible to secure a date for its first performance, but it has been suggested that it was imported by the Normans, or may even have been in existence before William's conquest. It is thought to have been used for the first time in 1286 for the execution of John of Dalton, but even then its use was only officially chronicled as late as 1541. From that date, the Halifax gibbet took no more than fifty-one heads, six of which belonged to women such as Sarah Lum and Anna Fairbank, who were both executed during the 1620s. The number of lives taken by the Halifax gibbet, however, pales in comparison with the number taken by the guillotine in France.

The English machine has been described in some detail and it certainly bears a striking resemblance to the guillotine. It comprised of two 4.57 metres (15 feet) high uprights crowned by a horizontal crossbeam. The blade was an axe head attached to a 1.37 metres (4.5 feet) wooden block which slid up and down between the vertical struts, and the axe itself was held in place by a wooden pin. This pin was attached to a long rope. All this was mounted on top of a raised stone platform 1.21 metres (4 feet) from the ground and is locally believed to have been brought out during times of considerable social unrest.

GIBBET LAW

The use of the Halifax gibbet was not limited to the town but was applicable throughout the entire parish. Its jurisdiction extended to cover the surrounding hamlets and villages such as Ovenden, Illingworth and Sowerby and many other estates belonging to ruling landowners. The gibbet is thought to have been introduced in order to deal with the regular theft of cloth and material; the area's main product at that time. Whether this is true or not, the device was used mostly as a form of capital punishment for grand theft; this was defined as anything to the value of 13.5 pence or over, and was calculated by four constables appointed from four separate towns within the parish.

There were three scenarios whereby a thief could find himself sentenced to death by the gibbet. If he was caught 'hand-habend' – with the stolen goods in his hands – or in the process of stealing, 'back-berand' – carrying the stolen goods on his back or person – or if the accused actually confessed to stealing.

The punishment of thieves was a very serious matter. This was not solely illustrated by the severity of the penalty, but also by the ancient custom of enforced prosecution. The Halifax authorities demanded official justice. If the victim refused to prosecute or it was discovered that they had attempted to handle the matter privately, then the victim would risk forfeiture of goods as well as conviction as an accessory to the crime.

THE EXECUTIONER WAS A BEAST!

Once the death penalty had been decreed, the condemned thief was taken to the machine on one of the three market days of the week. These fell on Tuesdays, Thursdays and Saturdays. The prisoner was often placed in the stocks to wait for the appropriate day. When that came the prisoner, accompanied by the bailiff, the clergyman and attending witnesses, would mount the raised platform. The 4th psalm was played on the bagpipes while the condemned looked up at the glinting blade that would soon seal his fate.

The executioner was rarely one man when it came to the Halifax gibbet. It was common for every person present to take hold of the rope that was fixed to the pin holding the blade in place. The 'collective' approach meant that no one person was fully accountable for the act and it went some way to creating a sense of community spirit. This was far from the strangest scenario. If the prisoner was guilty of stealing livestock, then that animal in question – be it a sheep, a horse or even a pig – was granted the honour of performing the execution. The rope would be tied to the creature and when it moved away from the gibbet the pin was released, freeing the hefty blade and allowing it to drop, thus completing the sentence. It is fair to say many executioners throughout history were animals, but it was never more true than in Halifax, West Yorkshire!

ESCAPING THE GIBBET

This most severe reprimand was not without its loopholes. In fact there were two known methods of avoiding death by the Halifax gibbet. Local law stated that if the prisoner was cognisant and quick enough, he could flee the scaffold as there were no restraints preventing escape. If the condemned was afforded a window of opportunity, then he had several directions in which to run in order to cross the parish border and so be beyond the jurisdiction of Halifax. If he chose north he was lucky, for it was a mere 600 paces to the boundary, if he chose south the distance grew to 1.6 kilometres (1 mile), but the unluckiest of all fugitives elected to go west, as freedom from decapitation lay 16 kilometres (10 miles) away! Those that reached the border were not eternally free from the gibbet curse, however, for if they returned to the parish at any time in the future they could find themselves upon that raised platform once more, facing the gibbet's blade.

This run for the border occurred on at least two ocassions. A convicted felon called Dinnis was successful in avoiding the drop of the axe and fled the parish. It is believed that while making his escape he was stopped and asked if Dinnis was to be beheaded that day. With a smile, he was said to have replied, 'I trow not' – meaning 'I think not' – and he continued on his way! One man who was not so lucky was John Lacy, who managed to leave the parish by way of Hebble Brook, only to return seven years later believing that he was in the clear. He wasn't, and on 29 January 1623 Lacy was promptly brought once again to the Halifax gibbet. This time there was no escape.

The only other known way to secure a reprieve was to avoid the third method of conviction, that of confession. Provided the suspected felon was not in possession of the stolen goods, a confession was required in order to obtain a conviction. Without this, the authorities had no option but to exonerate the supposed thief. This would seem to have been quite a glaring loophole, that is until one realises that, at that time, death itself was considered preferable to committing an act of perjury, as this was seen as a sin against God.

THE FALL OF THE GIBBET

From its early beginnings, death by the Halifax gibbet was the final act in the lives of many condemned thieves, but its reign over the West Yorkshire townsfolk came to an end in 1650, following closely after the demise of King Charles I. Many historians believe that the two were connected, as the country became caught up in civil war it is likely that pressure from parliament forced the cessation. Yet there exists no solid reason why the Halifax gibbet severed no more necks beyond this point.

There are, however, details of its final operation and the last victims thereof. On 30 April 1650, a double execution took place in the town of Halifax. The heads that rolled belonged to Abraham Wilkinson and Anthony Mitchell, who were arrested for theft several days before. According to the ancient tradition, four constables were summoned to verify the extent of their crimes. It was recorded that 14.6 metres (16 yards) of russet and 5.4 metres (6 yards) of cinnamon-coloured kersey – a kind of coarse woollen cloth – had been purloined along with two colts from a man called Durker Green which were all brought before the court to ascertain their value. With one horse alone priced at 48 shillings, the verdict was inevitable and, as it was a Saturday, they were taken to the gibbet that very day and swiftly dispatched.

As the blade fell down on the necks of these two thieves so did the curtain on the Halifax gibbet. The contraption was either dismantled or left to perish upon the raised dais in the market square; its finale pre-empting the overture of the French machine by almost 140 years. It would make a surprise return in the 20th century not to take heads but purely to turn them, as a full-size replica was built on the original site at Gibbet Street in 1974 before being dismantled again in April 2003.

THE GUILLOTINE

LIBERTY, EQUALITY AND FRATERNITY

In eighteenth century France, free thought and philosophical expression were the desires of the day, and it was into such an atmosphere that the most famous of all execution styles was born. The rights of everyone, even the unlawful man, were considered by the free thinkers who resided in the newly empowered people's parliament, the National Assembly. They wished to bring an end to the unnecessary suffering of the condemned. Thanks to an ancient penal code, there existed more than 100 capital offences and numerous cruel and sadistic forms of execution, including judicial torture known as 'the question', all of which were greatly in need of reform or, indeed, abolition.

While there was no real desire to abolish the death penalty, there was a belief that the practice could be cleaned up and made more efficient. The usual beheadings by axe or sword ran the risk of multiple swings by unskilled executioners. Hanging prolonged the agony by slowly strangling the victims and burning or the breaking on the wheel were both torturous and humiliating. A particularly gruesome example of such a long drawn-out execution came to serve as a major catalyst for change. The unfortunate victim was Robert-Francois Damiens, who had attacked Louis XV with a penknife in 1757. His punishment consisted of considerable torture behind the walls of the Conciergerie prison, followed by a public display of punishment. He was torn with red-hot pincers and had molten lead poured into his wounds, then he was hanged before being pulled four ways by horses in an attempt at dismemberment. This was only achieved after his limbs were 'loosened' by the executioner. Such appalling acts of judicial violence would soon have no place in a rapidly changing France.

Legend has it that the man charged with the conception of the guillotine was born following a scene of such barbaric suffering. It is said that Joseph Ignace Guillotin prematurely entered the world on 28 May 1738 when his mother, Catherine Martin, witnessed a man being broken on the wheel in the town of Santes. Despite such a traumatic delivery, it would be hard pressed to find a more philanthropic existence than that of Guillotin. After seven years of following Holy Orders, he turned his attention to medicine and graduated by 1770 with a thesis on the prevention of rabies, before being appointed as Doctor-Governor of Medicine in Paris. However, Joseph was in his fifties before he achieved true renown. In 1789, he was elected to the National Assembly where he presented his suggestions for reform, paving the way for the creation of his namesake: the guillotine.

THE PROPOSAL

Joseph Guillotin's election to the National Assembly in 1789 came at an ideal time. Revolution was in the air. Before he delivered his proposals, the Bastille had been stormed and King Louis XVI and his wife Marie Antoinette had been removed from the Versailles Palace. Just five days after the relocation of the monarchy, Guillotin delivered his proposals for penal reform. These consisted of six articles all aimed at ending the suffering of those involved in criminal proceedings. These articles endeavoured to re-evaluate judicial punishment, echoing Dumas' Musketeer sentiment of 'one for all and all for one'. They called for a single universal mode of punishment for the most serious crimes regardless of rank or estate and specifically, that this punishment should be decapitation by means of a simple and efficient mechanism.

Despite the shifting mood, change was not immediate. The assembly chose to adjourn on several occasions to consider the good doctor's proposals, reconvening over the next two years to ratify one or more of the articles. By 3 June 1791, the Assembly finally approved the article relating to decapitation and by 20 March 1792 all six articles had become law. Progress was achieved albeit in piecemeal fashion and now they had the legal capacity to implement the new penal code. Unfortunately, the Assembly had nothing to implement. A device which was in keeping with the humanitarian motives was needed. This would require the involvement of several men including one Dr Guillotin, who would be instrumental in its invention.

THE MANUFACTURE OF THE GUILLOTINE

Guillotin's idea of a simple machine may have been inspired by two events. He is thought to have witnessed the construction of a bridge for which a manual pile-driver was used that hammered the supports into the ground. There is also the belief that the theatre was his muse; specifically a stage production entitled *Les Quatres Fils Aymon* in which a simple beheading device was used for an execution scene. Without belittling the legend, it is realistic that the forerunners of the guillotine covered earlier in this book were greater influences. Similarly, while Guillotin was responsible for preparing the foundations for his namesake, his influence in its actual design was minimal.

The true designer of the guillotine was Dr Antoine Louis. An acquaintance of Guillotin, Louis was not only the royal physician but permanent secretary to the academy of surgeons, and he had some experience in developing innovative designs. He was initially asked to submit a report to the assembly focusing on the design of such a machine. He responded swiftly, suggesting the device should follow the example of the Halifax gibbet and Scottish maiden to ensure a quick and efficient mode of execution. He created a detailed technical specification echoing these machines, with one or two improvements. The proposed machine should allow for the immobilisation of the prisoner and this would be achieved in two ways. Firstly, the condemned would be secured to a tilting board called the bascule and secondly the head and neck would be held firm beneath the blade by the *lunette* or 'little moon'. The *lunette* was in effect a pillory which closed around the neck. This revamped head remover now had a design. Next, they needed someone to build it.

The first carpenter they approached was a Monsieur Guedon, who estimated the construction costs at a total of 5,660 livres. It would be made from high quality chestnut and include a 15-kilogram (33-pound) blade and a *lunette* made from iron. On 5 April 1792, his quote was passed to Claviere, the Minister of Taxes, who deemed the price too high. He called for a further costing from another carpenter. This led them to German-born harpsichord maker and inventor Tobias Schmidt, who resided in the Commerce-St-Andre district and was well known by the assembly for his countless submissions of inventions such as a fire escape ladder, hydraulic diving equipment and a modernised plough. He had even invented his own beheading machine, so was certainly qualified to undertake such a project. Schmidt returned with an estimate of just 960 livres, considerably undercutting Guedon, and on 10 April 1792 it was agreed that he would build the new appliance while Guedon was hired to construct the scaffold. Two weeks later the guillotine was be ready to take its first head.

THE TRIAL OF LADY GUILLOTINE

Schmidt got straight to work on the device, and by the following day he was ready to test its efficacy. Here, at his workshop on the rue Saint Andre-des-Arts, the guillotine claimed its first living victims. Schmidt obtained two sheep and two calves from the local abattoir on which to try out the crescent-shaped blade and, by all accounts, this trial run went without a hitch.

The machine now required human test subjects and to this end, Dr Michael Cullerier, the chief surgeon at Bicetre hospital was asked to provide Schmidt with fresh human cadavers as well as a more practical location for this preliminary analysis. On Tuesday 15 April 1792, a select group of witnesses gathered along with the doctors Guillotin and Louis to watch the posthumous execution of several corpses. The curved blade cut through the first neck with ease but with the second more muscular frame it failed to cleanly separate the head from the body, leaving strands of sinew and tendon still linking the two. With this grisly sight came the realisation that there was a clear fault with the machine and those entrusted to create this humane, efficient device withdrew to ascertain what the defect was and how best to correct it.

The answer lay in one of three possible alterations: the height of the uprights could be raised to increase the drop of the blade, the mouton – the crosspiece containing the blade – could be made heavier or the actual blade could be redesigned. Louis and Guillotin agreed that by focusing on the latter, the efficiency of the machine would be improved and so they chose to install an oblique blade to replace the curved edge. Further tests revealed that when the blade hit at a forty-five-degree angle it sliced cleanly through rather than hacking at the neck, leaving no ghastly connection between head and body. The trial runs were now complete and the necessary adjustments had been made, the machine was ready for action.

THE DEBUT

From commission to construction in just over a month, the development of the guillotine had moved almost as swiftly as the speed of execution it would soon deliver. However, for one man the wait had been agonisingly slow and painful. Nicholas-Jacques Pelletier, a highwayman found guilty of robbery and violent assault on the rue Bourbon-Villeneuve, had been waiting for ten long weeks for the arrival of his final day on earth. He was imprisoned until the simple machine had been devised. Finally, on the 25 April 1792, the guillotine was unveiled at the Place de Greve in Paris. It had been painted bright red – an unnecessary step as Pelletier's blood was about to provide it with a fresh coat! It was probably this thought, along with the protracted wait, that caused the prisoner – also clad in red - to faint upon seeing the new machine. He had to be carried up Guedon's scaffold, unconsciously proving the necessity of the *bascule* and *lunette*. His blackout would have rendered the old method of execution near-impossible.

To the humanitarians, the guillotine's debut was a success. It took just over two hours to assemble and the execution lasted only one minute, inflicting minimal suffering on the condemned. However, the general public were not as compassionate as their representatives in the National Assembly. The crowds that flocked to the first appearance of this new execution style were ultimately disappointed with the event. They berated its efficiency and called for a return to the (far from trusty) gallows. The guillotine's swift slice lacked drama; a boon in the eyes of the philanthropist but the people who were used to seeing pain and suffering at such events desired a horror show. Despite this conflict the guillotine would very quickly become a part of French culture, embraced by the ordinary men and women of the street. Black humour prevailed, with inappropriate merchandise such as toy guillotines sold to children, who executed mice for fun. Even members of the criminal community had dotted lines tattooed around their necks along with the words: 'Cut Here!' It may not have provided the horror show they wanted, but what it lacked in savagery the guillotine soon made up for in quantity.

THE REIGN OF TERROR

The guillotine soon became the instrument of the masses. Created for its swiftness and efficiency, it would prove perfect as the tool by which society would bring the aristocracy to its knees. Lines of unfortunate noblemen and noblewomen queued to be touched by the blade of Lady Guillotine as if partaking in some mass knighting ceremony. The revolutionary tribunal sentenced between 15,000 and 40,000 people to be cut by what was also nicknamed the 'National Razor'. Many of its victims had been found guilty of spurious crimes. The ultimate quarry came on 21 January 1793. King Louis XVI had already been ousted from his royal home and confined in the Tuileries Palace, but this was stormed by hordes of his subjects on 12 August 1792, whereupon he was charged, convicted of treason and sentenced to death after a three-day trial.

After this initial purge in Paris, the guillotine soon toured the country and then parts of Europe, dispensing its speedy sentence. While the device was a permanent fixture in the capital, copies were built to be transported from town to town. The dreadful drop of the blade was witnessed by Charles Dickens in nineteenth century Italy, and later featured in his novel, *The Tale of Two Cities*. This device could well have sported the improvements made by Leon Berger, an assistant executioner and carpenter, who between 1870 and 1872 developed a spring system that prevented the mouton from damaging the *lunette* after the drop, as well as a superior release mechanism for the blade. These refinements helped the guillotine endure well into the twentieth century.

The last public use of the guillotine in France took place on 17 June 1939, when multiple murderer Eugene Weidmann took to the scaffold in front of the Saint Pierre Prison in Versailles. It was subsequently ruled that all further executions should take place behind the closed doors of La Sante Prison and it was here that Madame Guillotine was incarcerated, along with the condemned, until her final performance on 27 November 1972, when she took the heads of Claude Buffet and Roger Bontemps. While these ended her reign in Paris, it would be another five years until she retired altogether, exacting her unique method of execution upon torture-murderer Hamida Djandoubi on the 10 September 1977. At long last, France abolished the death penalty in 1981.

THE SANSON
DYNASTY

The introduction of the guillotine in 1792 was supposed to symbolise a revolutionary commitment to equality for all – but ironically this did not extend to the executioners who used and maintained it on a daily basis.

In fact nowhere in Europe were executioners more shunned by society than in France. Many ordinary people saw executioners, or 'the borreaux' as they were known, as mystical beings rather than fellow humans. They were originally employed to carry out the king's work and so were seen as an extension of his divine right. For this reason the borreaux were viewed as simultaneously holy and unclean.

Executioners and their families were made to live outside city or town walls and local tradesmen often refused to serve them. They did not pay taxes and were exempt from military service. Marriage with other families was sometimes diffcult, and so members of the borreaux were legally allowed to marry their cousins in order to ensure the continuation of the bloodline. Their children were refused schooling, and so enjoyed the perks of private tuition. As a result the children of these families were often well-educated and comparitively cultured, many of whom spoke fluent English. Unfortunately though, the low position of their birth meant they had little or no choice but to follow the profession of their forefathers: that of professional killer.

Perhaps the most famous dynasty of French executioners were the Sansons, who supplied France with executioners for over 200 years. It all began, as many great stories do, with a romantic liason between an injured serviceman and his nurse.

CHARLES SANSON I

Charles Sanson de Longval was born in Abbeville in 1653. As a young man he harboured military ambitions, and so as soon as he came of age he entered the regiment of the Marquis de la Boissier. One day, while stationed at Dieppe, Sanson was riding through the countryside when he fell from his horse. The accident landed him in hospital, where he met and fell deeply in love with his nurse. However, this was no ordinary young woman. She may have been employed to save lives, but her father – Master Pierre Jouanne – was employed to take them. Charles was shocked to discover that his girlfriend was actually the daughter of the executioner for Dieppe and Rouen. Despite this bombshell, the relationship continued unabated, until

Sanson's regiment threatened him with dismissal for associating with such disgraceful company. Sanson immediately resigned from the army and prepared to leave the area. It was during a farewell visit to the Jouanne household that his plans changed forever, and with them the destiny of his children, grand-children and great-grandchildren to come.

When Charles arrived at the house the master executioner was busy conducting a torture session on his own daughter in order to discover the name of her seducer. Charles bravely owned up to the fact that it was him, and offered to marry the daughter in order to remove her from her violent father's clutches. Master Jouanne refused the offer of marriage because he was appalled at the thought of his daughter marrying into a family who would regard her with contempt. The only way Sanson could convince Master Jouanne to sanction the marriage was by promising to adopt the profession of executioner himself. So the sacrifice was made and Sanson became a headsman in order to ensure the hand of an executioner's daughter.

SANSON'S FIRST OUTING

At this time in France, the guillotine was but a twinkle in the nation's eye. The French establishment still favoured painful and torturous punishment over efficient decapitation. They broke their criminals on the wheel, asphyxiated them slowly on the gallows or decapitated them using a heavy axe.

Charles Sanson's first job as executioner came when he was involved in the torturous execution of a man named Martin Eslau. The records show that his new boss, Master Jouanne, insisted that his new assistant aimed a blow at the prisoner, whereby the unwilling rookie fell into a fit, to the jeers and taunts of the spectating mob.

Tragically for the young Sanson, his beloved wife died shortly after giving birth to a son. He was now a widower and single parent who was trapped in an occupation that horrified him. The reality of losing of his wife made him angry and bitter, and as a result the people of Rouen came to see him as a figure of terror. When a job offer came from Paris, Sanson jumped at the chance to leave behind this unwanted celebrity, as well as the scene of so many sad memories. Sometime during the latter part of 1685, Sanson arrived in Paris.

Charles Sanson eventually settled in to his gory profession, although his nerves sometimes got the better of him. One Madame Tiquet found herself on the wrong end of his shakey hands during her execution for the murder of her husband. The forty-two-year-old woman looked so graceful, dressed head to toe in spotless white, and her manner was so gentle that Sanson quite forgot himself. It took no less than three messy swings of the axe for Sanson to finally sever her head from its pretty neck.

At the age of sixty-four, Sanson's jittery nerves finally got the better of him and he was compelled to resign. He and his second wife moved from Paris to a small farm at Condé in the district of Brie. Where, one hopes, he lived out his remaining days in relative peace and tranquility. His eldest son, also called Charles Sanson, inherited the roll of executioner in 1703.

CHARLES SANSON II

According to reports, Charles Sanson Jr was a chip off the old chopping block, and so not at all suited to his profession. He was a mild-mannered and gentle man who married young and was able to provide his wife and children with a comfortable life through his career as a headsman. He carried out torture sessions and executions until his own death in 1726, when he left behind three children.

CHARLES JEAN-BAPTISTE SANSON

Charles Jean-Baptiste was the eldest son of Charles Sanson II. He inherited the job of executioner at just seven years of age. To many, the premature death of

Charles Sanson II would seem like the perfect opportunity for the mother of his children, Anne Marthe Debut, to break the cycle by refusing to allow her young child to take the scaffold. However, it was not to be. For reasons known only to them, Anne and her new husband, Francois Prudhomme, decided to actively encourage Jean-Baptiste to follow in his father's footsteps. The young boy had long acted as his father's assistant, enthusiastically holding on to the legs of his victims in order to afford his father a clean strike of the axe. However, to begin with, he was not strong enough to lift the axe himself. He had to be present at executions in order to legalise them, but two stand-ins were hired to actually carry out decapitations. Jean-Baptiste continued in this role until 1754, when an attack of paralysis, or palsy, meant he had to resign from the post. He never fully recovered. When Jean Baptiste eventually died, he left behind ten children, three daughters and seven sons. All his male children went on to become headsmen, but one child in particular, Charles Henri Sanson, became the most famous Sanson of them all.

CHARLES HENRI SANSON

Charles Henri Sanson was the eldest son of Charles Jean-Baptiste. He was a handsome and well-formed man of superior intellect and education. At the time of his father's death, Charles had already rejected the idea of entering the family profession and was studying to become a physician. However, destiny had other ideas and in 1788, at the age of just fifteen, he received the red cloak – the symbol of the Parisian executioner.

Charles Henri had an unusual talent for performance that would come in useful in later years. He became so well-known for his elegant manner and elaborate dress that he was banned from wearing blue because it was a colour reserved for noblemen. In protest, he began to wear even more gorgeous clothing made from a sumptuous green cloth. Ironically, these green garments were so stylish that he succeeded in making them fashionable with members of the royal court, who began dressing *a la Sanson*.

By 1792, the French revolution was gathering pace, and Sanson was experiencing difficulty dispatching with so many enemies of the republic. He asked for a machine to help him, and on 25 April 1792 the National Assembly obliged, presenting him with the brand-new guillotine. The crowds didn't like it at all, insisting loudly that he 'bring back the block', but Sanson himself was quietly impressed with its 'simplicity and absence of noise'. At the peak of the terror, Charles Henri Sanson executed over 300 men and women in just three days. He could decapitate twelve people in as little as twenty minutes. He famously had the honour of demonstrating his talent to King Louis XVI on the day of his execution, 21 January 1793. It was cold and wet when King Louis XVI made the two-hour coach journey to his place of execution. The king was silent for most of the trip, speaking only to recite psalms from the Bible. When the procession eventually arrived at the Place de Louis XV, the king stepped out of the coach, flanked by guards. He refused to allow the guards to undress or bind him, preferring to undo his necktie and loosen his shirt himself. Louis was confident as he mounted the scaffold, proclaiming these immortal words:

I die innocent of all claims laid to my charge; I pardon those who have occasioned my death; and I pray to God that the blood you are going to shed may never be visited on France.

The drums began to beat, and with one swift slice of the guillotine's blade it was all over. The king was dead, and the crowd began to shout over and over again 'Vive La Republique'! Charles Henri later confirmed in a letter to a newspaper that the king died with bravery and calmness of mind. Nine months later, King Louis's wife, the despised Marie Antoinette, also brushed shoulders with the guillotine. In fact, she trod on Sanson's foot as she mounted the scaffold, exclaiming, 'Monsier, I beg your pardon, I did not do it on purpose'.

FERNAND MEYSONNIER

Fernand Meysonnier was one of France's last official executioners. His career was a long one, lasting for over two decades. He began in 1947, at the tender age of sixteen, when he became apprenticed to his father, the Chief Executioner for Algeria during the period that the country was ruled by France. Over the next twenty-one years, he assisted at the execution of 200 men. His usual job was to hold the victim's head, but on two occasions he actually performed the execution himself, under the benevolent eye of his proud father. Because of the War of Independence raging in Algeria at the time he lived there, many executions were ordered by the French government, particularly of Algerian nationalists. Fernand continued in the job until the French finally lost the war. After the war had ended, Meysonnier left North Africa to work in Polynesia, returning to France in his later years to open a museum.

KEEPING IT IN THE FAMILY

Fernand's father Maurice Meysonnier was a communist who owned a bar and restaurant in Algiers. The family belonged to the 'pied noir' community – white French-speaking nationals who had been born in Algeria. This community was a tightly knit one, and the Meysonnier family became friendly with Henri Roch, another 'pied noir'. Roch was from a long line of executioners going back to the sixteenth century and had held the post of Chief Executioner in the colony for many years. When Fernand was born, Maurice asked Roch to become the child's godfather. On Roche's retirement, after World War II, Maurice himself took on the job as Chief Executioner in the city, thus linking his son to the macabre line of business that was later to shape his life. Maurice also continued to run the bar and restaurant.

As the War of Independence in Algeria escalated during the 1940s, many executions were ordered by the French government to quell the insurgents. Again, it was mostly Algerian nationals who met their end in this way. To cope with the demand, Maurice Meysonnier enlisted his son's help in carrying out the beheadings. Later, Fernand recalled: 'I remember the first time I witnessed an execution. It was very violent. It wasn't like killing a fly. This was a human being. It affected me greatly.' He went on to describe the event in detail:

> *Everything happened very quickly. Just three seconds separated the base of the guillotine from the blade raised above it. However, an hour of suspense and strained, pressing silence were unbearable. And when the blade dropped, I gave a shout. Then the blood gushed out of the wound, and several streamlets ran from the carotid artery.*

PERKS OF THE JOB

Despite his shock at the sight of the beheading, Fernand agreed to become his father's assistant in performing executions. He later denied that he had wanted to emulate his father, saying that it was more case of wanting to help his father carry out his job. 'My father needed someone he could trust absolutely,' he said. 'The important thing about the job was that absolutely nothing should go wrong.' In time, the young man became accustomed to the horror of the event, but the gravity of the situation never failed to impress him. 'I don't mean that these are things men can get used to,' he explained. 'However, when you know what your objective is, you concentrate on the job only.'

Despite the gruesome nature of the work, Fernand found that there were positive advantages in working as the assistant to the Chief Executioner of Algiers. 'I had good money,' he remembered. 'I could carry a gun. I had plenty of free time; the chief of police would greet me. And I had the goodwill of the whole of French Algeria.'

HOLDING THE DEAD MAN'S HEAD

Fernand Meysonnier began his career as a junior assistant. This involved waiting at the bar for a call from the prosecutor's office, and then packing up the guillotine equipment into boxes. In the evening, father and son would set off by lorry to the prison in Algiers, Oran, or Constantine, where the executions would take place. The guillotine was erected in the courtyard of the prison, and at dawn, the prisoner would be brought out.

Fernand's job involved tying the condemned man's ankles and thighs together with fishing wire. After this, the man's hands were handcuffed behind his back and his elbows were tied together. This method of trussing the prisoner meant that the man's head stuck out from his body, which made decapitation easier. Fernand proved reliable and trustworthy at this task, and before long was promoted to first assistant.

As first assistant, Fernand had to stand in front of the guillotine and pull the condemned man's head through the wooden half-circle, holding it until the blade came thundering down. This was not a particularly easy job. It was important to make sure that the prisoner was held in exactly the right place on the neck, otherwise the assistant himself could have an accident. On several occasions, assistants had had their fingers sliced off. Also, the prisoner had to be manoeuvred into position quickly.

'You must never give the guy time to think,' Meysonnier later recalled. 'Because if you do he starts moving his head around, and that's when you have the mess-ups. The blade comes through the jaw, and you have to use a butcher's knife to finish off the job.'

Fernand later recounted that once he had got the prisoner's head held properly in his hands, he would give the instruction to his father to let down the blade by saying 'Go, father!' Immediately the blade would fly down, there would be a cracking sound, and Fernand would find himself holding the dead man's head in his hands. The blood would spurt out 'like two glasses of red wine chucked three metres', as he later described it. Unphased by this bloody gore, Fernand would finish the job by throwing the head in the bucket beside him, and then he would help to clean up the blood, re-pack the guillotine and go home to work in the bar until the next execution order came in.

CONSCIENCE NOT TROUBLED

Father and son soon developed into a slick team, and before long they had notched up 200 souls on the death list of those executed for agitating against French colonial rule. At the height of the conflict in Algeria, there were five or six executions carried out every month, most of them Algerian nationals. Yet, in later years, Fernand was not troubled by his conscience. He declared that he believed each one of the men he helped to execute to be guilty, and had no regrets about beheading them. However, over time, his feelings about the death penalty changed. When interviewed in his seventies, Fernand explained that in certain cases, he thought capital punishment was too 'soft'; he felt that all prisoners should receive life sentences, since languishing in jail for forty years or more would be a more painful, lasting punishment than instant death, and thus more appropriate for mass murderers and the like.

WORDS OF AN EXECUTIONER

Once the war in Algeria came to an end, the demand for executions tailed off, so Fernand moved to

Polynesia, where he earned a living as a fly exterminator and bar owner. In 1992, he returned to France and opened a Museum of Justice and Punishment at Fontaine de Vaucluse, a pretty town in the south of the country. On display at the museum were such items as medieval torture instruments, a preserved head and notebooks owned by the last executioner to ply his trade in Britain, Albert Pierrepoint.

However, the museum was not a success, and eventually Fernand had to pack up the displayed items and store them in boxes in his basement. In a rather contradictory fashion, he then went on to write a book, '*Words of an Executioner*' whose aim, as he explained it, was to 'end this image of the bloody executioner of the Middle Ages'.

In his book, Fernand argued that the process of beheading 200 prisoners had not hardened him. He told a story about how once, in Algeria, a friend was trying to start a car with a handle and injured his head in the process. Fernand had taken him to hospital to have stitches, and while watching the process, began to feel nauseous. When he told the doctor that he felt sick, the doctor said it was probably because he wasn't used to the sight of blood. This the executioner found very amusing.

Fernand also pointed out in his book that he did not regret his career as an executioner. Although he took no pleasure in the job, he believed that punishment for the victims was necessary.

I executed a sentence, but no matter how guilty the sentenced was, I never felt hatred against him. At the same time, I never demonstrated weakness, because I thought about his victims, whom he probably tortured, and their relatives. I am proud that I was a punitive instrument of justice.

He added, "If the government entrusts us with this hard and sad duty, it means that we are considered just, honest, and not spiteful toward anyone."

However, Fernand also pointed out that there were times when he could not bring himself to do the job, as happened when several communists were sentenced to death for posting political leaflets in the streets. On this occasion, Fernand pleaded illness. 'I couldn't execute the punishment,' he says. 'I said I was unwell and stayed home.' Thus the executioner was not always as impartial and objective as he has claimed to be.

OFF WITH HIS HEAD!

In his later years, Fernand contracted liver cancer, but said that he was not afraid of dying. 'May I, the man who beheaded 200 criminals, be afraid of death?' he commented. 'This would be absurd.' In accordance with his light-hearted approach to his past, he also trained two grey parrots to sing The Marseillaise, France's national anthem, and to shout 'Off with his head – long live Meysonnier.' To some this might appear to be in bad taste, but he explained his action by saying that he was 'fond of a laugh'.

He continued to live quietly in Fontaine de Vaucluse, and with his neat appearance and the gentlemanly air of a respectable retiree, it was hard for local residents to believe that he had helped to dispatch 200 victims during his time as executioner's assistant. He was described as an opera and ballet lover, a champion of justice, a resourceful businessman' the founder of a museum and – last, but not least – a man with a 'humane attitude towards other people'. Little did they know that, far away in Algeria, the ghosts of 200 men haunted his past. Yet Fernand himself claims that the memory of the many executions he helped to perform does not trouble his sleep at night.

THE ROLE OF THE EXECUTIONER

It is an exorbitant power – to kill your fellow man. The whole thing happens like in a movie. They bring in the first one and then the second, and in twenty seconds, two people are decapitated. You come out with an incredible sense of power – only God can do that!'

Today, this is how Fernand describes his former life as an executioner. Yet he feels that this power was wisely used, at least in his case, arguing that the role of executioner is an honourable one, since the executioner simply carries out the law of the government in as humane, reliable and impartial a way as possible. What Fernand does not – perhaps, cannot – do is to look beyond the law and ask how culpable were the condemned men sent to the guillotine at a time when war prevailed. His story points up the fact that the executioner does not ask questions about the morality of the death penalty, but merely to carries out the letter of the law in the most competent way he can.

MARCEL CHEVALIER

Marcel Chevalier's name has gone down in history as the last executioner to ply his trade in France. He took up his appointment as Chief Executioner in 1976, taking over from Andre Obrecht, who had been in the post for over twenty years. However, in his new role, Chevalier only went on to perform two executions, that of Jerome Carrein, a child rapist and murderer, and Hamida Djandoubi, who had tortured and strangled his girlfriend to death. Carrein was put to death on 23 June 1977 in the town of Douai, and Djandoubi on 10 September 1977 in Marseilles. Both were beheaded with the guillotine, under the capital punishment laws that had been introduced during the French Revolution. In 1981, capital punishment was finally abolished in France, and with it the guillotine. The macabre post of *Monsieur de Paris*, as France's Chief Executioner was popularly known, also came to an abrupt end.

FRIENDS IN HIGH PLACES

Marcel Chevalier was born in Montrouge on 28 February 1921. Aged thirteen, he began work as a printer. After World War II, he met Marcelle Obrecht, the niece of Chief Executioner Andre Obrecht, and married her on 12 June 1948. In this way, Chevalier became connected to the small, secretive world of the execution business. Marcel and his wife went on to have two children, a girl named Dominique, born in 1952, and a boy named Eric, born a year later.

Beginning in 1958, Chevalier began working as an executioner. He performed about forty executions in total, and when his wife's uncle retired in 1976, he applied for the post of Chief Executioner, known in popular parlance as the '*Monsieur de Paris*'. The following year, Chevalier was required to carry out two executions in his new post, those of Jerome Carrien and Hamida Djandoubi, who had both been sentenced to death.

Hoping that his son would follow in his footsteps, Chevalier decided to give his son, Eric, an early apprenticeship into the job by allowing him to be present at the executions, so that he would understand what the illustrious position of Chief Executioner involved. Unfortunately – or fortunately, perhaps, depending on one's point of view – Eric never had the chance to take over the family trade, since the abolition of capital punishment meant that his father's work became redundant.

FIRST CANDIDATE

Chevalier's first candidate for the chop was a high-profile villain called Jerome Carrein, who had attracted the loathing of the French public because he killed an innocent eight-year-old girl, Cathy Devimeux. To add insult to injury, Cathy was the daughter of a woman who had had been kind enough to give him credit in a cafe. As it transpired, the killing of the girl was the final episode in Carrein's miserable life story.

Shortly after his birth, Carrein was abandoned by his father, leaving his mother to cope on her own. He left school at fourteen with no qualifications. By the age of nineteen, he was married to a sixteen-year-old girl, with whom he fathered five children. Family life was anything but harmonious; the penniless couple fought and drank, while their offspring struggled to survive as best they could. An aggressive drunk, after many scenes of domestic violence, Carrier was finally convicted of beating his wife with a chair, and received an eight-month prison sentence.

Madame Devimaux, the patronne of the bistro, had numerous children, one of whom, a pretty eight-year-old girl called Cathy, caught Carrein's eye. On 27 October 1975, Carrein waited for her outside her school, and asked her if she'd like to go fishing with him. Cathy agreed, and he led her down a country road towards the river. A passer-by from the village was surprised to see a beggar accompanied by such a young child, and followed the pair of them, but then lost sight of them. Cathy's chance of being saved was lost for ever, and her young life was about to come to an end.

Carrein led the child to a deserted spot and tried to undress her. When Cathy tried to fight him off, threatening to tell her mother what had happened, Carrein strangled her. Unbelievably, he then returned to the village and decided to go for a drink at Madame Devimaux's bistro. The distraught woman was desperately worried about her child. Carrien told her that he had seen Cathy early but left the child to return home on her own. However, he was not believed, and the police were called. The following day, Cathy's body was recovered and Carrein confessed everything. He was tried, convicted of murder and sentenced to death on 12 July 1976.

The execution of Jerome Carrein was carried out by Chevalier on 23 June 1977 at the prison of Douai. Like most French executions, it took place in the early hours of the morning, in this case at 4.30 a.m. On the very same day, the National Assembly of France announced the findings of the Peyreffite Commission, which advocated the abolition of the death penalty. However, it would be another four years before this became a reality.

LAST EXECUTION

Hamida Djandoubi, the last man ever to be guillotined in France, at Baumettes Prison in Marseille, was perhaps one of the most memorable victims of a system of capital punishment that had lasted so long. Born in Tunisia, Djandoubi was an immigrant to France, who had moved to Marseille to find work. By 1968, he was working in the city as a packer. However, disaster then struck. An accident at his workplace resulted in the loss of two-thirds of his right leg and he could no longer find work as a result. He then appears to have started working as a pimp, surrounding himself with young women whom he badly mistreated. This continued until one of his girlfriends, Elisabeth Bousquet, filed a complaint to the police against her former lover, claiming that he had treated her cruelly, kept her captive and tried to force her into prostitution. Djandoubi was taken into custody but later released, whereupon he decided to take his revenge on Bousquet.

On July 1974, in front of two other young women, he beat his former lover, burnt her body with lit cigarettes, and then took her by car to a suburb of Marseille, where he strangled her until she was dead. Too frightened to report what they had witnessed, the two girls remained silent until Bousquet's body was discovered in a shed by some children on 7 July 1974. At this point, the two witnesses decided to come forward and give evidence against Djandoubi, and he was duly arrested.

Djandoubi was tried at the court of Aix-en-Provence on 24 February 1977, charged with murder, torture, rape and premeditated violence. His defence tried to claim that the loss of his leg had driven him to become a violent alcoholic and altered his personality. However, the jury were not convinced, and on 25 February he was given the death penalty. He appealed, but the appeal was rejected.

The execution took place on 10 September 1977. Early that morning, Djandoubi was told that the president had not offered him a reprieve. Not long afterwards, at 4.40 a.m., Djandoubi was executed by the Chief Executioner of France, Marcel Chevalier. Four years later, capital punishment was abolished in France under President Mitterand and Justice Minister Robert Badinter, making Djandoubi the last person ever to be executed in the country.

THE END OF AN ERA

When his career as Chief Executioner came to an end, Chevalier became a printer. He gave several interviews about his experiences as an executioner, but when he found that the newspapers sensationalised what he told them, he gave up talking to the press.

There had been moves towards abolishing the death penalty in France for over 200 years, beginning in 1791 when a bill was presented aimed at abolishing it. It was supported by Robespierre, but did not succeed. During Napoleon's reign it continued to be in force, and was upheld during the nineteenth century despite campaigns by such leading lights as Aristide Briand and Jean Jaures to abolish it. In the twentieth century, during World War II, Marshal Petain supported the system of capital punishment by guillotine, refusing to pardon eight women due to be guillotined, but was lucky himself to escape execution at the end of the war. Charles De Gaulle, the new head of state, issued Petain with a reprieve, committing him instead to life imprisonment on the grounds of ill health.

The eventual abolition of the death penalty came about in 1981, largely as a result of campaigns by Robert Badinter, a staunch opponent of capital punishment and a lawyer who had tried to defend some of the last victims of the system. When Badinter became Minister of Justice, it became clear that the days of the guillotine were numbered, and in 1981 a bill to abolish the death penalty was finally pushed through the National Assembly, under the leadership of the newly elected President Francois Mitterand. The days of the guillotine had at last come to an end.

THE GUILLOTINE GETS THE CHOP

Marcel Chevalier's last job as Chief Executioner also marked the end of the guillotine as a method of capital punishment. There had been no public executions since 1939, when Eugene Weidmann, a man convicted of six murders, was beheaded outside the prison at Versailles, in what is now the Palais de Justice. This was a shameful occasion, in which the guillotine was badly assembled, the executioner Jules-Henri was alleged to be drunk and members of the crowd behaved in a disrespectful way. Desfourneaux, the Chief Executioner, was later reported to have argued with his cousin, Andre Obrecht, which involved a fist fight after an execution. Obrecht later took over as Chief Executioner, and when he retired, Marcel Chevalier took over his post. It was Chevalier who was in office when the death penalty was abolished in France in 1981.

The guillotine had been an eblem of progress since the days of the French Revolution – albeit a gruesome, violent type of progress. As compared to the hideously cruel tortures of the medieval period, this decapitation machine was at least more humane than the methods of capital punishment that had gone before – punishments that included burning at the stake, drawing and quartering, and many other horrific forms of killing.

n previous eras, methods of killing had varied according to the social standing of the victim: often, peasants and ordinary townspeople were tortured to death overmany days, for example onthe wheel, while higher-born individuals were beheaded by sword. Beheading often went wrong, however; a slip of the blade, and the victim might have to suffer several more blows before the head was finally severed.

In contrast to these primitive forms of capital punishment, the guillotine was – relatively speaking – a humanitariandevice,aproductoftheEnlightenmentideas of the age. For more than two centuries, it became the method for carrying out the death penalty in France, and improvements were made to the machine over the years. For example, wheels were added to the inner grooves so that the blade descended quickly, and a shield was put up so that the beheading scene was hidden from sight. Later, the authorities dropped the habit of erecting a scaffold so that crowds could see the event, and finally banned public executions altogether.

PART EIGHT

Hanged, Drawn & Quartered

Hanging, Drawing, Quartering

This horrific punishment was a product of the Dark Ages, when short life and brutal death were commonplace. Children died young, deadly diseases were rife and major criminals were summarily put to death for their crimes. The authorities believed that the worst offences were treasonable ones. Treason was not just confined to plotting the assassination of a sovereign, and in fact its definition varied depending on the monarchy ruling of the time. One could find oneself subjected to the noose followed by the knife for as little as forgery.

It was thought that the punishment should fit the crime and with treason being at the top of the Crown's list, ahead of such crimes as rape and murder, a suitably harsh penalty was required. During the unenlightened, unruly thirteenth century, a solution was finally found: that of hanging, drawing and quartering. This punishment was deemed so cruel that two sections of society were instantly exempt from it. Those traitors that bore title normally escaped the full penalty and were divided into only two parts, having their head separated from their body by axe before the general public. Female traitors also escaped this particular punishment and instead found themselves tied to a stake and burnt. The threefold punishment was deemed too immodest for them.

THE PROCEDURE

The three-in-one death penalty succeeded in ensuring that no stone was left unturned when it came to physical and mental punishment. To begin with, the victim was taken from their respective prison cell, often placed upon a hurdle which resembled a wooden sledge. The hurdle was a far from comfortable mode of transport considering the bumpy cobbles of medieval towns, but far better than the original practice of tying the prisoner to the tail of a horse and dragging them to the scaffold without any protection against the ground. Provided the victim survived this humiliating journey through the pelting throng of onlookers, he was hung from the scaffold by a half-penny halter until half dead. This undoubtedly damaged the throat enough to reduce any screams of agony to that of a whisper.

The executioner then cut the traitor down from the scaffold and carried him to a raised trestle table, where he was brought back to his senses with cold water so as to not deprive the crowd of their entertainment. This ensured that the condemned felt the full force of the law. As the victim fought for air against asphyxia, the executioner turned to the cache of weapons from which he would select the appropriate device for phase two.

The pain of this half-hanging would soon be superseded by what came next. The victim saw the executioner return holding a sharp cutting knife, which would be unceremoniously drawn across his stomach. Without any anaesthetic, this operation would have been excruciatingly painful, and would have surely had the 'patient' pleading for death's swift arrival. Unfortunately for some, it would not be forthcoming. For those that had not been granted the mercy of death or, at the very least, unconsciousness, arguably the worst part of this deplorable punishment would occur.

The executioner then selected a second instrument from his collection and extracted the intestines from the fresh wound at the stomach. The executioner preferred this method to using his hands, as the innards often proved too slippery to control. The victim's entrails would then be brought before his very eyes before being placed on a nearby fire. If the condemned remained conscious, then he would witness the executioner enter his chest to pluck out his heart, which soon followed the viscera onto the flames. This, then, would guarantee the death of the traitor.

Many experienced the ignominy of castration before the disembowellment took place. While this added to the agony and humiliation of the condemned, it did have a further if irrational purpose. The removal of the sexual organs represented the symbolic withdrawal of any opportunity for producing future offspring. Saying this, there is no account in existence that tells of a victim having been hanged, disembowelled and divided into five pieces having the opportunity to procreate!

The neck choked, the stomach torn and organs drawn, and yet still the punishment was not complete. Mercifully, the prisoner – now nothing but a mutilated corpse – would have left the land of the living, however, the crowd chose to stay put for the final acts. At this point, it was customary for the executioner to step aside, possibly to take a much-needed breather from the quite literally gut-wrenching work and allow someone else to deal with the beheading. This was because rather than using an axe to hack the head from the body, it was usual to use a surgical knife and so it required a more skilled hand than that of the executioner. The body would be placed in the coffin with the head raised on a block at the top edge of the wooden box and once the head was freed from the body it was passed to the executioner who would raise it up for all to see, holding it high at the four corners of the scaffold, before declaring, 'Behold the head of a traitor! So die all traitors!' This was met with undoubted cheers from the satisfied crowd who, without the technology to capture the affair, acted as official witnesses to the event. After the show had ended, the head made the return journey back to Newgate (or similar gaol), where it was parboiled in a concoction of salt water and cumin seed, and then placed on its own stake upon London Bridge to serve as a reminder of the comeuppance for all convicted traitors. This vile process ensured the head would be left alone by the circling gulls that were keen to feast upon rotting flesh.

This leaves the last step: quartering the body of the condemned traitor. Rather than a purely gratuitous act of deformation, this procedure was not without reason. The main purpose of the entire process, aside from punishing the convicted, was to act as a deterrent to any citizen of the land entertaining thoughts of betrayal in any guise. This division of the body created five sections including the head – to serve as promotional material for the Crown. The lack of a national newspaper or other media such as radio or television meant that these five pieces were needed to advertise the severity of the crime and remind people of the severity of the punishment. In effect, the traitor himself would be made to tour the kingdom, spreading the word that it was unwise to cross the king. Depending on the status of the individual, his quartered parts would travel across the county or even the entire country to locations chosen by the monarchy.

This was not the only reason for the final stage of this most brutal of capital punishments. The quartering of the body had a religious significance as well. It was the Christian belief that the body must remain intact to ensure successful passage to Heaven and so physical damage to the corpse would act as a further punishment post mortem.

In France, quartering would often be facilitated by horses. A wild stallion was tethered to each of the victim's arms and legs and then whipped into a gallop, thus wrenching the limbs savagely from the body. This was not always as easy as it sounds. As in the case of Robert-Francois Damiens in 1757, the four horses of his own personal apocalypse were not sufficient to tear out his limbs and so the executioner was forced to make cuts on the relevant joints to facilitate the quartering.

Today, there exists considerable divergence of opinion over the actual meaning of the term: hanged, drawn and quartered. There is two beliefs, both of which have an undeniable logic attached to them. The issue is primarily with the definition of the 'drawing' part of the procedure. Some believe the phrase should more accurately read: 'drawing, hanging, quartering' as they define drawing as the act of dragging the prisoner to the execution site. Some others disagree with this definition, believing instead that the word 'drawing' refers to the removal of the intestines from the body, much like the practice of preparing poultry prior to cooking it.

THE HANGED, DRAWN AND QUARTERED

The first recorded execution of this kind appears to have occurred in 1241 upon William Maurice, who had been convicted of piracy. Further information regarding this debut remain scarce, and many believe that it was in fact Edward Longshanks, during his sixty-eight year reign of England, who firmly established the threefold punishment as a penalty befitting traitors to the Crown. Also known as Edward the Lawgiver, he gave out this cruel sentence to two major opponents during his border conflicts to the North and West.

The first to feel the wrath of this boundary-breaking monarch was David, the Prince of Wales. His downfall came after he betrayed Edward (with whom he had grown up as a child) when he chose to side with his brother Llywelyn in the fight for Welsh independence. This treachery coupled with the loss of a worthy ally ensured a harsh punishment would be forthcoming. In 1283, David was hanged, drawn and then divided into four, and the quarters of his body were scattered throughout the expanding kingdom. This last Welsh Prince of Wales then joined his brother when their heads met atop stakes fixed at the Tower of London.

With the suppression of Welsh opposition, Edward I was then able to focus his attention to the North, where he came up against the Scottish nationalist William Wallace. After the defeat at the Battle of Falkirk in 1298, Wallace avoided capture for seven years until he was duped by Scottish knight John de Mentieth. Transported to London and found guilty of treason, the Scottish rebel was dragged to the Smithfield gallows in London on the 23 August 1305, where the rest of this sadistic sentence was carried out in full. Wallace's parboiled head decorated the Tower while his four quarters were sent to Newcastle, Berwick, Stirling and Aberdeen in an attempt to quash the Scots.

It was 200 years later when this most violent of judicial practices began to flourish once more. The sixteenth century saw great change in matters of religion initiated by Henry VIII's creation of the Church of England which, in turn, bred considerable discontentment among the clergy. Friar John Houghton was one of 105 Catholic martyrs who were hanged, drawn and quartered at Tyburn during the 1500s for failing to recognise the monarch as the supreme head of the Church.

The Carthusian priest made the hurdle ride to the famous execution site in 1535 where he was turned off the ladder in the customary way. A short time later he was sent crashing to the ground writhing in asphyxiating agony. Once stripped of his clothes, his belly was cut open and the executioner fetched out his bowels with the necessary tool – an image made all the more disturbing with the friar continuing to pray. After gutting, the executioner moved up to the chest cavity and, while in the process of wrenching out the heart, the friar was heard to exclaim, 'Good Jesus, what will you do with my heart?' Thankfully, these were his final words, but to make doubly sure the head was hacked off immediately afterwards and the torso was carved into four. One quarter of his corpse was suspended over the gate of the Carthusians' quarters in London.

THOMAS DOUGLAS: A GLUTTON FOR PUNISHMENT

It was not just active enemies of the king who found themselves fighting for air as their innards were forcefully ejected. The definition of treason could stretch to petty crimes, as Thomas Douglas discovered in 1605. He conspired with a man named James Steward in forging the King James I's signature. Their plan was to use this forgery to obtain the Great Seal of England with which they could then legally acquire land held by the Crown. The scam was discovered but while Steward was executed for his involvement, no solid case could be made to convict Douglas and he was allowed to go free. He failed to learn his lesson and foolishly continued with his swindling ways. He managed to fake the king's Privy Signet in letters to German royalty asking for capital. This plan was as successful as the initial one and he was sentenced to this vicious capital punishment, which was performed in all its grisly glory on 27 June 1605 in the Smithfield district of London.

THE GUNPOWDER PLOT

While Douglas's parts made their respective journeys to publicise the king's displeasure, there were seven fervent Catholic men planning to commit high treason. Their plot was an audacious one: they were going to blow up the Houses of Parliament, and with it the country's Catholic-hating sovereign, James I. Of course, this was the notorious Gunpowder Plot which resulted in the most famous victims of the three-act punishment. The authorities were informed by one of the conspirators who had little faith in the plan and they caught Guy Fawkes attempting to light the barrels of gunpowder on the 5 November 1605. Under torture Fawkes confessed the names of his co-conspirators and they were quickly rounded up and tried at Westminster Hall in January 1606. All seven men were given the brutal sentence to take place in two locations: St Paul's Church and the Old Place Yard, before the very Houses of Parliament they had attempted to destroy. The ferocity of this punishment must have gained much notoriety by the seventeenth century for Guy Fawkes found it necessary to cheat the full agonising process. He flung himself from the gallows thus snapping his neck to ensure he avoided the ordeal of living through the rest of the sentence. Fellow plotter Robert Keyes had the same idea. Unfortunately for him, the rope snapped and he was subjected to the full treatment; his intestines were torn from his body, allowing all to see that he did, in fact, have the stomach for such punishment.

In 1660, during the executions of those responsible for the 1649 execution of King Charles I – Major General Thomas Harrison was brought before the gallows and the assembled crowd of witnesses which included Charles II, the son of the executed king. Harrison swung from the gallows and after only a few minutes he was cut down, his oxygen-starved lungs gasping for air. He was then laid out on the boards where the executioner selected a cutting device to slit open the stomach and pull out his entrails. It is reported that on having his torso cut open and his slippery innards stolen from him, the major promptly sat up, leaned forward and struck his executioner across the head! The executioner – while surely surprised at this – did not delay in completing the punishment and swiftly removed the head of Harrison before burning his intestines in a nearby fire.

OVERSEAS AND OVERKILL

Hanging, drawing and quartering was not solely confined to England. The punishment was also adopted in Rhode Island in the United States. In 1676, the English colonist Joshua Tefft was executed at Smith's Castle for fighting alongside the Narragansett tribe of Native Americans versus the colonial leaders. This is considered to be the only time that this vicious sentence was carried out on US soil. On 21 July 1797, David McLane was hanged, drawn and quartered in what is now Quebec, but early nineteenth century Canada began to show signs of retraction. In May 1814, seventeen traitors to Canada in the 1812 war against America were given the threefold death sentence. However, ultimately only eight were executed without being quartered and the rest were given a reprieve. England, too, was becoming more moderate.

The practice of this disagreeable punishment was slowly being phased out during the late eighteenth and early nineteenth centuries. No doubt spurred on by the horrified reactions of those who witnessed the gory goings-on. Governments were concerned that they may be alienating their people with such judicial barbarism and so began to reduce the punishment, omitting the more gruesome aspects. Such an example of this commutation took place in 1817 when riots broke out in Derbyshire as a result of grievances against the high level of unemployment and general living conditions. To bring an end to this Midland melee the authorities sentenced the main agitators, Jeremiah Brandreth, Isaac Ludlam and William Turner, to be hanged, drawn and quartered. Their sentences were eventually commuted to one of hanging till dead, followed by a post mortem beheading. The condemned trio were hanged before the crowd outside Derby Gaol for a full hour before being cut down, where a local miner – not the official executioner – was called to don the mask for the decapitation. One hopes that the rope had done its job for this makeshift axeman took several swings at the first head before using a knife to finish the job. It is chronicled that the crowds fled the scaffold in horror at the mess that was this ineffectual display of justice.

In 1820, a similarly reduced capital punishment took place as a result of the Cato Street Conspiracy. Discontent towards social conditions caused a troubled few to plot the downfall of the government by murdering a selection of the Cabinet. The police caught wind of their designs and the gang of five, led by Arthur Thistlewood, were cornered by police in a house on Cato Street. They were all found guilty of high treason, but instead of facing the three dreaded steps to death they were all hanged before having their heads surgically removed while their corpses laid in their coffins. The records show that the three-phase punishment was slowly being phased out and this brutal tripartite execution was eventually omitted from the Statute Books in 1870 by the Forfeiture Act.

WILLIAM CALCRAFT

William Calcraft is best remembered as the hangman with the longest career and the shortest rope! Calcraft's method left a lot to be desired, and most condemned prioners would have counted themseves lucky to have been executed by his successor, the eminent William Marwood, who ridiculed Calcraft, with the statement 'He hanged 'em, I execute 'em.'

A journalist once asked Calcraft whether his profession ever gave him cause for agitation, and this fascinating exchange took place:

Calcraft: *'No, not a bit. Why should I be. I am only doing my duty.'*
Journalist: *'Still it is a very dreadful duty; and even as a matter of duty, few persons could kill a man without ...'*
C: *'Kill a man!, who kills a man? I never killed a man, they kill themselves. I merely put a rope around their necks and knock away the platform beneath them. I don't kill 'em; it's their own weight that does it.'*

CASSELL'S SATURDAY JOURNAL, 23 JANUARY 1892

In fact, Calcraft's use of the short drop method meant that quite often the victim's own weight *didn't* kill them, and he had to descend the gallows and add his own weight to the rope in order to cut short his victim's suffering.

William Calcraft was born in 1800, in Little Baddow near Chelmsford, Essex to 'humble but industrious' parents. One biographer describes him as an adventurous but impatient child, who had a great affection for animals, particularly rabbits, a passion which would last throughout adulthood. He left Essex for Hoxton, London, at the age of ten, and having 'graduated from the gutter, with a degree in petty crime', he began his working life as a shoemaker before becoming a pie salesman at public executions. This is how he became aquainted with the hangman Thomas Cheshire (Old Tom) and eventually Calcraft became apprenticed to him.

Calcraft's very first execution was that of the hated child murderer and sweatshop owner, sixty-one-year-old Ester Hibner in April 1829, who had to be put in a straight jacket for her execution at Newgate, because she proved to be such a violent prioner.

Calcraft received one guinea a week retainer from his London employers, plus one guinea for a hanging at Newgate and a further half a crown for a flogging. His earnings were greatly enhanced by hangings at other prisons, for which he could charge between ten and fifteen pounds. He was also allowed to keep the clothes and personal affects of the people he executed, which he sold to people such as Madame Tussaud to dress the models in her Chamber of Horrors. The rope used to hang a particularly notorious criminal could also fetch good money because people considered it lucky.

Between 1829 and 1874, William Calcraft is thought to have carried out between 400 and 450 hangings, and at least thirty-five of these victims were female. During this period capital punishment was carried out by high sherrifs for the area in which the sentence had been passed. Therefore the executioner was an employee of the local authority rather then the national government. Calcraft was made executioner in London and Middlesex, but he was also employed at Horsemonger Jail in Surrey and at Maidstone Prison. Later in his career Calcraft took his services all over the country, he apparently loved to travel.

TESS OF THE D'URBEVILLES

Elizabeth Martha Browne became posthumously famous for providing a sixteen-year-old Thomas Hardy with the inspiration for the character of Tess in his novel *Tess of the D'Urbivilles*, and the young man himself was present at her execution. Elizabeth was an attractive but ordinary woman of humble origins who grew up to become a housemaid and marry a fellow servant, John Browne. It was an unhappy marriage almost from the beginning, and the pair argued non-stop. The constant quarrelling came literally to a head when Elizabeth caught John in bed with another woman and, in a furious rage, struck out at him. John then beat her with his whip. In retaliation, Elizabeth struck her husband several times in the head with a wood-chopping axe, fatally bashing in his skull.

During her trial at Dorchester, Dorset, Elizabeth claimed that her husband had died when he was kicked in the head by a horse, but no one believed her story. She was swiftly found guilty and given a mandatory death sentence. Her case attracted much sympathy from the public in view of her attractive demeanor as well as the abuse she had suffered at the hands of her husband. However, no reprieve was granted and on Saturday, 9 August 1856, the executioner beckoned.

Calcraft travelled to Dorchester by train, arriving with his assistant the day before the hanging was due to take place. The gallows were erected outside the gates of Dorchester Prison that evening. The next morning a crowd of between 3,000 and 4,000 people had gathered to witness the momentous event. Given the circumstances, Elizabeth remained unruffled and appeared almost callous. She had chosen to wear a tight-fitting black silk dress and refused to be transported to the scaffold in the prison van, preferring to walk in the heavy rain. She climbed the first eleven steps where Calcraft pinioned her arms in front of her. He then led her up up to the trap. He had to be reminded to pinion her legs. In those days it was very important to ensure that a female prisoner's skirt was secured so that she retained her decency even in death. The rain rendered the white hood damp so that it clung to her features like a shroud. When Calcraft released the trap, Mrs Browne fell just 30 centimetres (1 foot) with a thudding noise. She struggled for a number of minutes as her body 'wheeled half round and back' on the end of the noose.

MARY ANN COTTON

On the 24 March 1873, William Calcraft was given the dubious honour of executing England's greatest mass-murderess, Mary Ann Cotton, at Durham Jail. Mrs Cotton was found guilty of murdering four husbands, a lover and a great number of her own children, bring the final body count to twenty people, possibly more. Originally, the deaths were put down to gastric fever and her friends and neighbours saw Mary as an object for pity. But as the number of dead family members began to mount up, it soon became clear that arsenic poisoning was to blame. By the time of her sentence, hanging was conducted in private, much to the dissapointment of thousands of people who would otherwise have flocked to see Cotton do the jig. *The Times* newspaper later reported that Cotton died slowly, Calcraft having miscalculated the length of rope required to cleanly break her neck.

Calcraft never admitted any failure in his duties as a hangman, and as an elderly man he would boast that he was 'capable of doing his duty with the most accomplished and practised person in his profession'. Given the number of disastrous mistakes he made over the years, one seriously doubts whether his contemporaries, or indeed any of his many victims, would have agreed with him.

WILLIAM MARWOOD

Remarkably, William Marwood was fifty-six years of age when he took over from the short-drop bungler William Calcraft as Britain's top executioner. He would go on to become something of a celebrity – perhaps the first of this type of high-profile hangman. He became so well-known in England that this popular riddle could be heard in homes all over the nation.

> Q: ' If Pa killed Ma, who'd kill Pa?'
> A: 'Marwood'.

William Marwood was born in 1818, in the village of Goulceby, Lincolnshire. He was the fifth of ten children of William and Elizabeth Marwood. William's father was a shoemaker, and following a brief apprenticeship to a miller, young William followed him into the family business. It was perhaps during his time as a fledgling cobbler that he aquired the passion for excellence of a master craftsman.

Marwood was a devout Methodist (although partial to gin) and saw himself as a servant of the world. It was in this spirit of servitude that, as he approached middle age, Marwood began to petition the High Sheriff of Lincoln for an opportunity to perform an execution. It was an extremely odd thing for a man of his age to do, especially for one with no experience even of the penal system, let alone the scaffold. It was extraordinary, therefore, that his request was ever granted, but granted it was, and on 1 April 1872 he was invited to Lincoln Prison to execute William Frederick Harry. It was to be the first time that the long-drop method of hanging had been used in England. He dispatched with Harry cleanly and efficiently and impressed everybody present (apart from the condemned, obviously) with the smoothness of his new method.

Marwood was a public executioner for a total of eleven years, and managed to accumilate a fair amount of wealth, owning several properties and other investments. Initially, he was highly regarded by his colleagues in the prison system, and is well-remembered for introducing a number of important reforms to the British execution process. He not only introduced the long-drop method, he also devised the table calculating the relationship between the victim's weight and the length of drop needed to efficiently break his or her neck. Up until this point, the short-drop method meant that the victim was often strangled to death slowly, and the process was deeply unpleasant from beginning to end, not only for the victim but also for the witnesses who were forced to watch. Marwood revolutionised hanging in England, and while it would never be a comfortable experience for anyone present, he at least rendered it quick and relatively efficient. Marwood had always been a keen student of anatomy, and this must have informed his craft to a large extent.

CHARLES PEACE

In some ways at least Charles Peace could be seen as Marwood's ultimate archcriminal counterpart. There were certainly similarities between the two men. Each saw their profession as an art form, and were regarded as talented craftsmen by their contemporaries. It just so happened that, where Marwood's chosen art form involved dispatching of criminals in the name of the crown, Peace chose burglary.

His great skill as a thief, and his almost super-natural ability to escape from the clutches of the law meant that he, like Marwood, made it into the collective public conciousness. He was even immortalised in literature by the writer Arthor Conan Doyle, becoming one of the few real-life criminals ever to feature in a Sherlock Holmes story.

By the time of his execution, Charles Peace was as famous a criminal in England as the American Jesse James on the other side of the Atlantic. On the surface, he appeared to be a well-dressed, violin playing, respectable man who travelled the streets by day, selling musical instruments and bric-a-brac. But by night he was a clever and prolific cat burglar and double murderer, whose many crimes struck terror into the heart of the nation.

Over the years, Charles Peace has become the inspiration for a whole host of archcriminal characters for artists, writers and dramatists alike: part artist, part scoundrel. Peace finally came face to face with Marwood at Armley Gaol on 25 February 1879 – a bitterly cold day. He went to his death in the conviction that he had been forgiven for his many sins, having set about atoning for them upon his capture and incarceration for burglary and murder.

Towards the end of Marwood's career it was noted that he was frequently drunk. In the beginning, he had taken great pride in his chosen vocation, even going to the lengths of having business cards printed with the words:

William Marwood: Public Executioner,
Horncastle, Lincolnshire

He also had a sign installed above the door of his shoe shop which read 'Marwood Crown Office', and his customers often came specifically to buy bootlaces from him, fascinated and amused by his other life. These were not the actions of a man ashamed of his work. However, it seems that the real nature of the job did cause him some agitation. In one conversation with the young James Berry, he said 'My position is not a pleasant one. No, it is not a pleasant one!'

The pressure of the executioner's job often means that they become heavy drinkers, and more than a few develop problems with alcohol. Hangmen such as Bartholemew Binns and Henry Pierrepoint used alcohol to steady their nerves before an execution, and to help with the guilt they felt afterwards. It is debatable whether Marwood drank for the same reasons, but it certainly indicates that his enthusiasm for execution had died a death.

JAMES BERRY

James Berry is perhaps one of the more likable characters on our list of British hangmen, but a lot of the information we have about him comes directly from his own diaries, so we have to take it with a pinch of salt. He became an executioner at a time when the Victorian public were generally fascinated with all aspects of death and crime. Therefore, at the height of his career, Berry became a household name, his notoriety even providing him with an effigy in Madame Tussaud's Chamber of Horrors.

A PASSION FOR ADVENTURE

James Berry was born in Heckmondwicke, Yorkshire in February 1852 to Daniel Berry, a respectable wool-stapler and his wife Mary Ann, formerly Kelley. As a young man he established himself as a passionate, headstrong and adventurous boy, who was quick thinking and imaginative, but also rather wayward.

At nine years old he was kicked in the face by a horse while 'playing hookey' from Sunday school. This nasty accident left him with a permanent scar on his cheek, but it did little or nothing to quash his impulsive, boisterous nature, and he seemed constantly to be getting mixed-up in schemes and scrapes. He was expelled from school after school for truancy and general cheekiness, and his frustrated parents, having run out of options, set him to work in the family business.

At sixteen years old, young, brave and still hungry for adventure, Berry ran away from home with a friend. The two young men made their way to Goole, intent on becoming cabin boys on a ship. Berry found himself engaged upon an old three-masted, fully rigged, wooden vessel whereby the captain, sceptical as to whether young Berry would cope with the life of a sailor, gave him a job. Within a few hours, Berry had discovered that a seamen's life was not all it was cut-out to be, so he borrowed five shillings from his captain (to by some clothes for sailing in) and set off for home.

JAMES THE CRAFTSMAN

For all his faults, James did show some talent. He was cunning and quick-witted, practical and enjoyed designing and constructing things. In his diary he writes fondly about making a monster kite with two plasterer's lathes and a calico front, and he describes the joy of seeing something he made actually work, a feeling only a true craftsperson can experience.

Berry eventually became a police officer in the Wakefield West Riding Depot. By this time, he had met, fallen in love with and married Sarah Ann Ackroyd. The police force was able to offer the man and his young family a rare chance for job security. He was effective in his new job, and 'had the fortune of bringing to justice several notorious criminals.' Berry was a brave officer, and often found himself right in the thick of the action, but he was also quick tempered. His impatience did not sit well with his seniors in the force. Berry was taken before his Chief Constable for insubordination, and although he was cleared of any actual blame, he had lost respect for the police force and resigned soon afterwards.

POSITION VACANT

On 4 September 1883, the English pioneer of the long-drop hanging method, executioner William Marwood, died. He had been instrumental in transforming the hanging process from the gory public spectacle of Calcraft's short drop, to a sombre, private and relatively efficient event governed by science rather than emotion. He was also an aquaintance of Berry's. By this time, James had left the police and become a boot salesman, but he was not making enough money to comfortably support his wife and their four children. He decided to follow in the footsteps of Calcraft and Marwood, who were both cobblers by trade, and applied for the vacant position. The work seemed to him 'distasteful' and he had no personal desire to kill for a living, but at least he would be able to feed and clothe his family.

Upon the death of Marwood, there were as many as 1,400 applications for the post of hangman. James Berry was among twenty individuals selected for interview at the Old Bailey. He assumed he'd got the job, and wrote a telegram to his family to this effect. Unfortunately for him, his potential employers had discovered that Berry suffered from occasional epileptic fits, and so they employed Bartholemew Binns instead.

Berry was disappointed at the news, but his family and friends had done everything within their power to stop him from getting the job. They even petitioned the home secretary to have his application dismissed, believing that his appointment as executioner would bring the family into disrepute.

Fortunately for Berry, Binns was quickly found to be both a bungler and a drunkard, and having subjected a number of his victims to a long, painful and desperate death by strangulation, he was duly removed from the job. Berry's day had finally come.

COLD FEET

James Berry's first execution took place on 31 March 1884 in Edinburgh. The prisoners in question were poachers Robert Flockart Vickers and William Innes, who had been charged with the murders of two assistant game keepers John Fortune and John McDiarmid at the Roseby estate in the Moorfoot hills.

On the morning of the 28 March, he paid a visit to the scaffold, where builders were still constructing the shed provided to render the execution private. He tested the gallows using bags of cement which were the same weight as Vickers and Innes respectively. He calculated the length of the drop required, using Marwood's long-drop table, and when his preparations were complete he spent some time pacing around the prison grounds in contemplation of the poor men who were 'nearing their end, full of life, and knowing the fatal hour, which made me quite ill to think about.'

Berry was beginning to feel uncomfortable with his responsibilities and he lost his appetite:

Nothing felt good to me, everything that I put into my mouth felt like sand, and I felt as if I wished I had never undertaken such an awful calling. I regretted for a while, and then I thought the public would only think I had not the pluck, and I would not allow my feelings to overthrow me, so I never gave way to such thoughts again.

When the time came for Berry to launch Vickers and Innes into eternity, the executions were done 'quick as lightning'. The magistrates, doctors and members of the press all admitted that James had done a stirling job, carrying out the sentence in a humane and efficient manner. It appeared James Berry had finally found his calling.

EXECUTIONER NUMBER 1

In his long career as hangman, Berry's most important contribution to the science of execution were the many refinements he made to Marwood's long-drop method. He is responsible for giving us the sub-aural positioned knot, placed under the left ear instead of the chin, which meant that the victim's neck was more likely to snap cleanly and quickly, shortening the victim's physical and emotional distress. Indeed, some of the practices introduced by him remained official procedure until the death penalty was finally abolished in Britain.

Berry carried out a total of 131 hangings during his career, with five of his victims being female – a fact which sometimes gave his concience more grief than he could manage. For the most part he proved himself more than capable of the job at hand, but there were occassions where circumstance let him down. One of these rare occasions was the astonishing execution of John Lee, who became known as 'the man they couldn't hang'.

THE MAN THEY COULDN'T HANG

In the days following his 'execution', John Henry George Lee became a national hero, the first man to cheat the gallows, not just once but over and over again! Lee had been a servant in the house of an elderly lady, Miss Emma Anne Whitehead Keyse, from Babbacombe, Dorset. John was already a known criminal and Miss Keyse saw his employment as a merciful act.

On the night of 14 November 1884, a housemaid was woken by the smell of smoke and went downstairs to investigate. She was extremely distraught to find the partially charred remains of Miss Keyse lying on the dining room floor. She had been hit over the head with a heavy object and had her throat cut before the killer doused the surrounding carpets and furniture with paraffin and set them alight. There had been no forced entry.

Unsurprisingly, John Lee's criminal record immediately made him the prime suspect, and the fact that hairs from the dead woman were found on his socks, convicted him. He was sentenced to hang at Exeter Gaol.

On the allocated day of his death, Lee was accompanied from his cell to the coach house by the chaplain, the governor and other officials. Berry strapped the prisoner's legs together, pulled the white cap down over his head, put on the noose, took a step back and operated the drop. Nothing happened. Berry jerked the lever once more, harder this time. Again nothing happened. He stamped hard on the trapdoor, but even when the wardens added their own weight, the trapdoor still would not budge. Berry removed Lee's morbid regalia and went to inspect the gallows. There was nothing obviously the matter and the contraption seemed to be working perfectly.

Berry once more ascended the scaffold, pulled the white cap down over Lee's head, put on the noose and pulled the lever so hard it bent in his hand. Again, the trapdoor stayed put.

By this time, the execution party were becoming seriously spooked. What could be causing the mysterious hold-up? Was John Lee in possession of psychic powers and controlling the scaffold with the strength of his mind? Or was there some satanic force at work? Lee kept his composure throughout this ordeal and he remained calm and quite in control, which must have disturbed Berry, the chaplain, the officials and the witnesses still further. In the end, they decided to call off the execution and inform the home secretary of the problem.

A NEW LEASE OF LIFE

Lee was led back to his cell and given a large meal of chicken, potatoes, muffins and cake. One can't help but wonder what ran through his mind while tucking into his dinner. In that position, most of us would feel like the luckiest person alive, but still Lee seemed unruffled, as if he knew the outcome all along. He was apparently surprised to learn that Berry, who'd been extremely disturbed by the day's events, had lost his appetite. Eventually, John Lee's sentence was commuted from death to twenty years in prison. He was eventually released in 1907 at the age of forty-three, and began a new life in America.

JAMES THE PREACHER

Berry continued to work as an executioner until 1891, when he hung up his noose for the last time. His years on the scaffold had taken their toll. He was drinking a great deal and had become more short tempered than at any other time in his life. He was also haunted by nightmares, prompting some contemporary historians to conclude that he suffered from some kind of post-traumatic stress disorder. In the years following his resignation, he toured the New World as an evangelist and gave lectures on phrenology (the science of determining a person's character and criminality by the shape of his head). He changed his mind about his belief in the death penalty, concluding in his diary that:

> *The law of capital punishment falls with terrible weight upon the hangman and that to allow a man to follow such an occupation is doing him a deadly wrong.*

Berry continued his evangelist teaching until his death in October 1913. It would have surprised the former executioner to learn that executions continued in Britain until 1964, convinced as he was that 'we shall never be a civilised nation while executions are carried out in prison.'

THE BILLINGTONS

One of the best known family of twentieth-century executioners were the Billingtons – James and his sons Thomas, William and John. As with many now obsolete trades, the fascinating skill of execution was often passed down from father to son, with each individual stamping his own unique style on the trade. Mind you it took more than family connections to secure the position of executioner, and the candidate had to have a good character and a clean slate. Even if the applicant got past the first interview, they still had to pass a written examination and take part in training courses. Despite being a depressing job with meagre remunerations, for many it still held a fascination and James Billington had always dreamed of becoming a hangman.

From an early age, James Billington was fascinated by the art of execution and experimented using a dummy on a homemade scaffold in his back garden in Bolton. He was of medium height and slight build, but was exceptionally strong. After completing his education, he dabbled in various jobs including working in a cotton mill, being a collier and also trying his hand at being a wrestler, but he could settle at none. In the late 1860s, James moved to Farnworth, where he set up in business as a barber. He started to frequent public houses and became renowned for his singing and outlandish drunken behaviour. However, meeting his future wife, Alice Pennington, made him see the light and he pledged to give up the drink. He even went as far as wearing the blue ribbon indicating that he was a teetotaller.

Billington married his beloved Alice in 1872 but the union was plagued with sadness. Not ony did the couple lose three children in infancy, but Alice died prematurely in 1890 at the age of forty, shortly after her husband had realised his dream of becoming an executioner. Determined to make something of his life, James Billington applied for the post that had been held by the somewhat celebrity executioner, William Marwood. His application was turned down, however, he managed to secure the position as the hangman for Yorkshire.

Billington's very first execution took place at Armley Gaol in Leeds on 26 August 1884, when he hanged a Sheffield hawker, Joseph Laycock, for the murder of his wife and four children. Just before Billington placed the noose around his neck, Laycock pleaded, 'You will not hurt me?' to which James replied, 'No, thaal nivver feel it, for thaal be out of existence i' two minutes'. Billington mastered the art of swift execution and soon gained himself a reputation for a 'clean, quick finish'.

In July 1891, Billington married for the second time to Alice Fletcher, who bore him two more children. He had three surviving sons from his first marriage, Thomas born in 1873, William born in 1875 and John in 1880. The year after his marriage, in 1892, he succeeded James Berry as the main executioner for London and the Home Office.

Billington went on to complete 147 executions, the last one taking place on 3 December 1901 with the hanging of Patrick McKenna at Strangeways Prison in Manchester. Ironically, McKenna was a friend of the Billington family, and they had once lived on the same street in Bolton. On this occasion, Billington's assistant Henry Pierrepoint assisted in the execution, and the night before they carried out the hanging Billington admitted that he would rather not have to carry out the deed on someone he was so familiar with, despite the fact that McKenna had murdered his wife.

Perhaps Billington's most interesting hanging was that of the poisoner Dr Thomas Neil Cream on 15 November 1892 at Newgate Prison. Just seconds before the trap door opened, Cream could be heard to say, 'I am Jack the . . .' but he never managed to complete the sentence. Although the authorities felt it was highly unlikely that the doctor was indeed the infamous Jack the Ripper, it certainly caused quite a stir at the time.

During his career, Billington developed a hatred for the media who seemed to hang around his barber's shop when he wasn't carrying out any executions. They would sit in the barber's chair and while having their hair cut try and coax Billington to give them some gruesome stories. He hated the intrusion and if he got wind of the fact that his customer was a newspaper reporter, he thought nothing of downing his tools and leaving the man half way through a shave or a haircut.

Bit by bit, Billington turned into a melancholy character and returned to drinking. He gave up his barber's shop and became the licensee of a public house in Bolton called the Derby Arms. He was once heard to say to one of his customers that being a hangman was like 'living in a bloody cage', and that it wasn't all that it was cracked up to be.

Billington died ten days after his very last execution on 13 December 1901. He had suffered a severe bout of bronchitis and at just fifty-four years of age he left a wife and five children.

THOMAS BILLINGTON

Thomas Billington was James's eldest son and loved nothing more than to assist his father in his executions. His role, however, was short-lived as he died of pneumonia in 1902 when he was just twenty-nine years old.

WILLIAM BILLINGTON

At the time of his father's death, William was living with his stepmother in the Derby Arms. William Billington took over where his father left off not only in the barber shop but as an executioner as well, often assisted by his younger brother, John. He assisted his father in fourteen executions and went on to carry out another fifty-eight on his own. He carried out the very last execution at Newgate Prison, that of George Woolfe on 2 May 1902 and also the first at Pentonville Prison on 30 September the same year. He was also responsible for the first executions at Holloway Prison, which was an establishment set up for women prisoners. William hanged two women Annie Walters and Amelia Sach on 3 February 1903 for the crime of 'baby farming'. This crime was one of the more distasteful aspects of Victorian England and was the practice of taking in unwanted babies in return for a commercial fee and either overcrowding or killing them.

William's career reached its pinnacle in April 1903 when he executed George Chapman at Wandsworth Prison, assisted by Henry Pierrepoint. Shortly after this William appears to have gone off the rails and took to drinking, resigning from his job as executioner and relinquishing his interest in the barber's shop as well. On 20 July 1905, he was charged with failing to maintain his wife and two children after they were forced to go and live in the Bolton Union workhouse. He was in and out of court and failed to keep his promises of financial support for his family. William died on 2 March 1952 in his early sixties.

JOHN BILLINGTON

Like his father and older brother, John was a barber by trade. He assisted his father in executions and in December 1903 carried out one himself at Liverpool, hanging Henry Starr for the murder of his wife at Blackpool. Unlike William, however, John was on the Home Office list of approved executioners and assisted in twenty-four executions and another fifteen as principal hangman. He died suddenly at the age of twenty-five, leaving behind a wife and one child.

THE PIERREPOINT FAMILY

HENRY ALBERT PIERREPOINT

Much like the Billingtons before them, the Pierrepoints were a dynasty of executioners. They took up the mantle from where the Billingtons left off and went on to dominate the role of the hangman during the first half of the twentieth century.

Henry Albert Pierrepoint was the first of the family to enter this ignoble and notorious profession. He had grown up reading stories about the executioners of the past, taking great inspiration from educated and literate hangman James Berry. Pierrepoint read his autobiographical work *My Experiences As An Executioner* and longed for the same. He dreamed of travelling outside his hometown of Huddersfield and saw the role of hangman-for-hire as a means to tour the country and the world. The ambitious young man persistently bombarded the Home Office with letters of application, expressing his desire to follow in the footsteps of Berry, Ketch and Calcraft.

He eventually received a positive response from the Home Office and, in time, he was invited to train at Newgate Prison. His first role, as assistant executioner to James Billington, came at the age of twenty-five. His first victim was twenty-three-year-old Marcel Fougeron on 19 November 1901 for the murder of Hermann Francis Jung. His involvement was deemed a success and it signified the beginning of a nine-year term of office as a judicial killer. During his career, he performed a total of 108 executions, acting as lead executioner for sixty-eight of them.

Very little information can be found regarding the majority of people who died by the hands of Henry Pierrepoint, but it is safe to say that his victims were an eclectic mix. There was Richard Wigley, who was hanged in Shrewsbury for the murder of his girlfriend, and the Indian student-cum-martyr, Madar dal Dhingra, who shot dead Sir William Curzon Wyllie – a colonial administrator in the foyer of the Imperial Institute. Pierrepoint also saw to the deaths of three baby farmers during his career. Baby farming was a Victorian phenomenon which involved taking in unwanted infants in return for payment. While the majority of these pseudo-adoption agencies used the money to care for the children, there were some despicable people who simply murdered the children in order to keep the money for themselves. Amelia Sach and Annie Walters – known as the Finchley baby farmers – perished at the hands of Henry Pierrepoint in what became the only double hanging of women in modern times. Pierrepoint also oversaw the final baby farmer death sentence in Britain on 14 August 1907 in Cardiff, when Rhoda Willis was hanged by the neck on her forty-fourth birthday.

The day before Rhoda's execution Henry was busy at work in Wandsworth Prison, London, overseeing another death sentence – there was clearly no rest for those who dispatched of the wicked! The condemned was one Richard Brinkley, who had attempted to swindle seventy-seven-year-old Johanna Blume out of her worldly belongings. The ingenious con involved tricking the old woman into believing that a folded piece of paper was a list of those keen to travel to the coast. She eagerly signed the register which unbeknown to her was, in fact, her last will and testament in which she made Mr Brinkley the sole beneficiary of all that she owned! His perfect scam began to flounder on the death of Johanna, when her grand-daughter contested the will. Realising that the witnesses, whom had been swindled in the same fashion, would be questioned, Brinkley decided he had no option but to kill them. He contacted the first witness, Reginald Parker, pretending to be interested in buying their dog. During the visit, he gave Parker a bottle of stout which was contaminated with prussic acid. This proved more than adequate, though Parker was not the victim. While Brinkley and Parker were inspecting the dog, his landlords, Mr and Mrs Beck entered the house and, on finding the poisoned chalice, sampled its contents and promptly died!

Three years later, Henry Pierrepoint's yearned-for career came to an abrupt end when, in 1910, he was involved in a drunken brawl with his assistant, John Ellis. Ellis accused Henry of being drunk on the job, whereupon a tirade of abuse flowed forth from Henry and, according to Chief Warder Nash, resulted in Henry knocking his aide off his chair. The incident was promptly reported to the Home Office which decided to remove him from the list of approved executioners. Henry did not go without a fight. Losing this post would have meant losing not only his considerable fee of £10 per hanging but also his much strived-for all expenses paid travelling about the country. He appealed directly to the home secretary stating that Ellis was in fact trying to undermine him, desiring for himself the position of chief executioner. This was to no avail and Henry never held the post again. Banished from his dream job, he kept the memories alive by writing about his experiences which were later chronicled in *The Thomson's Weekly News*. Henry Pierrepoint died in 1922, ten years before his son, Albert, was to follow in his footsteps.

THOMAS PIERREPOINT

Born in 1870, Thomas William Pierrepoint was the elder brother of Henry. Unlike Henry, Thomas did not aspire to be a hangman for his country. In fact, one could say he was roped into it by his younger brother! Despite not wanting a career in capital punishment, he clearly had a knack for the noose. He was only required to complete one of the compulsory two weeks of training at Pentonville, before being judged ready for service. This was surely due, in part, to some considerable personal training he had received from brother Henry inside a stable situated at the rear of his cottage.

Like his brother, widespread demand for his skills would see him spend considerable time in Ireland, although he went one step further in being named the official executioner for Eire after its independence was granted in 1923. During his time there, he carried out twenty-four executions at Dublin's Mountjoy Prison. He obtained a further feather in his cap across the border in Belfast, where he achieved the record for the most executions performed by one man. His victims included

William Smiley – considered an exemplary prisoner – who was sentenced to death for the double murders of Maggie and Sarah McCauley. Samuel Cushnan was dispatched on 8 April 1930 for the murder of postman James McCann, and similarly Thomas Dornan was found guilty of the murders of Bella and Maggie Aiken, falling foul of the rope on 21 May 1931.

Back in Blighty, Thomas continued to add to his tally of victims with some noteworthy individuals. On 19 December 1934, he hanged Ethel Lillie Major at Hull Prison for the murder of her husband, Arthur. She had poisoned his food with strychnine causing convulsions which were initially identified as epilepsy. Nearly two years later, Thomas executed another female poisoner, one raven-haired Charlotte Bryant, this time in Exeter. Bryant had been having an affair with a lodger and had decided to do away with husband, Frederick, using arsenic. The unfortunate husband's suffering was, yet again, misdiagnosed – this time as gastroenteritis – however, the post mortem examination revealed grains of the poison still inside Frederick's system. During her incarceration, waiting for the dreaded day of her demise, a remarkable change occurred; Bryant's jet-black hair had turned completely white. On Thursday 15 July 1936, her wait was over and she was promptly dispatched by Thomas Pierrepoint.

In 1940, Thomas reached the grand old age of seventy yet the frequency of his executions had far from diminished. However, questions were beginning to be asked regarding his ability to do the job by the governing authorities. Along with his age, there were concerns over his eyesight which was considered poor enough to render him potentially unfit for the position. After keeping a close yet discreet eye on Thomas, the Prison Commission decided against relieving him of his duties. There seems to have been sufficient positive feedback from other prisons to counteract the negative reports and this assisted in their decision. Also, the world as at war and, therefore, there existed an exceptional shortage of manpower. This played no small part in Thomas retaining his post.

Thomas went on to make a meaningful contribution during World War II. He was appointed as executioner by the US Armed Forces at Shepton Mallet Prison in Somerset. This was a jail exclusively for American servicemen who had flouted military law. Beginning with David Cobb on 12 March 1943 and ending with Aniceto Martinez on 15 June 1945, eighteen men were executed under the Visiting Forces Act, of which nine were convicted of murder, six of rape and three of both crimes. Of these convicts, sixteen were hanged within the purpose-built two-storey brick building containing the gallows and Thomas was in charge of thirteen of these.

Following this appointment, Thomas Pierrepoint left the post of his own volition, retiring in 1946 in his mid-seventies. With over forty years of service, Thomas had become the longest serving of all the Pierrepoints and had managed to notch up around 300 hangings throughout his career. While no verified statistics exist in full, it is known he carried out 235 hangings in England and Wales, of which thirty-four he assisted. Thomas died in 1954, ten years before the last hanging took place on British soil.

ALBERT PIERREPOINT

The third and final member of the Pierrepoint family to attain the position of Chief Executioner was Albert Pierrepoint, the eldest son of Henry. He would go on to surpass both his father and his uncle Thomas to become the most renowned member of the dynasty.

It was almost inevitable that Albert would follow in his father's footsteps. Even as an eleven-year-old schoolboy, he wrote that he wanted to be the Official Executioner when he grew up. He often stayed with his Uncle Thomas with whom he shared a close bond, and was permitted to read his execution diary whenever Thomas was away on business. It was not long before he would be recording one of his own. In 1922, Henry Pierrepoint, the first of the family executioners, died. A seventeen-year-old Albert took charge of his father's papers and diaries, which he poured over whenever possible. It could not have been clearer which career path young Albert had chosen to take.

At the beginning of the 1930s, Albert was working for a wholesale grocer delivering wares by lorry, earning an honest £2 5s a week. The thought of carrying on his father's legacy must have been at the forefront of his mind at this time for on 19 April 1931, he wrote to the Prison Commission offering his services much as Henry Pierrepoint had done some thirty years earlier. In the autumn of that year, after being told that no vacancies existed, he received an official letter inviting him to an interview at Strangeways Prison in Manchester.

After successfully completing a week's training at Pentonville Prison, and much to his mother's dismay, Albert Pierrepoint's name was added to the list of assistant executioners on the 26 September 1932. However, at this time the execution business was quiet and Albert did not receive his first experience, or his first payment of £1 11s 6d until 29 December, when he accompanied his uncle to Dublin's Mountjoy Prison to assist at the hanging of Patrick McDermott. He continued in this supporting role for a further nine years, learning the ropes chiefly from his uncle until 1941 when, on 17 October, Albert Pierrepoint stood at the gallows for the first time as chief executioner administering the death penalty to one Antonio 'Babe' Mancini. His nerves must have been tested on this momentous occasion. Legend has it that the condemned gangster and club owner had the gall to shout, 'Cheerio!' as the hood was placed over his head!

DOUBLE LIFE

Together with his career, there was also progress in Albert's personal life. He had been courting a woman called Anne Fletcher who helped run a sweet shop only two doors down from his own workplace and on 29 August 1943, the couple married and quickly settled into their new home in Newton Heath, Manchester.

It was with this relationship that Albert's attitude towards his chosen line of work was made abundantly clear. Albert believed that his role as death bringer to the condemned was a responsibility which bore no relation to his personal life. Just as he covered the heads of those he hanged, so did he place a figurative hood over his work when at home. This even included keeping his true profession a secret from his wife, Anne. The couple never discussed his other, darker career. However, with the many impromptu and unexplained trips he took, Anne was soon able to piece together the puzzle, yet he never confronted her husband.

Albert's creation of this separate life was his way of coping with the distasteful nature of his work. He also had a unique attitude towards the victims of the noose. He was not interested in the crimes they had committed but remained utterly focused on the part he played within the criminal justice system. When the deed was done and the rope was made taut the price had been paid and, in Albert's eyes, they were now innocent.

SWIFT JUSTICE

This detachment and commitment to providing the prisoners with a humane and dignified death led Albert to develop the efficiency of his executions. An advocate of the variable drop method, he made his own calculations from the height, weight and physical condition of each convict as to the length of rope rather than blindly following the official table provided by the Home Office. These made-to-measure 'designer' ropes resulted in the clean separation of the second and third vertebrae, granting a quick and clean kill rather than slowly strangling the condemned with a rope that was too short or, if the rope was too long, causing complete decapitation.

Albert also improved the speed of the ceremony. He believed there was no sense in prolonging the agony for either the condemned or the executioner and attendant witnesses. His father, Henry, had averaged a time of about thirteen seconds during his time as chief executioner but Albert soon smashed this time by almost half in a bid to lessen the suffering of all those present. From cell door to trapdoor, Albert dispatched James Inglis in seven and a half seconds on 9 May 1951 at Strangeways Prison.

NAZI HANGINGS

These humanitarian modifications soon came to the attention of the Armed Forces. With the defeat of the Nazis in 1945 and the resulting war trials, the military were in need of someone who could implement the punishments they had imposed and, at the behest of Field Marshal Montgomery, Albert was promptly called to Germany to apply his distinctive no-nonsense execution style. Flying out on the 11 December 1945, Albert Pierrepoint would face his biggest test as an executioner in just two days.

The visiting executioner was taken to Hameln Prison in the heart of the British-controlled section of

Germany, where those convicted of crimes against the Geneva Convention of 1929 were being held. Famous for the legend of the Pied Piper, Hameln once again saw another mass execution when, on 13 December, Albert Pierrepoint led thirteen war criminals to their deaths in just one day!

The unlucky thirteen included three women. The pick of the bunch was Irma Grese. Known as the 'Bitch of Belsen', she was the supervisor at the Ravensbrueck, Auschwitz and Bergen-Belsen concentration camps. Despite being only twenty-two years old and the youngest guard to be executed for war crimes under English law, her sadistic nature was fully developed and had been wholly realised through the treatment of her prisoners, whom she randomly shot in cold blood or had mauled by half-starved dogs. She showed no remorse, calling for Pierrepoint to be quick with her fatal farewell. She clearly was not aware of Albert's reputation!

After the women came the men, and they took the gallows in pairs in an effort to stay on schedule. Albert came face to face with Josef Kramer who had been given the macabre moniker – 'The Beast of Belsen'. He had been the commandant of Bergen-Belsen camp and remained at his post as the Allied Forces broke through the gates, even offering to give them a tour!

As soon as the courts reached their verdicts the condemned were made ready for punishment with immediate effect. The convictions came thick and fast and over the next four years, Albert made a further twenty-five trips to Germany and Austria to act as executioner. In one day, there were thirteen hangings, which was followed by forty-seven in one week and by the end of this tour of duty he is thought to have executed as many as 200 Nazi war criminals.

Not only did he have to cope with witnessing so much death so close at hand but throughout this purge of convicted war criminals, he had to endure the attention of the press back at home – something that appalled his plain and private sensibilities. These principles were not shared by the War Office and in 1946 it provided the British media with the name Albert Pierrepoint as a symbol of Great Britain's professional handling of those responsible for the atrocities. Anonymity was a thing of the past for him now, no longer able to throw a veil over his profession, he was lauded as a national hero – plain hangman to pseudo-super man.

FRIEND AND FOES

One positive outcome from his own 'war effort' was the money which allowed Albert to quit the grocery delivery business once and for all. Still requiring a second job to make ends meet, the Pierrepoints decided to buy the lease on a pub called Help The Poor Struggler in Hollinwood, Oldham, which did a roaring trade. They were never short of patrons who no doubt yearned for a pint pulled by the hand which pulled the lever on the Beast of Belsen.

Throughout the 1950s, Albert's inimitable style of execution saw to the necks of some of the most infamous criminals in British history. He applied the last death sentence in Eire to Michael Manning and, two years later, saw to the death of Ruth Ellis, the last woman to be hanged in Britain.

On 9 March 1950, Albert executed Timothy Evans for the murder of his daughter, despite subsequent discovery that in fact serial killer and self-confessed necrophiliac John Reginald Christie was the true perpetrator. Evans would eventually receive a post-humous pardon in 1966. Christie failed to escape the noose and Pierrepoint was available to oversee his execution on 15 July 1953. Earlier that year, Albert travelled to Wandsworth Prison to dispatch Derek Bentley for the murder of Police Constable Miles. Another case steeped in doubt, it was later realised that Bentley was in fact under arrest at the time of the killing, resulting in another belated pardon in 1993. These wrongful executions were to slowly alter

Albert's view on the efficacy of execution, although one specific moment in his career would go further than any other to affect a change in his belief.

Throughout his career, Albert's strategy for coping with the job was serving him well. With every prisoner he took to the gallows, he was always able to emotionally distance himself. This was business not personal. Yet in 1950, both sides of his double life were forcibly slammed together when he was entrusted with the execution of his friend, James Henry Corbitt. Corbitt was a regular in Albert's pub and the two – known to each other as Tish and Tosh – would often perform songs to the crowds inside. On 28 November 1950, convicted of the murder of his mistress, Tish and Tosh met again at the gallows. No longer able to disregard the details of the condemned, as Corbitt's body fell through the trapdoor, a tear must have fallen from Albert's eye.

RESIGNED

In the winter of 1956, Albert was called to Strange-ways Prison to preside over the hanging of Thomas Bancroft. Leaving his wife to look after the pub, he made his usual trip and subsequent preparations for the convict's smooth demise. He was then told that the condemned had been afforded a reprieve – a rare occurrence and Albert's first experience of such a reversal in England. He claimed his full fee of £15 but this was denied and eventually a mere £4 was offered to cover his expenses. Suitably affronted, Albert appealed to a disinterested Prison Commission, prompting him to tender his resignation. While this was the official reason, Albert was growing tired of the role. The combination of the aforementioned events must have all factored towards Albert's resignation which came in a year in which not one execution was performed in Britain.

After this decision to stand down from his post, he held talks with the press to run a series of articles entitled *The Hangman's Own Story* but this was ultimately quashed by the Home Office. They even considered charging Albert with contravention of the Official Secrets Act. He did eventually get to tell his uniquely captivating story as Britain's most swift and efficient executioner in 1974, with his autobiography entitled *Executioner: Pierrepoint*. In it, he revealed his concluding thoughts as to the validity of capital punishment declaring that it, 'achieved nothing except revenge'.

Executions continued in Britain for a further eight years after his resignation. Albert Pierrepoint's tireless efforts would never be surpassed. During his twenty-four years of service, from 1932 to 1956, he was credited with an unverified 450 executions, including seventeen women and some 200 Nazis after World War II. He lived out his final years in a nursing home located in the coastal town of Southport in Lancashire and passed away on 10 July 1982 at the age of eighty-seven.

PART NINE

THE ELECTRIC CHAIR

THE ELECTRIC CHAIR

During the nineteenth century hanging was the most common form of capital punishment in North America. However, following a steady stream of gruesome deaths this execution technique had become out of touch with members of an enlightened society, who saw it as barbaric. While the executioners of Britain were mastering the long drop method, those in the United States were regularly decapitating prisoners or causing them to be slowly strangled to death. This was the case of poor Roxalana Druse who, in 1887, took a full fifteen minutes to perish.

By 1887 the search for a new, more humane way of dispensing punishment was well under way, but we need to travel back to 7 August 1881 for the initial spark of an idea. It was on this day that a dentist and former steamboat engineer, Alfred P. Southwick witnessed a drunk old man named George Smith stagger towards a live generator in Buffalo, New York.

He touched an exposed terminal, killing him instantly. Southwick's imagination lit-up: perhaps electricity was the civilised alternative to hanging society had been looking for. After discussing the idea with fellow doctor George Fell, as well as conducting some preliminary tests on stray cats and dogs, Southwick visited his friend Senator McMillan. McMillan spoke with Governor David Bennett Hill regarding the prospect of presenting the idea to the state legislature (the authorising body responsible for the death penalty) for consideration. In 1885, Hill put forward the case for electricity as a suitable substitute to hanging, but the state legislature was deaf to the idea.

AC VS DC

The foremost pioneer of electricity was the Wizard of Menlo Park: Thomas Alva Edison. The inventor had managed to harness the power of electricity, building his first plant in 1879. While his DC (or direct current) was successful in controlling electricity, it was not without its drawbacks. Edison's system was a complicated one. Direct current channelled electricity in only one direction, requiring commutators to ensure that the flow always went the right way. DC power was also a poor traveller; the necessary volts could only be maintained over small distances, necessitating countless expensive power plants. However, during the 1880s a replacement for direct current, called alternating current (or AC), was discovered. This negated the use of numerous generators to maintain voltage. The breakthrough was made by Nikola Tesla, a Croatian scientist who was employed by Edison and knew the inherent problems of direct current. AC offered a marked improvement because the current altered its direction many times per second, creating a magnetic field that allowed for a constant supply of power even over great distances. Tesla approached Edison with this new development, but the Wizard of Menlo Park dismissed the idea, and so Tesla left his employ to find a willing investor. It did not take him long. Shortly after securing patents for the AC system, a man named George Westinghouse, who had made his money with the invention of the railroad airbrake, revealed an interest in Tesla's product. Westinghouse gave Tesla the necessary financial backing, making alternating current a true rival to Edison's DC power.

As Westinghouse was preparing to overtake Edison with his new improved current, Governor Hill had managed to stir up enough support from the state legislature to issue Chapter 352 of the Laws of 1886, authorising the appointment of the New York State Committee to explore potential alternatives to hanging. Electricity was high on this list of possible alternatives and this worried both Edison and

Westinghouse, for neither man wished their product to be associated with death. They believed that consumers would not wish to have the same current in their homes as was used to fry violent felons in the death chamber. Edison was faced with another DC-specific problem. His technology used very thick copper cables to channel the current and, in 1887, copper prices were going through the roof. AC power was becoming more and more popular and the high costs and poor mobility of his DC power forced Edison to take action.

Edison orchestrated a systematic and calculating attack on Westinghouse's AC product by publicly associating it with danger, death and execution. He hired a man named Harold Pitney Brown to find a way to prove that AC was lethal in comparison with his 'safer' DC technology. Brown invited the press to watch AC tests performed at Edison's laboratory in West Orange, New Jersey. Small animals were lured onto a metal plate wired up to a 1,000 volt AC generator. The fatal shocks these animals received were just the clear message Edison desired: AC power kills. The attending reporters had a field day. They coined the phrase 'electrocution' following the demonstration. The smear campaign was well and truly underway.

Edison followed up this PR stunt with a publication entitled *A Warning*, which compared the two currents and included a list of all the AC victims. Early the following year the Gerry report was published. The commission appointed in 1886 to examine the ways in which execution could be made more efficient released their findings in what was a ninety-five page detailed analysis named after Eldbridge T. Gerry, who chaired the committee. It suggested that of all the methods, electrocution was the way forward and a proposed bill for the amendment of the Criminal Procedure Code was attached. On 8 May 1888, Senator Henry Coggleshell was able to get the bill passed. Less than a month later the New York State Legislature enacted chapter 489 of the laws of 1888, for the use of electricity of sufficient intensity to cause death for capital offences committed after 1 January 1889. Electrocution was now a legal form of capital punishment, but how best to apply this power? In order to answer this question, the Medico-Legal Society was charged with finding a device fit for the purpose. But for Edison and Westinghouse, there existed a more pertinent question: which current would it use?

Edison continued his denigration of Westinghouse's alternating current with added fervour. Harold Brown sent an article to the *New York Evening Post* the day after the electric bill became law, in which he described the death of a boy who had touched an exposed telegraph wire using AC. From June to December 1888, Brown continued to conduct his public experiments, drumming up hostility towards alternating current in the home and promoting its use for capital punishment. They invited both the press and the Electrical Board of Control. Brown and his assistant, Doctor Peterson of Columbia University, began their demonstrations by administering a series of shocks to a large dog using direct current, illustrating that the power only tortured the animal. Brown then finished the beast off with a shock of AC power, proving that it was the more deadly. They claimed that Edison's invention would not be up to the task of performing the pain-free execution the Medico-Legal Society was seeking. Brown and Peterson went on a multi-city tour throughout New York State, buying cats and dogs from school-children for twenty-five cents each to execute using AC power. Not only were domestic animals subjected to electrocution, in an increasingly theatrical show, calves, horses, a circus elephant and even an orang-utan were killed with electric shocks in a bid to persuade the public of AC's lethality.

The underhanded efforts of Edison and his associates finally paid off in 1889, when the committee finally chose Westinghouse's alternating current as the electricity provider for the electric chair – the

Kemmler? It soon became apparent that this was part of George Westinghouse's defence strategy. Edison's opponent had funded the plea in a bid to postpone the use of his alternating current by calling the electric chair unconstitutional. The appeal was rejected by the Supreme Court on 23 May by Chief Justice Melville Fuller, but Westinghouse had not finished. He hired another pricey lawyer – Roger Sherman – to prevent the death of Kemmler and protect AC power's domestic future. During this case, New York State called both Edison and Brown as witnesses to prove that the execution style was not a breach of United States law. On 23 July, Edison gave evidence which helped sway the decision in favour of the State. He dismissed accusations that electrocution was too unpredictable to be used on mankind, while continually associating the electric chair with Westinghouse at any conceivable point in the proceedings. Yet again, Westinghouse's lawyers failed to convince the court and the appeal was formally denied on 9 October 1889, condemning both Kemmler as well as Westinghouse's investment to a deadly fate.

On the morning of 6 August 1890, the time came for the electric chair's debut performance. The press and the public waited with baited breath to see how the new device would function upon the doomed Kemmler. Of the twenty-five witnesses invited to watch the proceedings, fourteen of them were doctors, including Alfred Southwick and George Fell, who were there to see their idea put into practice. The man given the responsibility of sending Kemmler to his death was Edwin Davis, who was actually the prison electrician. He had tested the machine on a horse the day before to ascertain what voltage would be sufficient to cause the death of the prisoner; 1,000 volts for a duration of seventeen seconds was the verdict.

Early that summer morning, a suited Kemmler was led from his cell to the death chamber. He appeared quite calm. As Charles Durston, the prison warden, nervously ensured that the straps were in place, Kemmler told him to take his time and not to hurry. Before the hood was lowered over his head, he was asked if he wished to say anything. Kemmler responded by wishing everyone good luck in the world. Durston then moved away from the chair and gave the signal to Davis who pulled the switch, sending the calculated current through Kemmler's body. The seventeen-second surge of power must have felt like a lifetime for the onlookers as the seated figure strained against his bindings. The body went limp as the power was cut and two physicians, Doctors Edward Charles Spitzka and Charles F. Macdonald, approached the chair to examine the prisoner for signs of life. Unfortunately for all present, they found some. Kemmler's heart was beating and despite such an ordeal he was still breathing.

The doctors called for the current to be quickly turned back on. Davis doubled the power to 2,000 volts and allowed the electrocution to continue for a massive seventy seconds. During this extended jolt, Kemmler's body thrashed and flailed, his blood vessels ruptured, causing his body to catch fire. Many of the spectators fainted or fled the viewing room in disgust. Once more, Spitzka and Macdonald checked for Kemmler's vitals. It was over – the chair had finally done its job. The ordeal had lasted eight minutes and the chair received mixed reviews. While there was public outcry at the unpleasantness of the proceedings. Witnesses reported an aroma of burnt flesh and the sound of crackling, but there were those who believed it a success. George Fell praised the performance of the prototype, assuring the press that the condemned felt no pain whatsoever. Westinghouse, among others, commented that they would have done better to use an axe. In his eyes, they were no further on from medieval head chopping. Some even said it was worse than hanging – the method it had sought to replace.

A JUMPY START

Despite such an inauspicious start, the electric chair soon became the number one method of capital punishment in the United States. Following a series of successful executions in the spring of 1891, with the deaths of James Slocum, Harris Smiler, Schichiok Jugigo and Joseph Wood at Sing Sing Prison, the technique was successfully pronounced as a clean and progressive successor to the rope. Slight modifications were made, including a thickening of the wires along with an increase in voltage, which seemed to ensure the immediate death of the prisoner.

However, further problems occurred on 27 July 1893 with the execution of William Taylor. The first jolt of electricity caused his legs to rip through the ankle restraints but failed to kill him. A second charge was called for by the warden, but the burst of power had blown the AC generator, causing an enforced stay of execution. Taylor had to be removed from the chair and kept alive with a cocktail of chloroform and morphine while the generator was repaired and the system made ready for a repeat attempt. An astonishing one hour and nine minutes later, the still living body of William Taylor was brought back to the chair for his second surge, which managed to eliminate the faint and final vestiges of life. It seemed that the chair was actually far from humane and a long way from Albert Southwick's idea of a quick and pain-free death.

Throughout these early years there were persistent teething troubles with the chair's performance, however, it seemed to flourish in the face of such failings. Ohio and Massachusetts followed New York's lead before the close of the century. New Jersey was next in line, approving its use for capital punishment in 1906. The following year, New Jersey built its first death row: a simple design consisting of six cells at one end of the building and a death chamber at the other. The chair was built by a man called Carl F. Adams who ran Adams Electric. His version differed slightly from the one in New York. Instead of a switch for administering the deadly dose of alternating current, the Adams chair used a rheostat dial which could be turned up or down. The New Jersey chair was also built with comfort in mind, incorporating adjustable head and armrests.

The first to experience the 'comforts' of this chair was a thirty-seven-year-old Italian immigrant named Saverio Di Giovanni. The squat and stocky man had been found guilty of shooting and killing a fellow Italian and, after a trial lasting only two days, a jury took a mere fifteen minutes to recommend the death penalty.

Di Giovanni spent just one month on the newly constructed death row at Trenton State Prison and made the final walk to the death chamber on 11 December 1907 where, at 5.57 a.m, Edwin Davis acted as legal executioner and turned the dial executing the bound and hooded killer with a sixty-second jolt of 2040 volts.

Back in New York, the prisons were still having problems administering a swift and smooth execution. In 1903, Frederick Van Wormer was sent to the electric chair at Clinton State Prison and the necessary shocks were applied. However, when the body was being prepared for post mortem examination, it was discovered Van Wormer was still breathing! A call to the executioner revealed that he had gone home, and he had to be summoned back to the prison to finish the man off! By the time the state 'electrocutioner' arrived, Van Wormer had already died from his half-execution. In what was to be a most grisly and macabre application of the law, Wormer's corpse was placed back in the chair and electrocuted with 17,000 volts for a full thirty seconds. Such horrors would plague this apparent improvement in capital punishment throughout the twentieth century, yet it continued to be the most popular form of death penalty in America with at least twenty states adopting the procedure.

THE PROCEDURE

Although the electric chair fried its first victims, the process was continually refined to improve its efficacy as a humane and painless form of capital punishment. Each state that had adopted this form of execution had at least one death chamber in which a chair was kept. Each chair differed slightly from other models in name as well as in design. Yellow Mama was the moniker given to the chair in Alabama owing to the colour it had been painted, thanks to the nearby State Highway Department. Other states christened their chairs 'Old Sparky' or 'Gruesome Gertie'.

The routine was fairly similar no matter what state you were in. First the prisoner's head was shaved in anticipation of the electrodes that would connect the condemned to the electricity generator. These electrodes consisted of a 10-centimetre (4-inch) diameter wooden cup containing a 8-centimetre (3-inch) diameter metal plate which was covered in a layer of natural sponge. This sponge was soaked in a saline solution or, in more modern times, treated with a gel known as Electro Crème, which aided the conductivity of the current.

In the very early days, the condemned was then bound to the chair with leather straps across his ankles, chest and arms, against which the prisoner would strain as the current flowed through his body. However, a prison inmate called Charles Justice, while on cleaning duty, noticed that these leather bindings were a possible root cause of the burning that had sullied previous executions, and suggested that the straps be made of metal instead. This improvement seemed to minimise burning and so the authorities decided to reduce Justice's punishment, allowing him to be paroled from Ohio State Penitentiary. He gained his freedom thanks to his eye for design, but he was free for only eleven years. He was later convicted of theft and murder and returned to prison where on 9 November 1911, Charles Justice was bound with his own creation and efficiently executed.

Thanks to numerous failed attempts to humanely execute prisoners such as Williams Kemmler and Taylor, electrocution usually consisted of multiple shocks. The first jolt of alternating current was between 700 and 2,400 volts, which travelled around the body for anything from fifteen to sixty seconds. Its dual purpose was to induce unconsciousness (believed to take a mere 240th of a second) and to stop the heart. To avoid the sight and smell of burning flesh, the current was minimised to about 6 amperes. Anything above this level ran the risk of cooking the body. Once the first shock had coursed through the victim's body, the power would be cut and an appointed physician would check the prisoner's vital signs. It was often necessary to apply a second jolt, normally a lower dose for a shorter length of time. An average of only two minutes elapsed from the first flick of the switch to the prisoner's eventual demise.

HUMANE DEATH?

The electric chair was certainly a fast method of despatching capital criminals, but what of its humane and painless status? To ascertain whether the volley of volts provided a civilised and constitutionally sound death, the effects of the procedure required study. Along with the destruction of brain cells and the central nervous system, the electric current causes total paralysis. Every muscle in the entire body locks tight in an enforced contraction. This may sound as if the level of pain and suffering experienced by the prisoner is minimal, however, there is much evidence to suggest that the electric chair is not quite the compassionate device that the authorities have encouraged people to believe it is.

The electric current is so potent that the prisoner's skin begins to turn bright red. It swells and stretches while smoke rises from the electrodes. If the body heat is allowed to rise, it can result in the prisoner bursting into flames, particularly if the seated convict is sweating profusely. It has even been known for a prisoner's eyeballs to pop out of their sockets with the force of the jolt. To add further insult to fatal injury, the death-row prisoner is forced to wear a nappy, as one of the many unpleasant effects of electrocution includes involuntary defaecation and urination as a result of the bowel and pelvic muscles contracting. Such facts do not paint a merciful picture of the electric chair and considerable doubt must enter the minds of those who have witnessed these terminations. Are these condemned men and women cognisant during their ordeal?

An early confirmation came in 1946 when seventeen-year-old Willie Francis met with Gruesome Gertie – the name given to the electric chair in the state of Louisiana. As the electricity sent his body into convulsions, the attendant witnesses heard him shriek from underneath the hood, 'Stop it! Let me breathe!' Young Francis was quickly removed from the electric chair and it was later revealed that the execution had failed on account of the chair being poorly prepared by a drunken official. This was the first time a prisoner had survived the electric chair and been able to speak about his ordeal. Francis is reported to have admitted to feeling burning at the points where the electrodes were attached to his skin, and he likened the taste in his mouth to that of cold peanut butter. Clearly, the victim was conscious during the electrocution.

POWER CUT

Such evidence fuelled protests against the electric chair, and as the peace-loving philosophy of the 1960s took hold over the nation, opposition towards the hot seat grew ever stronger. The Adams-built electric chair of New Jersey was quickly retired after its final performance in 1963. Prisoner visits to the death chamber were becoming less frequent. There were forty-two electrocutions in 1961, and this number dropped until 1967, when there were only two deaths at the electric chair throughout the United States.

A complete cessation of executions followed while the authorities waited for the Supreme Court to decide the electric chair's fate. The public's growing abhorrence of the process had to be taken into account and the highest court in the land was forced to examine whether or not electrocution violated constitutionally set human rights. During this time the only active electric chair in the world was in the

Philippines, and this was making a name for itself by delivering 'justice' to such notorious criminals as the three men found guilty of gang-raping actress Maggie dela Riva. Yet even the chair in Manila became unwanted furniture in 1976.

In this same year, the Supreme Court of the United States came to a decision regarding two cases: those of Furman and Gregg versus the state of Georgia. In both cases the presiding judges upheld the State's legal rights to administer the death penalty. This saw a return to capital punishment and the power was returned to electric chairs throughout the country. This second wind began with the execution of John Arthur Spenkelink on 25 May 1979. The resurgence of the chair did not begin well. Controversy surrounded the convicted killer's death. There were reports that a fight broke out in his cell, resulting in Spenkelink's neck being broken, thus rendering the electric chair superfluous. Dead or alive, there appeared to be no escape for death-row inmates from the electric chair in its second term of office. However, state after state began to review their association with this form of capital punishment. This rethink saw Texas and Oklahoma among others turn their back on the device in the 1980s in favour of a more efficient, merciful method.

THE DEMISE

The 1990s fared no better when it came to instilling public faith in the electric chair. Countless examples of botched executions continued to crop up all over the country, hindering the attempts by many authorities to sustain the life of the deadly 'harmchair'. Three significant executions acted as nails in the coffin for electrocution as capital punishment, all of which occurred in the state of Florida. The first took place on 4 May 1990. The victim, Jesse Tafero, suffered a fate worse than death when the natural sponge customarily placed between the electrode and the top of the head was replaced with a synthetic one. This caused the current to flow at a mere 100 volts, torturing him instead of humanely terminating the prisoner's life. Those present witnessed 30-centimetre (12-inch) high orange and blue flames rise from the hood. The power was switched off, allowing the prisoner to take several deep breaths before the current was allowed to flow several times in succession, finally seeing off Tafero. Seven years later, during the execution of Pedro Medina on 25 March 1997, witnesses once again saw the prisoner burst into flames. An enquiry into the affair revealed the fault lay with corroded metal in the helmet. Others believed it was again down to the sponge, which was thought to have been devoid of saline solution. Whatever the reason, the Supreme Court saw nothing to deem the practice as cruel or unusual and so the chair was allowed to strike again.

Two years later, in July 1999, 127 kilogram (20 stone) Allen Lee 'Tiny' Davis sat in Old Sparky and was electrocuted by 2,300 volts at 7.10 a.m. The observing press and prison guards saw blood pour from beneath Davis' hood, covering the front of his white shirt.

The prison officials blamed the blood on a simple nosebleed, popular thought suggested that the helmet housing the electrode was poorly fitted to the prisoner's head. Once more the Supreme Court was forced to decide whether the method was unconstitutional. Despite evidence to suggest that Old Sparky had faulty components, the attendant justices voted four to three in favour of the Floridian chair. It lived to fry another day, but the confidence in this method of judicially appointed death had disappeared.

Louisiana ended its affair with Gruesome Gertie in 1991. She had performed a total of eighty-seven executions since her creation. Kentucky and Tennessee soon followed suit, retiring their chairs in 1998 and turning to lethal injection as their preferred method of execution. With the exception of Nebraska, which still uses the electric chair as its sole method of execution, the remaining states in which electrocution is still practised do so only if the prisoner prefers the spark over the syringe. The last time the chair was used as a compulsory means for killing was on 10 May 2002 upon cop killer Lynda Lyon Block, in the southern state of Alabama. Dressed in a white prison outfit she gave no final words before Yellow Mama gave her two jolts, bringing an end to her life.

At the time of writing, the final execution to take place in the United States upon the electric chair was that of forty-five-year-old Daryl Holton, who chose to wear the electrodes on 12 September 2007. His life was extinguished after two surges of 1,750 volts. Block and Holton were two of only ten victims that went to the chair during the twenty-first century. The few remaining electric chairs now await their own death sentence, and with them the practice which saw to the executions of almost 4,500 men and women in little over a century.

PART TEN

THE GAS CHAMBER

THE CREATION –
THE IDEA

As the twentieth century got underway, capital punishment in the United States was rapidly changing. The changes stemmed from an abhorrence to the noose, which had been in use since the early settlers set foot on American soil. Hanging was seen as behind the times for a far more civilised society and creative individuals began to look beyond the rope for a suitable alternative. As we have seen, electrocution proved to be a viable alternative to hanging in such states as New York, Ohio and Florida. However, Edison had failed to persuade the authorities in the major western states to go electric. Despite the growing popularity of the electric chair, states such as California, Nevada and Arizona felt that the new device did not offer a pain-free method of execution and so it was not a practical choice for them.

Another alternative was not found until the 1920s. With World War I only a few years past, those who aimed to discover a fresh method of execution looked to newly developed techniques used on the battle-field. Major Delos A. Turner of the United States Army Medical Corps had observed the use of gas during the conflict and saw potential. During World War I, gas – usually hydrogen cyanide or prussic acid – had been launched by artillery in shells or thrown by hand in canisters. When the gas was released it caused a variety of unpleasant results. The fumes attacked the respiratory system, induced panic attacks and caused the skin to turn purple and the tongue to swell. Turner thought if the gas could be modified to act quickly rather than killing the victim slowly, then those states which refused to electrocute their violent criminals would have another practical solution.

Scientists took the Major's proposal and put it to the test, performing experiments on cats to study the effects. These unfortunate felines were forced to in-hale the fumes from hydrocyanic acid and their swift deaths indicated that lethal gas could indeed be applied to humans as a humane form of execution. After some initial debate, in 1921 Nevada's state legis-lature voted in favour of using gas as a replacement for hanging or the firing squad, and they became the first state to adopt this cleaner, swifter method of execution.

The first victim to undergo this new form of execution was twenty-nine-year-old gang member Gee Jon who had been found guilty of murdering rival gangster Tom Quong Kee during the notorious Chinese Mafia wars. Despite his lawyers insisting that the process breached the eighth amendment, Gee Jon failed to acquire a stay of execution and his fate was sealed. The only remaining question was how to apply the gas.

The Nevada authorities discussed piping the harmful vapours into the gangster's cell, but this idea was rife with flaws. There would be no way to ensure the containment of the lethal fumes and so it would risk the lives of other prison inmates and staff. In addition, there was no sure way to dispose of the toxic fumes which would linger unseen in the cell block. They soon realised that a stand-alone purpose built chamber had to be constructed in order to allow total control over the deadly gas. Boilermakers, The Eaton Metal Products Company of Salt Lake City and Colorado, were then engaged to design an appropriate piece of equipment that could safely despatch a prisoner with no harm coming to any witnesses. The company came up with a suitable design for a gas chamber along with a generator to create the gas and a safety guide on how to operate and maintain the machine.

At 9.30 a.m. on 8 February 1924, Gee Jon was strapped into the chair in the gas chamber at Carson City, Nevada. The condemned was seen to struggle as the gas enveloped him, but after six minutes, Gee Jon ceased to resist. With no ability to confirm a definitive time of death, the chamber remained closed for a further thirty minutes to ensure completion of the sentence.

Colorado followed Nevada's lead in 1933 with their own unique gas chamber. Prison warden Roy Best paid a visit to Nevada's chamber in May of that year and came away thinking one seat was not enough. He gave The Eaton Metal Products Company $2500 to build a three-seater model for Colorado which became known as 'Roy's Penthouse'. However, it was replaced by a more slim-line single seater in 1955. The first victim of the Nevada's chamber was William Cody Kelley, who was strapped to one of the three seats on 22 June 1934. The convicted murderer would be just one of a growing number of executions in the United States – judicial murders peaking in 1935 at 199 – as the gas chamber joined electrocution and hanging as a practical and accepted method of capital punishment.

With Nevada and Colorado proving that the gas chamber worked, other states began to look into a chamber and generator of their own. The state of California was keen to upgrade their death penalty and so liaised with The Eaton Metal Products Company to obtain assurances of improved efficiency. Earl Liston, the designer of the chambers already installed and operational in Nevada and Colorado, was adamant that the device was the quickest form of capital punishment with the ability to kill a man cleanly in about fifteen seconds. Ex-prison warden of San Quentin, James B. Holohan, who had seen many a disturbing death by hanging, managed to get elected to the State Senate. In 1937, he supported the move to make California the seventh state to adopt the gas chamber.

Before the Californian chamber took its first human life, the authorities demanded a trial run of the $5,000 device, and in March 1938, in front of thirty witnesses at San Quentin Prison, a small reddish brown pig was gassed for the sake of humanity. The sacrificial swine remained caged upon one of the two seats as sixteen cyanide pellets were dropped into a bowl of sulphuric acid. Far from being a swift and silent death, the pig thrashed and squealed for almost three and a half minutes as the deadly fumes attacked its respiratory system.

The press who were invited to attend the procedure in the hope that they would promote its use, wrote damning reports on the testing – describing the process as torture rather than a means for humane execution. Yet despite the fact that the Californian pig was not as co-operative as the Nevada cats, there was enough support for the chamber to get the go-ahead.

The first prisoners to succumb to the deadly fumes of the Californian gas chamber were Robert Lee Cannon and Albert Kessell, who were also destined to be the first double gassing. The pair were sentenced to death for their involvement in a riot at Folsom Prison in which a warden, Clarence Larkin, was stabbed twelve times. On 2 December 1938, thirty-nine witnesses took their seats behind the thick, bullet-proof glass to watch the demise of the two men, who took their fate in rather high spirits. As the thick smoke rose from beneath their seats, Cannon was seen to mouth, 'Nothing to it!' before his eyes rolled back in his head and he fell unconscious. Far from the fifteen seconds promised by chamber designer, Earl Liston, Cannon's death took twelve minutes. His partner in crime took a further three and a half minutes to be pronounced dead. The lack of speed and mercy was noted by, among others, the attending chaplain, Father George O'Meara, who had presided at over fifty hangings. He claimed that the new technique was the worst thing he had ever seen and called for its immediate abolition.

Such protests failed to dissuade the Californian authorities and Cannon and Kessell became the first in a long line of convicts gassed within its borders.

California went on to execute a total of 196 convicts over the years. They also became the first to gas a woman when Eithel Leta Juanita Spinelli passed away in a cloud of fatal fumes on 21 November 1941. The Eaton Metal Products Company went on to create similar chambers for Mississippi and Maryland, who acquired their Eaton gas chambers and generators in 1954 and 1959 respectively. Of the eleven states that opted for the gas chamber, only Missouri did not contract the Denver-based boilermakers to make their model. Throughout the latter half of the twentieth century, countless protests and legal cases have insisted that the procedure was cruel and unusual and, therefore, unconstitutional. As a consequence only five states now offer the gas chamber as an alternative to lethal injection. These are Wyoming, Maryland, Missouri, Arizona and California.

THE CHAMBER

The cubicle in which a death-row inmate breathes his last is a bleak and foreboding place. Like something from a work of science fiction, the gas chamber is a highly complex piece of apparatus, including valves, gaskets and other essential fittings, for what is the simple exercise of gassing a man (or woman) to death. These rooms are chiefly manufactured by one company but they differ slightly from state to state. The chamber situated in the basement of San Quentin Prison, California, is octagonal in shape measuring 1.8 x 2.4 metres (6 x 8 foot) and painted an eerie pale green and is fitted with two chairs which are bolted to the floor and plainly marked A and B. The six-sided example in Mississippi varied in size as well as shape. It was slightly larger than its equivalent in California, reaching almost 2.7 metres (9 foot) high at its centre point and 1.9 metres (6 ft) in diameter. Before its final bow on 21 June 1989, with the execution of convicted murderer Leo Edwards, the chamber within the red-bricked maximum security facility at Mississippi State Penitentiary was made of welded, riveted steel and painted – inside and out – with an aluminium acid resistant coating. The entrance to the cell was through a rubber sealed door which, when closed by a worm-gear and wheel mechanism ordinarily found on marine vessels, helped form an airtight system. The bullet-proof glass windows, through which the visiting witnesses would view the proceedings, were fixed into steel, gasketed frames. All edges to these apertures were coated in thick petroleum jelly as a further guard against leakage.

Inside the pressurised chamber there were additional security measures to prevent any hazardous gas leaks. Nothing was left to chance, even down to the light fittings which were explosion-proof models to safeguard against any errant spark that could ignite the combustible fumes. A manometer (used to measure the pressure of gas) consisted of a tube filled with mercury which was fitted to the interior of the chamber so that the execution staff could keep an eye out for any pressure leaks. Along with this instrument, a vial of phenolphthalein solution was placed inside to monitor the presence of gas within – an essential piece of equipment when it came to the post execution extraction of the gas. The liquid inside the vial turned red when the room was completely clear of the lethal asphyxiate.

Beneath the seats of the chamber, a bowl was

placed, above which, suspended on the end of a thin rod, hung a muslin bag containing on average twenty-four pellets – also known as briquettes or eggs – of sodium cyanide.

THE PREPARATION

While the gas chamber had found its way into the judicial systems of eleven separate states throughout the United States, from California in the west to Maryland on the Eastern Seaboard, the procedure followed by the prison officials is much the same wherever you happen to be. The Eaton Metal Products Company had, with the exception of the chamber in Missouri, the monopoly on the devices throughout the States which helped to ensure uniformity. The Colorado boilermakers also created a common code of practice to deal with the deadly gas before, during and after an execution, ensuring that the strictest safety measures were in place.

Despite its simple objective, the gas chamber is a complex piece of equipment and has to be meticulously prepared before every execution. Full and rigorous structural checks are made, together with verification that there are no blockages in the plumbing and piping. The pressurisation of the chamber is tested, as well as the calibration of all gauges such as the manometer, before the condemned takes their seat. Outside the death room itself, safety precautions include emergency breathing apparatus, special hydrogen cyanide first-aid kits and emergency vehicles on standby. In Mississippi, a surprising safety measure included the evacuation of the guard tower at the prison entrance, in order to prevent any risk to watchmen from the deadly gas expelled from the chamber's nearby chimney.

As for the prisoner, they are granted a last meal of their choice, and shortly before the call to the chamber, they are visited by the prison warden and the prison chaplain. In many prisons, on the day of their death the condemned are moved from the main block to a private concrete cell on Death Row. These cells measure less than 1.5 x 3.4 metres (5 x 11 feet) and contain a toilet, a mattress and two guards who remain with the convict throughout the day and night. After what must be a fitful night's sleep for the inmate, he or she is prepared for execution. The prison uniform is replaced by a plain white shirt and pocket-less blue jeans so that the gas has no place to collect and, for the same reason, the shoes are removed. The presiding doctor then affixes a stethoscope and heart monitor to the prisoner and confirms their clarity of mind. This is a prerequisite for execution, as the law demands that all death-row inmates must be fully aware of their imminent fate. In the early years of the gas chamber, there were ways of forcefully obtaining this lucidity. In 1954, a soon-to-be victim of the chamber had to be given electroshock therapy to be made suitably conscious of what was about to befall him.

While the prisoner is being prepared, the executioner is in the mixing room creating a deadly cocktail of diluted sulphuric acid made from 3.6 litres (6 pints) of acid and 7.2 litres (12 pints) of warm distilled water, and the chamber is brought to a constant 26°C (78.3°F). This was not to make the experience of the condemned any more comfortable but to ensure the hydrogen cyanide, the gas ultimately responsible for the ending of the prisoner's life, does not reach its condensation point of 25.7°C (78.3°f) and thus turn to a liquid, which could dangerously develop on the windows, walls and floor of the chamber.

THE EXECUTION PROCESS

The barefoot convict then makes his final journey escorted by prison staff and, entering through the chamber door is seated in one of the perforated chairs placed over the contraption containing the sodium cyanide crystals. The prisoner is securely strapped across his ankles, thighs, arms and chest in the faint hope that the restraints will minimise the many uncontrolled spasms his body will be forced to endure when the time comes. Once the convict is firmly fastened to the chair, the attached stethoscope and heart monitor leads are fed through small apertures into the viewing room, so that the physician can observe the prisoner's vital signs and confirm the all-important time of death. The prison guards then vacate the cell. The slam of the steel door sounds the death knell for the victim inside. The nautical-style wheel is turned, locking the door tight against its rubber seal and forming the airtight container ready for the final component – the gas.

The executioner then sends a freshly mixed blend of sulphuric acid and distilled water through tubing which leads to the bowl beneath the inmate. Once the receptacle is full, the curtain is opened for the invited parties to witness the completion of the sentence. As part of an official execution, the press, select family members and representatives of the prison and legal system are permitted to view the dramatic affair and hear the prisoner's final statement. Once the last words have been uttered, the signal is then given to the executioner who removes the locking pin and turns the gas valve lever, causing the rod to rotate and tip the bag of briquettes into the bowl beneath it. This allows a chemical reaction to take place between the sodium cyanide and the diluted sulphuric acid creating deadly hydrocyanic gas or hydrogen cyanide. Instantaneously, thick plumes of white smoke begin to rise from the bowl and envelop the prisoner.

WAITING TO INHALE

As the expanding cloud of lethal asphyxiate fills the room, the prisoner instinctively struggles to find clean air or worse, attempts to hold his breath. However, this natural action only serves to prolong the agony so prison officials advise that the condemned to inhale as deeply as possible to speed up the process and hasten the arrival of unconsciousness. One has to ask how humane is a device that calls for the victim to effectively contribute to his or her death. The prisoner blacks out on average between one and three minutes after the chemical reaction. Death takes as little as ten or twelve minutes to occur.

Obviously, first-hand accounts of the gas chamber are rare. However, victims' reactions to the lethal fumes tend to follow a similar pattern. Whether or not the seated and strapped inmate holds his breath in a vain attempt to survive, he or she will eventually be forced to inhale the deadly asphyxiate and will – in a relatively short space of time – succumb to its toxicity. Through irregular breathing combined with the overall feeling of terror, the victim will often begin to hyperventilate and suffer from extreme headaches and a feeling of nausea. Before consciousness is lost, the prisoner will experience a loss of balance, too. The cognisant state of the victim during the gassing has been compared to the effects of a heart attack or epileptic seizure. The prisoner will begin to drool, looking and feeling as if he is being strangled to death as his skin turns purple and his eyes begin to bulge. The condemned will feel pain in the arms, shoulders, back and in the chest as the body gives in to hypoxia; a condition whereby the brain and other essential tissues are starved of oxygen. The manner in which the gas attacks the prisoner's vital organs and nervous system breeds doubt as to whether this method of execution was as humane and merciful as various authorities have proclaimed.

POST EXECUTION

Once the prison's physician has confirmed the death of the condemned, the exhaust fan is switched on and the fumigation process begins. The venomous vapours are removed from the cubicle via the connected chimney. Adherence to this post-execution procedure is of paramount importance to ensure the health and safety of those involved. The extraction process lasts for fifteen to twenty minutes. The chamber undergoes five full air changes in order to guarantee that it is completely clear of hydrogen cyanide.

Only after this will the first members of the clean-up team enter the death cell, and they will be wearing the requisite oxygen masks and full chemical suits complete with air packs. This is in case any traces of the noxious gas linger behind after the extensive decontamination of the air, and also because the solutions they use to clean inside the chamber are themselves toxic. Anhydrous ammonia is sprayed throughout the interior via an injection system hooked up to the air intake manifold. This highly poisonous neutraliser, which has a sweet scent reminiscent of almonds, ensures that the chamber remains a deadly place to be for at least an hour after the execution. The post-death squad scrub down the inside and all instruments are meticulously cleaned with further disinfecting agents. The acid mixing pot used to create the diluted sulphuric acid is filled with caustic soda to render it safe.

The corpse is examined just as closely for signs of hydrocyanic gas before being carried out. Procedure 769 calls for the cleaners to ruffle the hair of the body to ensure that all remnants of the toxic gas are removed before it is taken away. All items of clothing are removed from the corpse and incinerated before the body makes the penultimate journey to the undertaker and lastly into the possession of a relative.

CHAMBER OF HORRORS

Despite many rigorous and strictly followed procedures, many errors have occurred, leading to widespread doubt that this method of execution is humane or merciful. One of the first took place during the chamber's formative years with the double execution of Pete Catalina and Angelo Agnes in 1939. It was claimed by the prison officials to be the quickest and most humane execution they had ever conducted.

The truth was that the gas chamber leaked lethal fumes during the process, causing the witnesses to flee in horror!

On 18 July 1949, Leanderess Riley, a one-eyed, hearing-impaired thief, shot a man named Walter Hills in the back while making his getaway from an armed robbery in Sacramento. Barely breaking 1.5 metres (5 feet) and weighing a slight 56 kilograms (124 pounds), Riley cut a sorry figure at his trial, but his guilt was undeniable and he was scheduled to die in the gas chamber on 25 August 1950. However, the execution was delayed by some years as the appointed doctors assigned to determine the sanity of the prosecuted could not agree on his mental state. The court hearing that followed voted in favour of the death sentence for the diminutive Riley, and he soon found himself in his own private concrete death-cell waiting for the chamber to be prepared. When the sun came up on Riley's last day and the prison guards came for him, he was found clutching the bars of his cell, crying with fear. He struggled and screamed all the way to the chamber and the officials had considerable trouble strapping Riley in to the chair. Twice the petite prisoner managed to pull free from his bindings. The second time occurred after the lever had been pulled to create the chemical reaction. This allowed the spectators to witness Leanderess, with his hands over his face, trying in vain to prevent the fumes from taking him. He died at 10.16 a.m. on 20 February 1953.

Seven years later, one of the most clear-cut signs that the method was flawed came with the execution of Caryl Whittier Chessman. Chessman became known as the Red Light Bandit after he was found guilty of impersonating a policeman and shining a red light into parked cars before physically attacking the passengers within. His death sentence was a highly controversial one. At the time there was a ruling known as the Little Lindbergh law of 1933, stating that any conviction which involved kidnapping with bodily harm should receive the death penalty. The prosecution at Chessman's trial claimed that when Chessman dragged his victims out of their vehicles to sexually assault and kill them, this was effectively kidnap. The judge and jury agreed, and the Red Light Bandit was sent to San Quentin where he spent twelve years on Death Row. He filed numerous self-prepared appeals and successfully avoided eight execution dates until Governor Edmund Brown refused him a ninth.

Chessman's execution was fixed for 2 May 1960, before which he informed the press that he would nod his head if he suffered any pain from the inhalation of lethal asphyxiate. He was strapped into one of the two chairs inside the chamber as all eyes remained fixed on the reaction of the condemned. The lever was pulled, and the sodium cyanide pellets dropped into the sulphuric acid, setting in motion an irreversible sequence of events. The sixty witnesses present watched as the prisoner was seen to nod his head several times as he unwillingly inhaled the lethal fumes. There it was: the abolitionist's first-person proof – albeit from a career criminal – that the gas chamber inflicted pain upon those unlucky enough to experience it. Still it was over thirty years before California called time on the gas chamber, allowing more examples of botched executions to occur. Robert Pierce and Smith E. Jordan were found guilty of killing a taxi driver from Oakland. On the day of their executions Jordan was found in his holding cell spurting blood from a self-inflicted wound to the neck. Rather than delay the proceedings, the prison guards made a makeshift bandage from a prison shirt and he was dragged, kicking and screaming to the chamber. The attending witnesses looked on in horror as Pierce, still bleeding profusely from the neck, wrenched his right arm free from the straps as the cloud of killer gas enveloped him. Thankfully, the hydrogen cyanide fulfilled its purpose before Pierce was able to free his remaining hand, sparing the spectators from further wild gestures and gesticulations.

In Mississippi on 2 September 1983, Jimmy Lee Gray, who had been sentenced to death for the rape and murder of three-year-old Deressa Jean Seales, died not because of the deadly gas filling his lungs, but through banging his head against a metal pole inside the chamber. The horror show took more than eight minutes to bring down the convicted killer, and was met with such disdain by the witnesses that officials had to clear the viewing area. Rumour has it that the reason for this inefficient display came down to the executioner, Barry Bruce, who was drunk on duty. Less than ten years later, in Arizona, Donald Eugene Harding took over six and a half minutes to succumb to the hydrogen cyanide. Throughout this time, the prisoner was seen by the onlookers to spasm uncontrollably, his body turning red and purple, which so repulsed the witnesses that many complained later of post-traumatic disorders.

THE END OF THE GAS CHAMBER

The 1990s saw the number of inmates gassed dwindle. David Edwin Mason met his maker in a cloud of lethal fumes in San Quentin on 24 August 1994 for the murders of four elderly women some fourteen years previous, yet soon after this California stopped using the gas chamber. This move was prompted by the American Civil Liberties Union, which accused the state's Department of Corrections of violating the constitution by applying cruel and unusual punishment upon 375 prisoners with capital convictions. This accusation was heard before Judge Marilyn Hall Patel in San Francisco, who agreed with the Union on 5 October 1994 and ruled the gas chamber was in breach of human rights. If there was any doubt as to the propriety of this decision, a panel of three judges at the Court of Appeals unanimously upheld the ruling two years later on 21 February 1996. Three years later, in Arizona, the most recent execution using the gas chamber occurred. The victim was Walter LaGrand – a German national – chose these fading fumes over lethal injection as a protest against the death penalty and, befitting the antiquated and flawed technique, took a lengthy eighteen minutes to die.

As well as the humane costs, the gas chamber had become financially untenable. Many of Eaton Metal's chambers were now more than seventy years old and were in dire need of new parts or total replacement. The seals, essential for the safety of the witnesses and staff, were hardening and they were in danger of leaking. Rather than refit these cubicles with new seals, the authorities began to favour lethal injection. This is not surprising, considering the cost of building a brand new chamber today is approximately

PART ELEVEN

LETHAL
INJECTION

LETHAL INJECTION

The United States has always endeavoured to adopt the most humane method of execution the age had to offer. The electric chair was seen as an improvement to the gallows and the gas chamber was preferred by many of its states as a merciful alternative to the chair. With the same objective, they arrived at the most recent means to an end: lethal injection. A far cleaner and quieter method of despatch, this harmful hit is now the most common form of capital punishment in the country, with thirty-seven of the thirty-eight 'death states' offering it as an option. Only Nebraska abstained in favour of the electric chair.

Lethal injection was first discussed in the late nineteenth century as a result of considerable advances made in medicine. Julius Mount Bleyer, a doctor from New York, advocated its use as a more humane alternative in 1888, but he failed in his bid to see it used in his lifetime. The invention of electricity stole the limelight, and indeed the right to replace the gallows. It was not until a full century later that lethal injection at last outshone Edison's creation.

The reason for its resurgence in the late 1970s came down to abolitionists insisting that electrocution and gassing were cruel and unusual in their technique and, therefore, violated the eighth amendment of the American constitution. The supreme court case of Furman vs Georgia brought an immediate cessation of all American executions in 1972, while authorities debated and deliberated on the legality of electrocution as a means for capital punishment.

There was immense pressure on all the death states to discover a new and improved system. In Oklahoma, state representative and Republican William J. Wiseman was seeking help from medical experts to unearth a much-needed replacement. Not only had the electric chair fallen out of public favour there, but the Oklahoma model was also in dire need of repair – thus providing a financial incentive to finding a fresh method of execution! However, Wiseman met with disapproval from the Oklahoma Medical Association, which felt any participation by those that had sworn the Hippocratic Oath stating 'never to do harm' would be impossible.

When all seemed lost, Wiseman received a call from Jay Chapman, the state's medical examiner. Chapman had invaluable experience of executions, having been present at many in the neighbouring state of Colorado. He had witnessed first-hand the grisly horrors of electrocution and was, therefore, keen to assist any with search for an alternative. He upheld Bleyer's original claim that injection of a lethal formula would provide a humane method of execution. What Chapman did not possess was any solid pharmacological training, but he would be the man to invent a procedure of execution that has seen the death of hundreds of people and still is very much in existence to this day.

Chapman dictated to Wiseman how he saw the basic procedure of taking a life by lethal injection. This became known as Chapman's Protocol. He advocated an intravenous saline drip placed in the arm of the prisoner, through which a fast-acting barbiturate should be injected. This was followed by a shot of a drug with paralytic properties. Chapman's protocol was given suitable backing by Doctor Stanley Deutsch, the then head of Oklahoma Medical School's Anaesthesiology Department, and Wiseman quickly had the lethal injection bill passed by the state legislature.

In fact, Oklahoma was not the first state to apply this new technique. The day after Wiseman had successfully passed the bill in Oklahoma, Texas followed suit. It would provide the location for the first lethal injection in the United States. On 7 December 1982, Charles Brooks was led into the death chamber at the Huntsville Unit of the State Prison and was injected with a lethal dose of barbiturate, becoming the needle's first victim and the first execution in Texas since 1964.

The prisoner given the dubious honour of this drug debut was a convicted murderer hailing from Fort Worth, who had been found guilty (along with his partner, Woody Loudres) of kidnapping mechanic David Gregory. They bound and gagged him in a motel room before shooting him in the head at point-blank range, and for this Brooks was given the death penalty. A stay of execution was denied and after a last meal of steak and chips followed by peach cobbler, the prisoner was prepared for execution. Having converted to Islam while incarcerated, Brooks said a prayer to Allah before the drugs were pumped into his bloodstream at 12.09 a.m. He was pronounced dead seven minutes later in what proved to be a reasonably efficient affair, devoid of first night nerves. This success suggested that a bright future was in store for lethal injection. The practice was eagerly snapped up by other states – twenty-seven legislatures had adopted the new method by 1994 and a further ten states had adopted it by 2004.

THE PROCEDURE

Chapman's Protocol forms the basis of a much simpler practice than that found with the gas chamber, and the use of needles ensures a more medical environment than that of the electric chair or indeed the gallows. Witnesses need not fear shocking skin discoloration or 30-centimetre (1-foot) high flames shooting up from the heads of the victims. The new method promised to be a far more civilised than its predecessors.

The prisoner is afforded his choice of last meal and is visited by a spiritual advisor while he waits for the officials to arrive. Then the prison's personnel fix heart monitors to the body of the condemned and strap him or her into a gurney, or trolley. A drip or cannula is then inserted into a suitable vein in the arm with a second put in the other arm as a back-up in case the primary line fails. This part of the procedure often proves difficult as many a convict cannot provide a healthy vein thanks to serious drug abuse.

The patient-cum-prisoner is then wheeled into the death chamber invariably covered from neck to toe in a white sheet. The drips are linked up to tubes leading into an ante chamber, which is separated by a wall or curtain from where the actual execution takes place. It is from here that the technicians will administer the doses.

Currently, the sequence of drugs is manually injected into the condemned, but this has not always been the case. In 1979, Fred Leuchter invented an automatic, computer-controlled device which, by a system of syringes, plungers and pistons, was able to administer the correct doses at specific intervals. It comprised of two modules. The control module with its on/off switch was duplicated, to hide the true identity of the executioner. The delivery module contained a series of syringes filled with the deadly doses and saline solution, which was used to flush out the intravenous tubes between each stage. It proved highly successful and was first bought by New Jersey. In total, seventeen states purchased a Leuchter machine; each one was built in the basement of the inventor's house. However, the bubble burst on this successful invention when, in 1990, Leuchter testified on behalf of Holocaust denier, Ernst Zundel, during which his lack of training was revealed. With only a Bachelor of Arts to his name, Leuchter had no scientific nor pharmacological training and this revelation saw many states dispose of the machine.

Once the prisoner is in place, bound to the gurney and fully connected to the ante chamber, up to three injections of fast-acting drugs are allowed to flow in through the drip inserted into the arm. The first drug dispatched is sodium thiopental also known as sodium pentothal, which is an anaesthetic used in surgical operations. However, rather than the usual dose of between 3 and 5 milligrams per kilogram, (causing a loss of consciousness in less than forty-five seconds) the prisoner is given a 5-gram dose in order to ensure a complete coma state.

The second injection follows soon after an intermediate saline flush. The second stage sees the prisoner's muscles paralysed, thanks to a 100-milligram dose of a drug called pancuronium bromide, or Pavulon. In some states, this jab is considered enough to do the job, as the dose can result in the collapse of the diaphragm bringing death by asphyxiation. In other states, a third injection is required to complete the execution. A lethal dose of potassium chloride is then administered to the prisoner in order to force a cardiac arrest. Known as an electrolyte – a solution that conducts electricity – the drug raises the electrical charge of the heart cells, rendering the heart unable to contract.

Whether two or three injections are used, the execution should last anything between seven and eleven minutes with death being pronounced within twenty minutes of the first injection. However, not all executions using this new method managed to achieve this average and not all prisoners went as peacefully as Charles Brooks in Huntsville, Texas.

Since its first use in 1982, the three-dose practice has come under fire for being unnecessarily cruel. Many believe the legally required death of the inmate could just as easily be obtained by one single dose of barbiturate, negating the need for the second and third injections that are considered to cause immense pain. An overdose of sodium thiopental would mean that the prisoner would simply slip into a coma and eventually stop breathing. However, this one-shot deal is fraught with difficulties. Using a single drug to kill the prisoner would mean the injected inmate could take up to forty-five minutes to expire. During this time, without the pancuronium bromide to paralyse the muscles, the prisoner would be prone to involuntary muscle jerks that could disturb the witnesses. Currently, the single-injection method has yet to be used, and the relevant states prefer to stick to a sequence of two or three drugs.

POOR SHOTS

While there is much evidence to suggest that injecting a series of deadly chemicals into a prisoner's bloodstream is the most humane method of execution yet discovered, there have been many examples to indicate that this clean and clinical form of execution is actually far from humane.

There are oppotunities for error throughout the procedure, and consequently potential for inflicting pain on the prisoner. Firstly, the personnel responsible often lack expertise necessary for properly injecting the deadly doses. In any other scenario involving the use of these drugs, highly trained doctors would be in charge. However, because the practice of lethal injection is concerned with taking a life, it clearly contravenes the Hippocratic oath. For this reason, the American Medical Association (AMA) forbid their members from participating. This means that there exists a greater chance of error, as potentially less-qualified staff are required to do the job. The injection process is not just a case of pressing a plunger. Each dose of every drug used must be tailored to each inmate. Too small a dose of sodium thiopental runs the risk of an early return to consciousness, and thanks to the paralytic properties of pancuronium bromide, the prisoner would likely suffer immense pain yet appear calm and at peace. While in this deceptively serene state, the condemned would be prone to asphyxia and, when the final fix of potassium chloride was introduced, intense muscle cramps and burning sensations would occur.

One of the first examples of a flawed injection process occurred on 14 March 1984 in Texas, when David James Autry was wheeled into the execution chamber inside the state prison. With such an auspicious start to the method two years previously, the execution of this convicted murderer came as a shock and brought doubt upon the efficacy of the practice. The prison officials in charge of the affair were unable to bring the prisoner into a state of complete unconsciousness. The first two doses reacted with one another to form a solid, which restricted the flow into Autry's bloodstream. He was seen to suffer for the duration of the execution which lasted a full ten minutes.

Another potential problem inherent in executing a prisoner by lethal injection is the difficulty in finding a suitable vein in which to insert the necessary drips or cannulae. Many of the men and women who find themselves on death row have been previous intravenous drug users, and as a result have damaged or weakened the veins needed for the needle-based execution. Such a problem was faced by the executioners of serial killer Stephen Peter Morin on 13 March 1985. Due to a previous heavy drug habit, it took forty torturous minutes for them to find a suitable vein – they even resorting to looking in his leg. A year later, when a similar anxious search took place, the technicians received assistance from the prisoner himself – Randy Woolls – who kindly found a usable vein for them!

It took several officials almost an hour to attach drips to the arms of Rickey Ray Rector in Arkansas on 24 January 1992. The curtain to the witness room was drawn and yet witnesses later reported audible sounds of suffering. The technicians were about to resort to using a knife on the condemned's arm to reveal an available vein until one was finally found in his right hand. Even this unbearable experience was surpassed when, on 2 May 2006, it took almost an hour and a half to execute Joseph Lewis Clark. The prisoner, who had murdered twenty-two-year-old David Manning during a robbery at a Toledo gas station, only had one usable vein, thanks to a life of drug addiction, and had to forego the back-up intravenous line. The convict was used to authorities taking their time as he had been waiting on death row for more than twenty-one years! When the time eventually came, he exhibited many signs of pain and suffering. He struggled with prison officials before the director of Ohio's Department for the Rehabilitation and Correction, Terry Collins, chose to close the curtains to the witness area. The spectators reported that Clark raised his head from the gurney to which he was strapped and moaned, '... don't work ... don't work' – surely the clearest indication yet received that the process is flawed. As recently as 24 May 2007, an execution by lethal injection went well over time due to missing veins, but this was down to something other than drug abuse. Christopher Newton, a thirty-seven-year-old criminal who was convicted of the aggravated murder of a cellmate, weighed a whopping 120 kilograms (19 stone). This made it almost impossible for the team of technicians at the Southern Ohio Correctional Facility to locate a vein. Ten attempts and two hours later they finally managed to complete the intravenous insertion and finish the job, though not before allowing poor Newton an unofficial and fleeting stay of execution: the ordeal took so long they afforded him a toilet break!

Poor dosage levels and ruined or remote veins have not been the sole cause of error. On 3 May 1995 in Missouri, Emmitt Foster suffered during his execution due to a much simpler mistake. When the first of the three drugs was injected into the convict's blood-stream, Foster failed to fall into the pentothal-induced deep sleep but instead began to gasp for air and convulse upon the gurney. Immediately, the curtains were drawn to hide any further signs of pain and anguish from the observers, and it would be a further half hour until the curtains were opened to reveal a corpse for them to officially witness. But what had transpired behind those closed curtains? Why had Foster failed to respond to the anaesthetic properties of the initial drug? It transpires that the error did not lie with the levels of the sodium thiopental, or with its timing but with the bindings used to restrain the prisoner to his gurney. The leather straps had been secured so tightly upon Foster that it had restricted the flow of the sedating serum, limiting its effect upon the body. The reason for the slow action of the drug was spotted by the attending coroner, William Gum.

Another example of incompetent execution took place on 13 December 2006, when convicted killer Angel Nieves Diaz failed to succumb to the initial dose of anaesthetic even after more than thirty minutes. The execution technicians decided to inject a second dose of sodium thiopental into the fifty-five-year-old man's bloodstream but this brought no coma-like state. Instead, witnesses present at the event reported seeing the Florida prisoner pull grotesque faces for up to twenty-four minutes after the injections began. Yet despite such first-hand accounts the prison officials said Diaz felt no pain during his execution and put his unusual reaction to the double dose down to a liver disease. This conflicted with the findings of the medical examiner, Doctor William Hamilton, who during the autopsy found his liver to be in normal working order. What he did find were chemical burns on both arms, which he judged to be evidence of poorly inserted drips. The needles from each intravenous drip had penetrated the desired veins but had gone through the other side and into his flesh. As a result of such malpractice, the final fix had been administered into the soft tissue rather than into the bloodstream. This severely reduced the effects of the sodium thiopental. Two days after these findings, Governor Jeb Bush suspended all executions in Florida and appointed a commission to look into the constitutionality of the technique. This state moratorium has since come to an end thanks to Bush's successor, Charlie Crist, who lifted the ban to sign the death warrant for Mark Dean Schwab on 18 July 2007.

The use of lethal injection as a death penalty in the United States is far from black and white. The country is far from united when it comes to this method of execution, with courts finding it unconstitutional in

Missouri, California, Florida and Tennessee, while Arizona and Oklahoma have had their rights to the judicial jab upheld. Not all the detractors of the lethal injection are opponents of the death penalty. There are many who believe that the method is too merciful, and offering such a pain-free technique removes the deterrent.

While the United States continues to be the main user or, possibly, abuser of the procedure, it is not the only country that offers the injurious injection as a means to an untimely end. Taiwan was the first country outside the United States to allow the lethal injection to be used, but has yet to actively take a life using this method. The first non-American land to 'shoot up' their capital convicts was China, and this began in 1997, some fifteen years after the first US death by lethal injection. Since then, Guatemala and the Philippines have both followed suit, debuting their noxious needles in February 1998 and 1999 respectively. Thailand joined the list with a multiple execution in December 2003, when four men were sentenced to death for drug trafficking and murder.